The World Encyclopedia of
MODERN GUNS

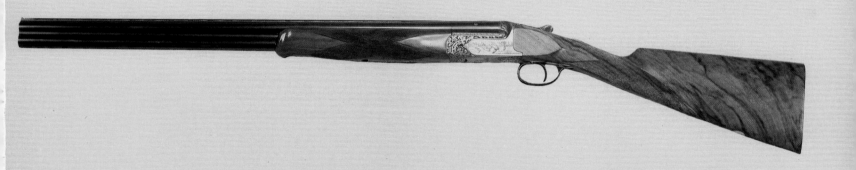

The World Encyclopedia of
MODERN GUNS

A.J.R.Cormack

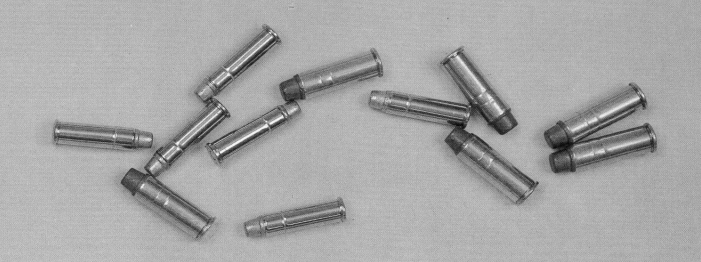

OCTOPUS

First published 1979 by Octopus Books Limited
59 Grosvenor Street London W1

© 1979 Octopus Books Limited

ISBN 0 7064 0974 4

Produced by Mandarin Books Limited
22a Westlands Road Quarry Bay, Hong Kong

Printed in Hong Kong

CONTENTS

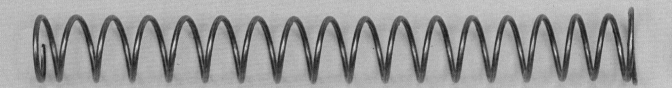

Introduction

Although firearms have in their short history had a major affect on the development of the world as it is today, they have also generated intense interest for less prosaic reasons. The technological developments in the fields of materials and production techniques have been mirrored and indeed in some cases led by those firearms. The great innovators in the area of gun development such as Colt, Wesson and Browning must rank along with designers from other fields as geniuses.

Early firearms were not only possessed for their power but also as a symbol of status. This resulted in a trend that continues today of decorating the piece in what is often an extravagant style. This has led to early examples being exhibited for the skill of their decoration.

The status symbol is exemplified by not only the presentation of a pair of shotguns to a head of state but also the supply of a gold-plated submachine gun to a sheikh's personal bodyguard.

The basic history of the firearm from those using the simplest cannon ignition to the complex modern caseless ammunition types is described and illustrated in this book. The famous designers, constructors and manufacturers, many with names well known across the world, have each been examined to show their place in the history of the art of gunmaking.

The technically inclined will find that a large number of cutaway drawings, all specially commissioned, are included so that the internal construction of both guns and ammunition can be examined. The development of rifling along with its affect on accuracy is also studied.

The sportsman, be he a target or game shot, will be able not only to view some fine examples of sports firearms in general but also the shotguns in particular.

Finally, for those who, like many of us, just like to be able to appreciate the genius of the artist and gunmaker there is a large number of colour illustrations. Famous collections such as the Tower of London, Holland and Holland, and the Victoria and Albert Museum have all provided examples of what is best in design and construction.

A. J. R. Cormack
Edinburgh, 1979

Early Development

Once upon a time when tired of battle, or perhaps realizing that defeat seemed near, the weary armies could retreat behind the walls of their castles or towns and try to sit it out. Medieval towns flourished behind massive encircling walls. Safety was not threatened by weapons, and the worst enemy was death by starvation or disease.

The baron built his castle walls so thick and defended them so well that he had little to fear. The architecture of the country was dictated by the ability of the walled town or castle to keep out the enemy. The main weapons of war were the bow and arrow, pike and sword for the infantry, and the lance, battle axe and club for the cavalry. The artillery had to make do with catapults and ballistae. If captured, the gentleman of war, the knight, had a short spell in captivity until his ransom was paid. The serfs were there to act as the forerunner of cannon fodder. War was a sport to many and the knight practised it at the joust and the bowman at archery contests.

The invention of the firearm and the cannon changed things dramatically. Although it took some time to develop

them to any extent, they made the knight's armour and the castle wall wholly obsolete. First, however, there was the need to produce a means of propelling the projectile and this required an explosive. Gunpowder, as it came to be known, was a low grade explosive which burnt sufficiently slowly to act as a propellant for the projectile.

The coming of gunpowder

The inventor of gunpowder is a shadowy figure shrouded in the vapours of his experiments. Pestle in hand, he grinds the ingredients together in a mortar while mouthing suitable incantations. A likely candidate for the title of inventor is Berthold Schwarz, or Black Berthold. Berthold (his real name was Constantin Anklitzen) was a Franciscan monk in the town of Freiburg in Germany. It is said that his fellow monks named him Schwarz because he dabbled in the 'black arts'. The stories of how he died are many and various. Some say the monks locked him up because they disapproved of his work; others that they executed him or, most probable, that he blew himself up in his enthusiasm. In all cases the influence of the Devil is strongly suspected.

Another claimant is Marcus Graecus, or Mark the Greek who, it is said, wrote a work called *Liber Ignium* (*The Book of Fires*) which recorded the composition of gunpowder. But the book was not original. It was a translation of another work and came after other writings on the subject.

To manufacture a successful gunpowder it was necessary to mix three main constituents in correct amounts. The three ingredients were sulphur, charcoal and saltpetre. The first two were well known for many years before the invention of gunpowder itself, and sulphur was known to be an ingredient of incendiary mixtures. These nasty concoctions were known as Greek Fire and contained pitch. They were thrown by catapult and sling inside the enemy's houses and stocks so as to burn down his defensive perimeters. The use of this can be dated from 700 AD. Greek Fire has managed to cloud the picture for historians of warfare for 'weapons that belch forth fire and noise' could refer to a gun or equally a catapult load of Greek Fire. It is known that some of the later mixtures included saltpetre. But at what point did the mixer achieve a formula that led to the first big bang? Having done this, when was the importance of the three primary ingredients recognized and the pitch and other additives omitted?

The addition of saltpetre is considered of crucial importance. Arabic descriptions of saltpetre are detailed and without doubt they knew of the substance as early as the first half of the 13th century. There is, however, little evidence that Arabs knew of its combination with the other two ingredients. In any case their writings are thought to have been copied from others, probably Chinese. The Chinese give recipes for various incendiary mixtures in the book *Wu Ching Tsun*, and these contain saltpetre. The work can be dated from the middle of the 11th century. The original work was considerably embellished by an enthusiastic author at a later date to include the cannon in the hope of claiming its invention for his homeland. As this original work was of such an early date it is probable that the process of experimentation and development would, if for no other reason than luck, eventually hit on the formula for gunpowder.

Whether the Chinese did or did not develop gunpowder and then spread the knowledge to the Arabs and thence to Europe may be debated, but one fact emerges clearly – the description of true gunpowder by an Englishman called Bacon in 1268. The earliest work in which he refers to it is *De Secretis Operibus Artis et Naturae* which dates from the middle of the 13th century. Bacon seems to have decided that the knowledge of gunpowder was not safe with the world so he concealed the charcoal ingredient in an anagram. His later works *Opus Majus* and *Opus Tertium* of about 1268–70 give the complete formula. All works give graphic descriptions of the 'thunder and lightning distressing men's ears' and 'terrible flashes'.

As has been noted, a gunpowder mixture was first used as an incendiary or possibly a firework and therefore the composition was of little importance. When, however, it was used as a propellant the composition became more important as consistent burning was required. The composition was not standardized, as gunpowder will, within limits, work quite well whatever quantities of charcoal, saltpetre and sulphur are used. The composition varied from date to date and country to country until the 18th century.

By 1600 the main problem with the powder was the very hygroscopic qualities of saltpetre, which led to even the most carefully kept powder becoming damp and useless. This was particularly a problem at sea. One solution was to make the very fine powder into grains that were less liable to absorb moisture. The manufacture of 'corned powder' as it was called was done by mixing the constituents wet and then allowing them to dry. The result could be sorted into grain sizes that were reasonably constant. Thus, not only was the damp problem

Above: Driven into submission by cannon bombardment the burghers of a Belgian village surrender the keys of their township. At a stroke, the invention of cannon made thick stone walls of little use against concentrated attack in war.

Below: This painting from about 1400 shows an armoured foot-soldier firing a matchlock cannon. The barrel is attached to a pole and mounted on a monopod. It was a development of this type of weapon that would eventually lead to the appearance of the shoulder arm.

lessened, but also, because the grain sizes were uniform, the powder was more liable to give consistent results.

One interesting avenue of research was explored in the attempt to make the powder waterproof. It consisted of heating it until the sulphur melted and sealed the mass against damp. There can have been few volunteers to carry out this dangerous business, however, and it is likely that premature explosions discouraged this practice.

To provide a further control to the burning of the powder, and so that it could be used in the stronger actions that were becoming available, 'prism powder' was manufactured. This, as its name indicates, was in the shape of prisms often with a hole through the centre. The hole increased in area as the grain burnt and balanced the reduction in area of the outside of the grains, so giving a more uniform pressure. The use of a special charcoal enabled manufacturers to reduce the amount of sulphur in the powder and thus promote a slower burning rate which was useful in large-bore guns.

The one problem with black powder that remains, even in its present form, is that it leaves a large amount of extremely corrosive residue in the gun barrel and breech. A sample of black powder has been found to produce, through burning, more than 55 per cent solid matter. The problem in the early days of the muzzle-loader was

that this fouling rapidly coated the bore with a hard deposit that made the loading of successive projectiles progressively more difficult. Yet this did little to detract from its efficiency as a propellant. Mute testimony to this efficiency are the ruins of castles visible throughout the countryside.

Although today black powder, which gives off smoke, is no longer used as a general propellant (except in special cases such as with the so called 'rubber bullet' anti-riot round) a resurgence of interest in the muzzle-loader has led to an increase in its use. But it is still a dirty and corrosive substance requiring scrupulous cleaning of the weapon after firing.

Development of smokeless powders

In the middle of the 19th century a concentrated period of development occurred which led to the discovery of the modern smokeless powders. Before smokeless powder could come into being it was necessary to develop other types of explosives, in particular nitrocellulose and nitroglycerine.

Nitrocellulose was developed simultaneously by two men. Christian Schonbein working in Basle and Rudolf Bottger working in Germany discovered in 1845 that mixing cotton with a mixture of nitric and sulphuric acids produced cellulose nitrate. When processed and washed to remove the

surplus acids it became nitrocellulose or, as the propellant became known, 'guncotton'. When the result was enriched with additional nitrogen it became the basis of a smokeless powder. This type of powder is known as a single-base powder.

Ascanio Sobrero, an Italian working during the same period as Schonbein and Bottger, discovered that a mixture of sulphuric acid, nitric acid and glycerine produced glyceraltrinitrate or nitroglycerine. Although nitroglycerine on its own is useless as a propellant because of its very high burning rate, it formed the basis for the explosive dynamite. But the blending of nitroglycerine and nitrocellulose can form a suitable explosive to be used as a propellant. This type of powder is known as a double-based propellant.

The first smokeless powder was developed by Captain Schultze in 1864. It was a single-based powder which had a fairly fast burning rate that was unsuitable for rifles and pistols but was ideal for shotguns. Schultze's powder became famous and was produced in large quantities for the shotgun cartridge.

In 1884 Paul Vieille developed Poudre B (Powder Blanche, white as opposed to black). This powder became standard with the French for military use. Alfred Nobel developed Ballistite in 1888 and cordite became available the following year. Smokeless powder had come of age and with it the development of the firearm took a leap forward.

Powders based on these ingredients are in use to this day as propellants in both sporting and military cartridges. The powders came in almost every shape imaginable except the true ball. Ball powder, which is now being used more and more, especially in the United States, was developed by the Western Cartridge Company before World War II. It is manufactured by mixing a protective colloid that pre-

The forerunner of the armoured corps: a mounted knight equipped with a small matchlock cannon. This drawing from the second quarter of the 13th century is more likely an artist's impression of possible armament than a practical weapon.

vents the grains reforming and encouraging the formation of balls of powder. The balls are easily sorted for size and pour very easily during the loading of the cartridge.

At the present time many experiments are being carried out to find substitutes for powder. Liquid propellants have been tried but with only limited success. The area that is attracting most interest is that of caseless ammunition, which adds problems to the producer of powders. The direct action of the heat of the chamber on the propellant means that the ignition temperature has to be raised without incurring too many problems in the primer ignition. The impact resistance of the propellant block can be increased but once again burning problems can occur. There is little doubt however that smokeless powder is here to stay for the foreseeable future.

Early cannon

Apart from the problem of finding a suitable propellant the other necessities for the firearm were all to hand. Wood and iron abounded and there were men with sufficient skills in the working of both. Illustrations seem to indicate that the prime purpose of these first weapons was against fortifications rather than infantry, although the infantry version was not long in following. The cannon, as these first guns were called, were named after the Latin word for a tube, 'canna'. It is probable that the first cannon were not firearms but, in effect, giant fireworks. Some pictures show bamboo tubes bound with wire as a reinforcement although whether they were designed to project much in the way of a missile is not certain.

The date on which the first cannon are mentioned in an identifiable form is 1326 and by 1350 there are illustrations of weapons. These later illustrations are the ones that concern the small arms and sporting gun development as they show wooden tillers attached to the tube barrel. Some are definitely too large to fire hand-held and it may be assumed the tiller was rested on the ground, but others are of a size that would enable a soldier to lift and fire them. Writings of the 1380s specifically mention handguns. The use of multiple loads or superimposed loads can be dated from the late 14th century. The superimposed load was the loading of alternate layers of powder and projectile down the barrel and igniting the front one first. As the flash passed back the projectiles would, in theory at least, depart one after the other.

The ignition of the propellant charge was the area in which most develop-

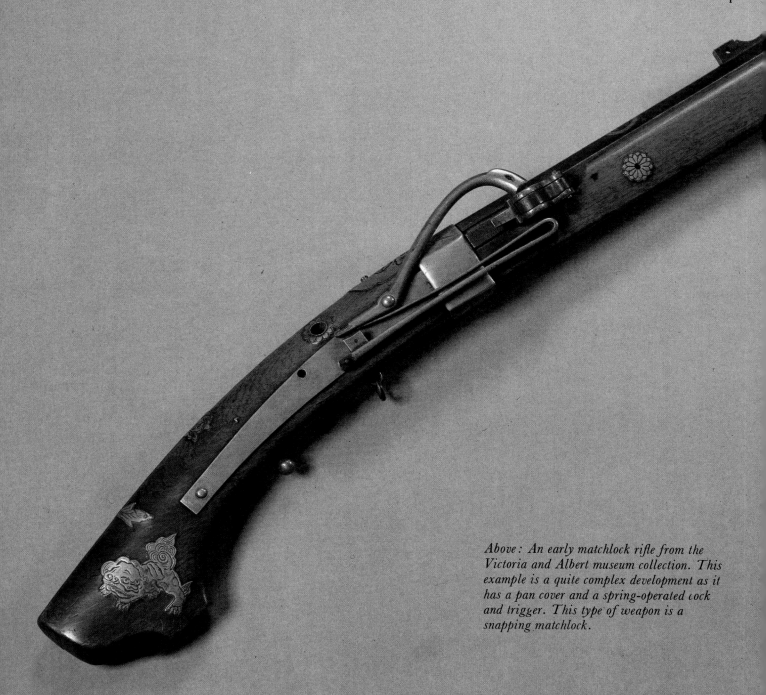

Above: An early matchlock rifle from the Victoria and Albert museum collection. This example is a quite complex development as it has a pan cover and a spring-operated cock and trigger. This type of weapon is a snapping matchlock.

Below: This ornate French matchlock dates from about 1600. The stock is extensively inlayed with horn, with patterns inscribed upon it. The shape of the butt has been determined more by considerations of style than practicality.

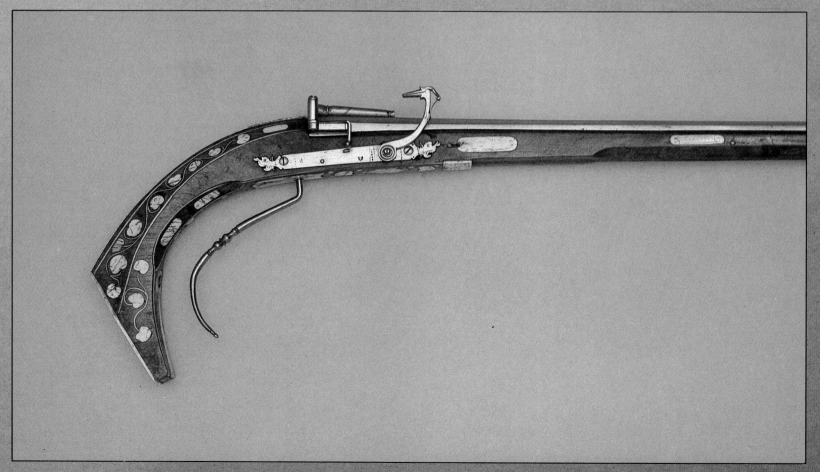

Above right: A trigger-controlled matchlock. In this weapon the match is clamped in the cock so that the glowing end can be lowered into the pan. The pan has a simple cover that can be moved by a lever. This would allow, in theory at least, the weapon to be fired even in the heat of battle.

Below: The matchlock musket has a very modern construction with its shaped stock, banded barrel, sights and ram rod, but its ignition system firmly identifies it as a historical weapon.

ment occurred for many years. The first system was on the firework principle in that the charge was lit from the front of the barrel. As this must have been at best a somewhat nerve-racking business someone, probably with his own safety in mind, drilled a hole at the back of the tube. This hole, or touch hole, allowed the firer to dip the hot end of a slowmatch into the priming powder in relative safety. The system has naturally assumed the name of cannon ignition.

There is little doubt that the early soldiers whose job it was to handle the firearms of the period were not to be envied. For a start, the reliability of the barrels was suspect. Not surprisingly, the gunners were more often than not serfs and the knights stood well to the rear. The cannon ignition system posed other problems, too. The powder had to be kept dry, the priming had to be kept in the hole and, as if this was not enough, in wind and rain the slowmatch had somehow to be kept alight. The habit of keeping a small fire lit so that one could make sure of the match must have given enemy archers a convenient target.

Once the match was lit, how could accurate aim be taken while trying to hold the stock, look at the target and at the same time apply the match to the touch hole? Even if the aim was, by some freak of chance, true, the propellant was so variable that the projectile was just as likely to drop not far from the muzzle as it was to wing its way through the air. The conclusion seems inescapable that in these early days at least the bow and arrow were infinitely more to be feared in warfare. But this state of affairs was soon to change, and change dramatically.

Evolution of hand weapons

Although cannon ignition was still in use with the hand cannon until the 1400s and, in the case of the cannon itself, much later, another system was under development from the day when an enterprising soldier attached the match to the hand cannon for ease of holding. The touch hole had graduated into a pan and had been moved to the side of the weapon. Soon a lever was added to the side and the match held in such a way that when the lever moved down it went into the pan. That was the matchlock in its simplest form.

Below: A 17th century German matchlock musket. Notice the intricate decoration, an indication that, as with many surviving weapons of this type, it had a wealthy owner. Many of these muskets were acquired or even gifted as symbols of importance.

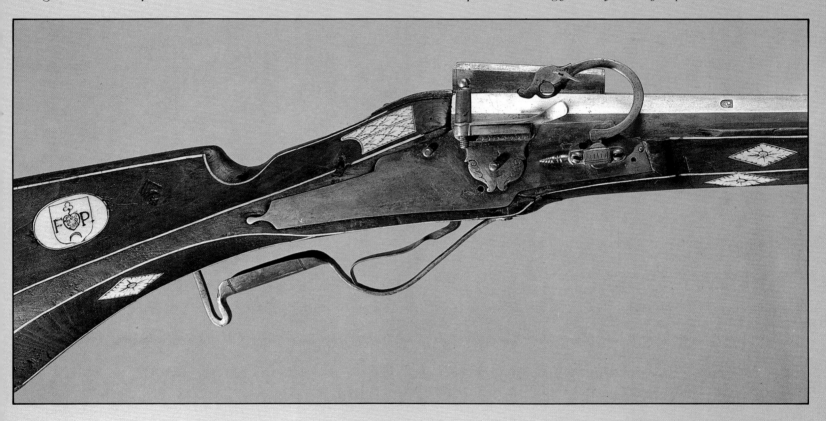

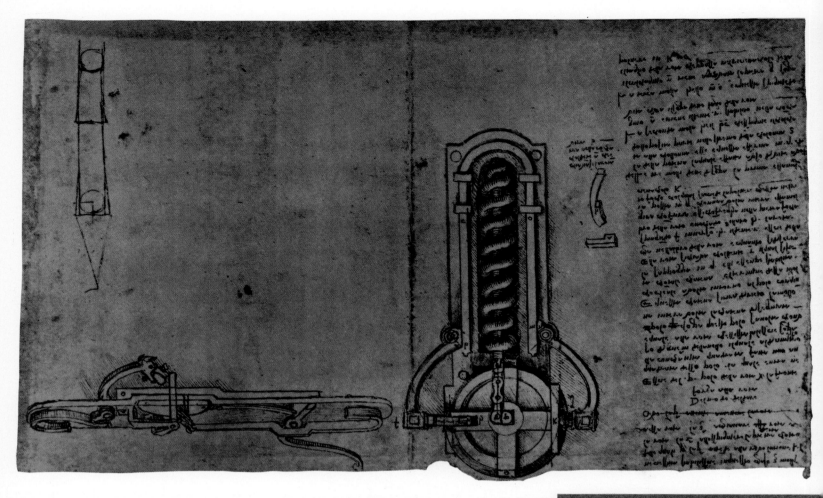

The trigger followed when the lever was extended so that it could be pulled into contact with the pan. Finally a pan cover was used to keep the priming in the pan and dry as well. The hand cannon was now truly a weapon of war.

The last development of the matchlock was the snapping matchlock in which there was for the first time in a firearm a trigger mechanism (although many crossbows had complex triggers). The arm that held the match was under the pressure of a spring and snapped forward into the pan when the trigger was pulled. The hand cannon was now a practical weapon able to be aimed, albeit approximately, and the powder charge ignited with some regularity. The main disadvantage of the system was the match itself which had to be kept lit – no mean feat in battle on a windy day.

Two independent areas of knowledge were combined in the early 1500s to provide a form of ignition that dispensed with the match. The clock-making industry was by then well advanced in the use of clockwork types of mechanism. Clock-making was probably one of the most advanced areas of engineering of the time and it is not surprising that the wheellock

should involve the spinning of a striker wheel driven by a spring. The fact that iron pyrites could be struck against a metal to produce streams of sparks was well known and this was used to light fires.

The combination of these two pieces of knowledge possibly took the form of a tinder lighter at first rather than that of a firearm, but as early as 1508 Leonardo da Vinci illustrated a wheellock applied to a gun. Traditionally the invention has been ascribed to Germany and, indeed, there are a number of very early surviving examples from there. The wheellock was not manufactured in any number until 1525–30.

The action of the wheellock was as follows: the lever that gripped the match had instead the pyrites at its head; the priming pan was primed and the spring wound; the lever was lowered so that the pyrites rested on the wheel; when the trigger was pulled the wheel revolved striking sparks from the pyrites into the priming pan and firing the gun. The reliability of the system was improved when flint was substituted for the rather fragile pyrites. Many early wheellocks had a duplicate arm with a reserve piece of pyrites. Some locks even had a reserve

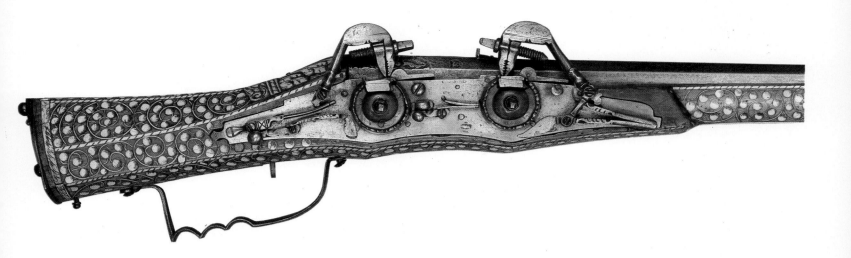

Opposite: The concept of the wheellock, and for that matter many other advances in firearms designs, was projected by Leonardo da Vinci as early as the beginning of the 16th century. Also illustrated here in one of his drawings is a complex trigger mechanism.

Above: A simple but basically unreliable method of firing more than one shot from a single barrel was to superimpose one load on top of another. The loads could then be fired by different locks which were positioned opposite the appropriate load. This early example uses wheellocks as the method of ignition.

Below: A highly decorated matchlock pistol from the Victoria and Albert Museum collection. It illustrates the ultimate in ornate design. This pistol, as well as being a practical weapon, is a work of art. It is most unlikely that it would have been often fired. It was probably a token of wealth and prestige.

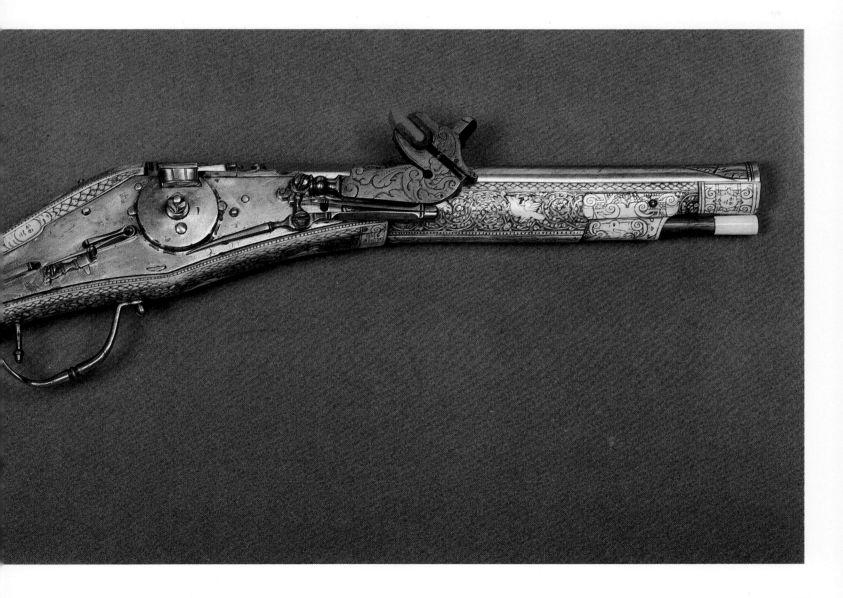

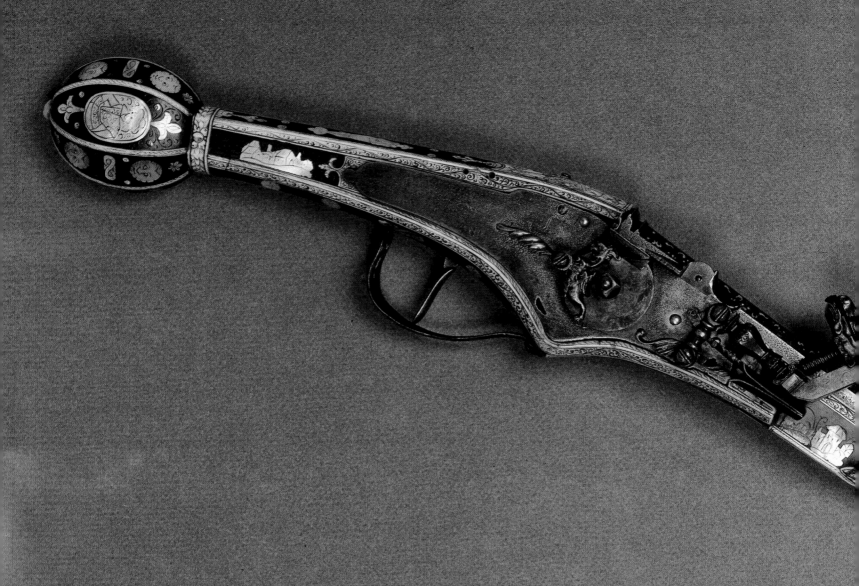

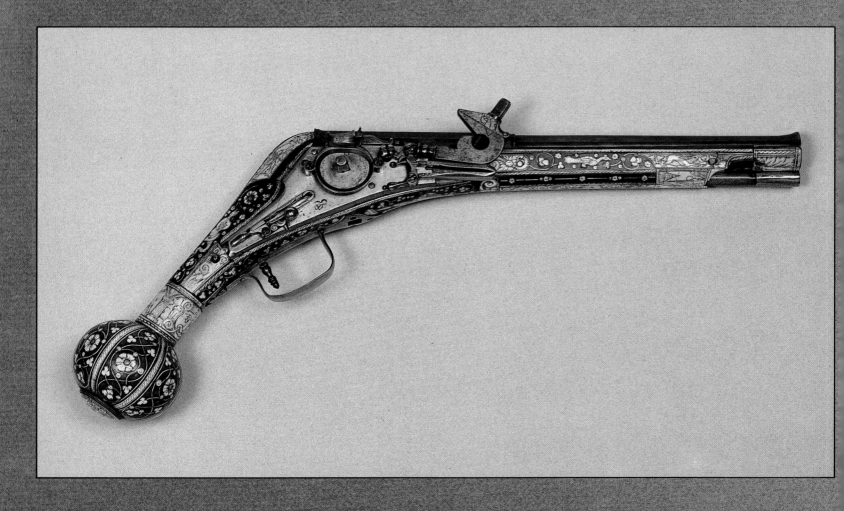

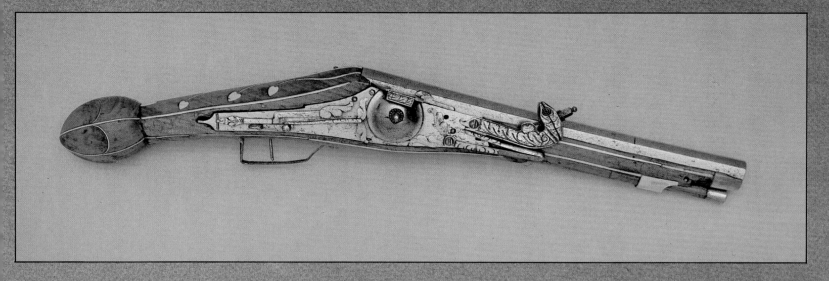

Left: A wheellock pistol with attractive and ornate decorations.. The ball butt displays human figures and buildings while the fore end shows animals and houses.

Above: A late 16th-century wheellock pistol attractively stocked in walnut with simple metal inlays. Less ornate than many of its type, this would have been a practical weapon although the butt, with its almost 'straight line' design and ball end, must have been uncomfortable.

Opposite: The prominent ball butt and oddly placed trigger must have made aiming this pistol extremely difficult if the owner wished to fire it.

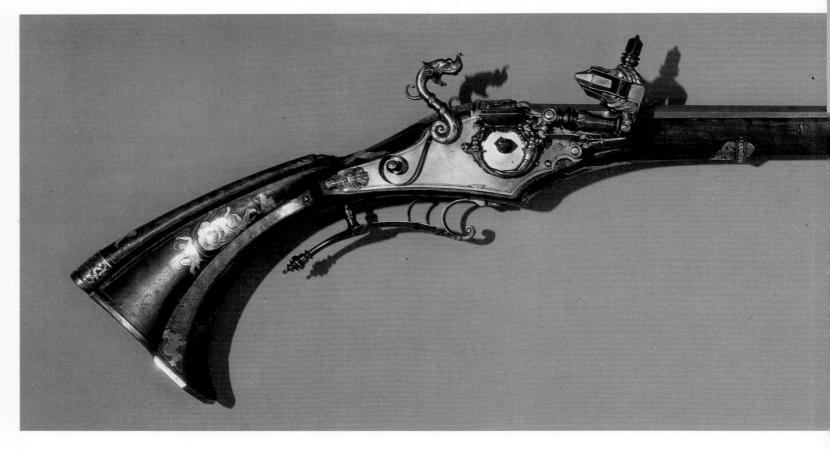

match lock fitted in case of ultimate failure or possibly just in case the firer lost the lock winding key.

The wheellocks that have survived are, in many cases, of the highly decorative type and not in the least suitable for the common soldier. The wheellock was therefore not a general issue weapon. It had a somewhat delicate mechanism and a loose winding key. As with many new devices it became the toy of the rich and those that survive have in many cases been handed down in families through the years.

The next major change occurred when the pistol became a practical possibility and double-barrelled versions as well as superimposed load types were developed. Also, because of the ease of concealment of the pistol, gun laws were passed for the first time by Emperor Maximilian I. Some rulers went as far as to ban the production of concealable pistols. Disastrous results from the accidental firing of a pistol were much publicized.

There would seem to be little connection between a Dutch hen and a firearm, but the 'snapshaan' or 'peck-

Above: It is a comment on the reliability of the older types of ignition system that duplex locks combining two methods were sometimes used. This long gun made in about 1620 in Italy combines wheellock and matchlock ignition. The decoration has earned this gun the name 'Naughty Gun'.

Below: A Miquelet pistol showing the externally mounted lock mechanism. The ramrod is double-ended and can do duty as a simple ramrod (right-hand end) or a bullet extractor (left-hand end).

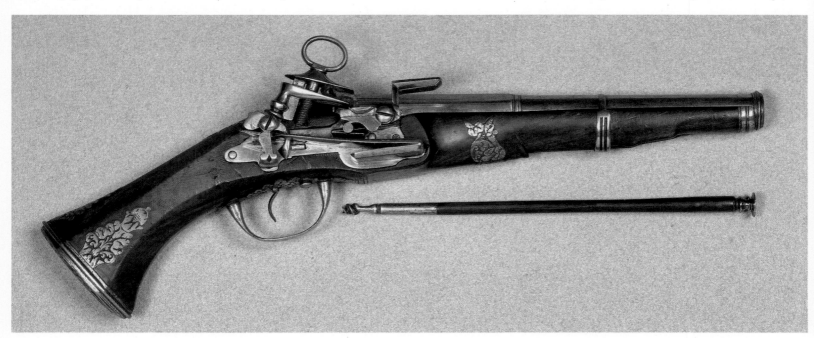

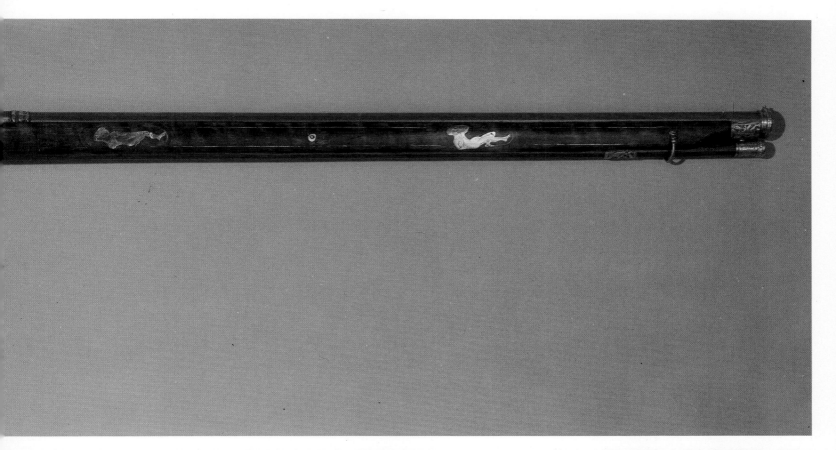

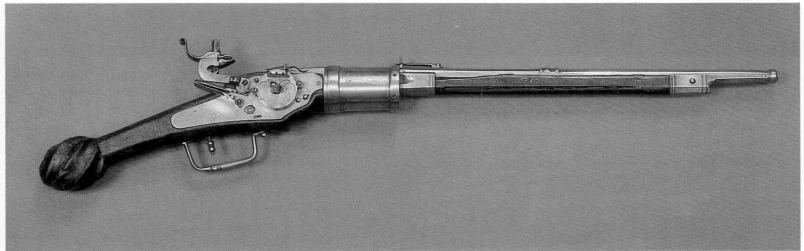

Above: A wheellock revolver. This pistol, while still being hand-rotated and having the problems of priming multiple chambers, was a practical attempt at a multi-fire weapon. The ball butt has been ornately carved, which can have contributed little to an already uncomfortable grip. This pistol is from the Tower of London collection.

ing hen' gave its name to the next development in the lock system. The Snaphance or Snaphaunce dispensed with the complex spring-turned wheel of the wheellock and substituted a much simpler mechanism. The basis for this early form of flintlock, and for that matter all flintlocks, was the striking action employed when using a flint and steel by hand. The cock, which on the wheellock had contained the pyrites or flint, was spring loaded in the manner of the snapping matchlock. The steel was hinged over the priming pan so that when struck by the flint it pivoted back directing the sparks into the pan. The pan cover was a separate unit and on later pistols complex linkages were used to open it

as the cock fell and the frizzen or steel was driven back. The Snaphance originated traditionally in the Netherlands but other parts of Europe have claims just as valid according to some experts. One thing is certain: the lock was first manufactured in the 1640s.

A parallel line of development was taking place elsewhere. The Mediterranean coast saw the evolution of another type of flintlock known as the Mediterranean or Miquelet lock. The Miquelet was an odd combination of advanced and retrograde features. The internal mainspring of the Snaphance was deleted and a massive external spring substituted, which could be considered retrograde. But the development which was really important

Above: These pistols from the Wallace Collection in London are of Italian manufacture in the period 1650–60. The decorated locks are of the Snaphance type. These pistols exhibit the use of metal not only for construction but also for decoration.
Right: a Miquelet lock pistol with a profusion of metal inlays. The butt shape, while allowing scope for decoration, is not altogether practical. The barrel is sharply tapered, terminating in a bell-mouth. This became known later as a Blunderbuss barrel.

Left: The lock of a British Brown Bess musket. It is shown with the pan cover closed and the trigger in the firing position.

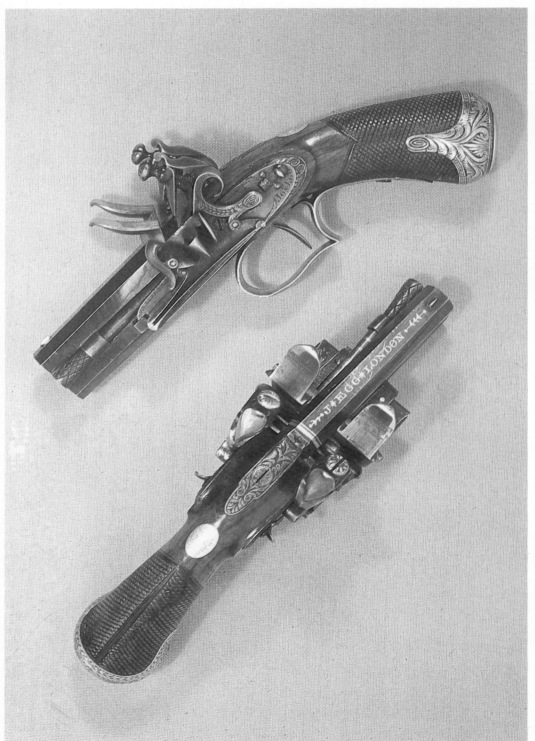

Above: A good example of a flintlock is this Millar's Patent detachable cannon lock. These locks were removed from the guns for safety and to prevent damage. Part of the gunner's job on board ship was to have the locks ready to fit if danger loomed.

Left: The epitomy of high-class pocket pistols were of the type manufactured by J. Egg in 1823–24. These over-and-under double-barrelled flintlock pistols, while perhaps being a little bulky because of the twin locks, would give any gentleman a feeling of security. The finish and decoration is in the tradition of the best hand-gun.
Opposite: A pair of brass-barrelled flintlock pistols. These pistols from the Victoria and Albert Museum collection were made by Moore and display interesting ornamentation. The opposite side of the woodwork to the lock also has interesting decoration.

was the combination of the frizzen and pan cover. It may appear obvious today, but this apparently simple discovery was a major step towards the final flintlock development. The frizzen was manufactured in an L shape so that the base covered the pan. When the vertical face was struck by the flint, the hinge allowed the pan to become open and the sparks to be directed into it. This development, brought about probably by the Spanish, made firearms reliable even in adverse conditions.

Other developments in the Normandy area of France led to the final form of flintlock. This lock is known as the French or true flintlock and combines the best features of the Snaphance and the Miquelet locks. The internal spring of the Snaphance was amalgamated with the combined steel and pan cover of the Miquelet. Additionally, and of just as much importance, was the change of the sear from a horizontal action to a vertical one. This important step led to the adoption of the half-cock position which en-

abled the weapon to be carried relatively safely but also to be brought quickly to full-cock for firing. The true flintlock was to remain in use for both military and sporting use well after the general adoption of percussion ignition at the beginning of the 19th century.

The division of development into the three groups, Snaphance, Miquelet and true flintlock, is to some extent arbitrary and the terms are of modern application. The development was fragmented and various combinations of the features outside these groups are to be found.

The use of fulminates

The foundation of the final development that was to bring the ignition system into the present day was the fulminates, particularly gold, silver, platinum and mercury. These fulminates are extremely sensitive to both temperature and percussion. As their burning rate is extremely high they are of no use as propellants. This fact was overlooked by early investigators who suffered blackened faces and burst

gunbarrels to say nothing of the disaster caused by an explosion. Samuel Pepys recorded the 'flash and bang' of the explosion of small quantities of fulminate in 1663. Experiments such as putting a small amount in the bottom of a teaspoon and heating it over a candle abounded, as did the stock of teaspoons with neat holes in the bowl!

The problem was solved by a Scottish clergyman and involved using the fulminate as an initiator or primer and the normal black powder as the propellant. The Reverend James Forsyth took over the Church of Belhelvie in Aberdeenshire in 1790 after the death of his father. With good duck shooting in the locality, Forsyth was soon struck by a problem. When the trigger of a flintlock was pulled there was the flash of the priming then, after a short delay, the propellant ignited. This flash frightened the birds and the delay made wing shooting very difficult indeed. Forsyth determined to improve the action and experimented with fulminates. He soon identified the two main requirements: safe storage and

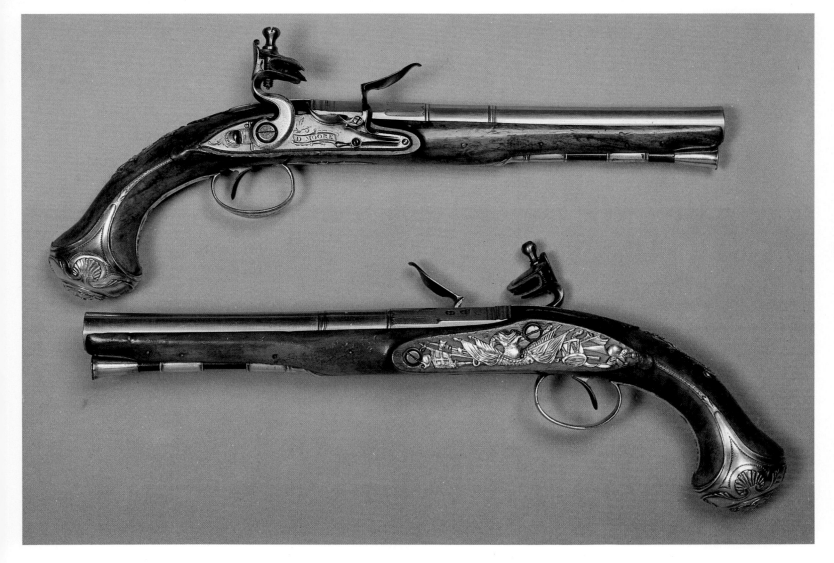

Right: With the advent of the rifled barrel the flintlock pistol became an accurate close-range weapon. This pistol by Hess of Zweidbruken was manufactured in the mid-18th century. The use of a detachable shoulder stock was to be copied by Mauser and Luger.

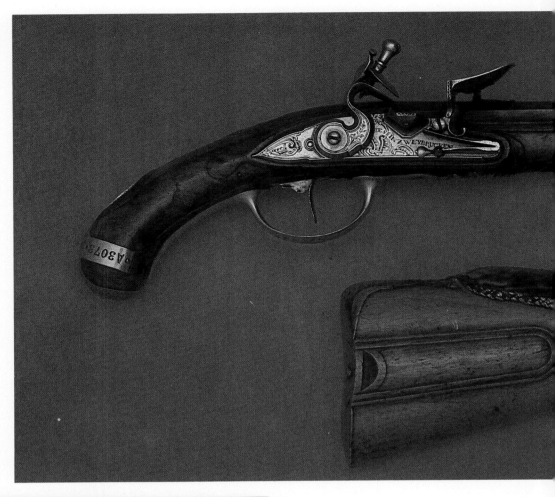

Below: A simple robust Austrian flintlock manufactured in about 1680. The hammer is forward and the trigger is in the fired position.

Below: Although manufactured at a much later date this flintlock has decoration that is typical of the 17th century. This style of metallic decoration was favoured by Bulkan and Turkish makers.

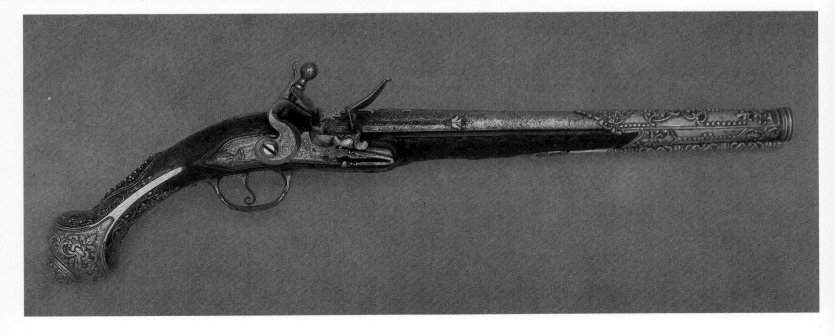

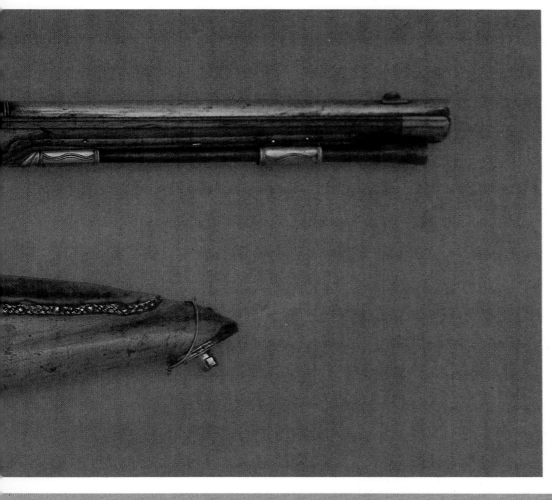

Below: A percussion pistol of the military type, one of the muzzle loading sort. The rammer under the bottom pistol has a 'corkscrew' type attachment for withdrawing an unfired ball.

J. S. Pauly patented an early centrefire breech-loading system. These cased pistols use the Pauly system, which was patented in 1812. The decoration and presentation are of the highest quality.

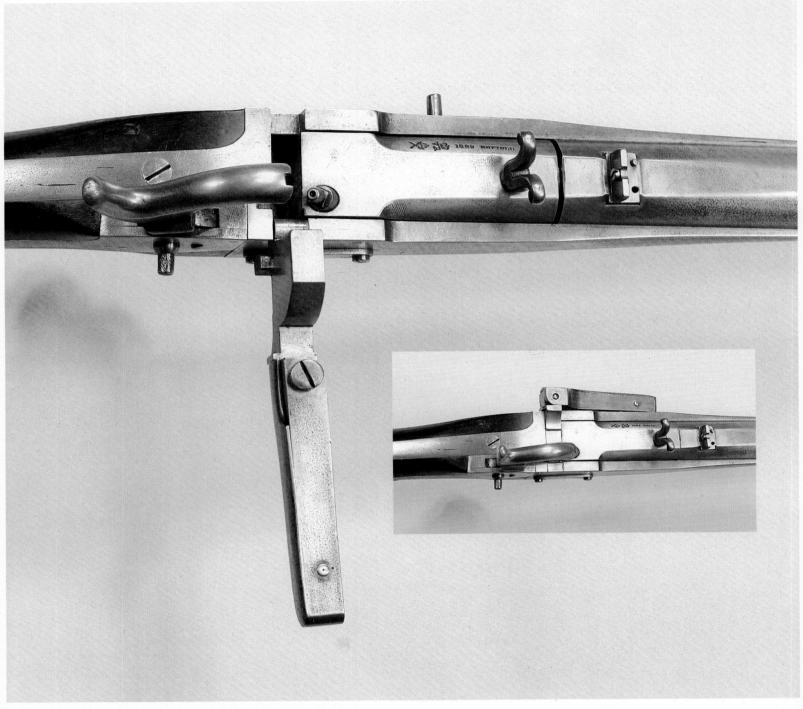

exact measurement of the amount of fulminate.

His first solution was a magazine attached to the gun with a sliding top, the operation of which measured the required amount into the position for the hammer to strike it. This was superseded by the 'scent bottle' lock, so-called because of its shape. The fulminate was contained in the base and when the bottle was turned over on a pivot the fulminate was measured into the top and left there as the bottle was returned to the vertical position. This lock gave a practical percussion ignition system. It attracted some support from the government of the day and Forsyth himself used the services of

James Purdie to manufacture firearms of his design with his lock. But the lock was not a military possibility because it was fragile.

A patent was taken out in 1807 and became a master patent covering not only the 'scent bottle' but a variety of pinfire and centrefire applications. This, unfortunately, held back the work of others and slowed finalization of the type.

The last use of a percussion compound before the cartridge evolved took the form of a percussion cap. A patent was taken out by Joshua Shaw in the United States in 1822 although he had been working on this much earlier. And there were attempts by

Above: Many attempts were made early on to manufacture efficient breech-loaders. Most suffered problems of inefficient sealing of the breech. This particular example in the Tower of London collection is lever operated.

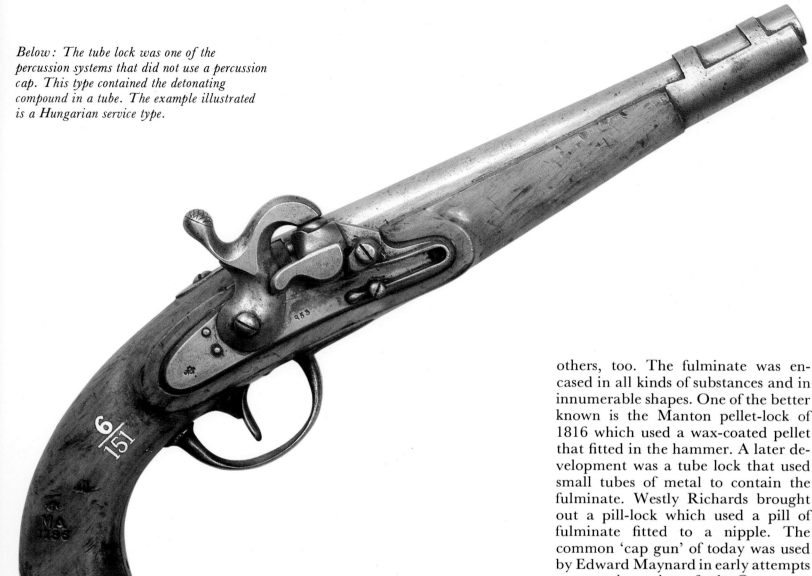

Below: The tube lock was one of the percussion systems that did not use a percussion cap. This type contained the detonating compound in a tube. The example illustrated is a Hungarian service type.

others, too. The fulminate was encased in all kinds of substances and in innumerable shapes. One of the better known is the Manton pellet-lock of 1816 which used a wax-coated pellet that fitted in the hammer. A later development was a tube lock that used small tubes of metal to contain the fulminate. Westly Richards brought out a pill-lock which used a pill of fulminate fitted to a nipple. The common 'cap gun' of today was used by Edward Maynard in early attempts at repeating-primer feeds. One enterprising inventor, perhaps more correctly described as intrepid, used a straw from which the correct length was cut with each shot. But Joshua Shaw's patent was the true percussion cap which would take the world into the cartridge era.

Below: The Forsyth 'scent bottle' lock, so-called because of its shape. It was the forerunner of all percussion systems. Although too fragile for military use many sporting guns used the system.

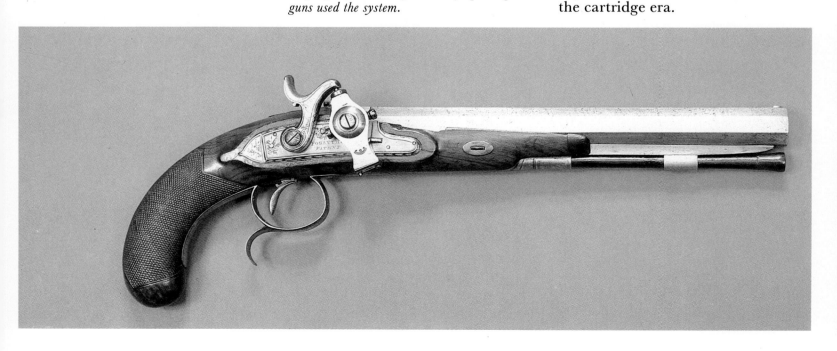

Inventors & Manufacturers

The history of the world has been changed significantly by relatively few famous names. Numbered amongst such people are some of the world's firearms designers and manufacturers. To include all manufacturers and designers would fill a very large book in itself and therefore some names that may have claims to fame may not be included here.

When the Reverend James Forsyth invented the percussion system he started the development of the modern firearm. In America the cowboy, Red Indian and bandit used the guns of Colt, Winchester, and Smith and Wesson. These names applied not only to the company but also to the founder and often the designer as well.

In the field of sporting guns the name of the manufacturer is often a guarantee of excellence and, to some, a symbol of status. To hold and use, let alone own, guns from such makers as Holland and Holland, Purdey or Dickson is a pleasure in itself for many people. And the target shot will know well the firms of Hammerli, Walther and Anschutz, while on other parts of the range pistols, rifles and shotguns from Ruger, SIG and High Standard will almost certainly be in use.

While soldiers may not know, nor really care, who makes their rifles or submachine guns, it is testimony to great designers such as Browning, Stoner and others that firms such as Armalite and Fabrique Nationale have flourished. Some weapons have even become known not by the set of figures and initials often imposed by governments but by the manufacturer's name. One such weapon, for example, is the Sterling submachine gun.

This list has, of necessity, to be heavily selective, yet most of the famous, infamous and important personalities and companies are described in this chapter.

Anschutz

In the 19th century Zella-Mehlis enjoyed a reputation for manufacturing high-quality firearms. Such firms as Walther made it their base and in 1856 Julius Gottfried Anschutz set up a factory there to produce high-quality sporting and target weapons.

The firm expanded and achieved a name for excellence. The two world wars interrupted the flow of target and sporting guns and with the Russian occupation of the Thuringia area the factory was destroyed and its staff dispersed.

It was not until 1950 that Max and Rudolf Anschutz, who had run the factory during the war but who resided in the West, set up a new factory in Ulm. This concern, now run by Dieter Anschutz, has specialized in the production of .22 target rifles and .177 target air rifles. The weapons have not only won many gold medals in all forms of competition but also hold many world records. Sporting rifles, all of the highest quality, are also produced.

Armalite

Occasionally the name of a manufacturing company becomes almost a generic term. It happened with the Colt-produced M16, which had been designed and developed at Armalite.

The Armalite business was formed by Charles Dorchester and George Sullivan to produce a line of sporting firearms that would embody the new techniques and materials available in the 1950s. It became part of the Fairchild Engine and Airplane Company in 1954. The first weapon designed by the original company in 1947 was not produced.

Armalite employed Eugene Stoner, a talented ex-Marine, who became their chief engineer and one of the top designers of the century. An early success was the American government's interest in the development of a survival rifle which led

Opposite: John Moses Browning, the greatest gun designer of modern times. With help from his brother he designed and manufactured prototypes of every type of weapon, both sporting and military.

33

the company to concentrate primarily on the military market.

One of their projects was the AR10 rifle. Although never produced in large numbers it was to be the basis for the AR15/M16 rifle. This, as with all weapons designed by Armalite, was not produced by them but by another firm. The development of the 5.56mm cartridge by Remington and the AR15 led to the licensing of Colt in 1959 to manufacture guns which achieved the highest production of any Western weapon. A weapon produced in prototype form was the AR16. This was after Stoner's departure in 1961 and was to be developed into the AR18.

Astra Unceta y Cia

The name of Astra has been associated with their 'water pistol' shaped handguns for many years, but with the introduction of a superior .357 revolver they moved into the class of weapons often held to be the preserve of the Americans. The quality is what one would expect from a top Spanish firm and compares favourably with any in the world.

In 1908 Pedro Unceta and Juan Esperenza set up a company to produce firearms. Unceta handled the administration and Esperenza the production side of the company that bore their names. In 1913 the company changed its name to Esperenza y Unceta. The name of Astra was registered as the company trade mark in 1914 and in 1926, as the family of Unceta were the major shareholders, the name was changed to Unceta y Compania. Astra was added to reflect its importance as the name by which the products were known to the public. The company became Astra Unceta y Cia.

The pistols produced by the company were manufactured initially under a series of different names, often dependent on the intended market. The first was the Victoria, a simple blowback design. This was followed by the first of the 'water pistol' types, the model 400 that was marketed under the Astra banner. This pistol and its bigger brother, the 600, were used extensively by the German forces during World War II. So highly regarded were these weapons that the Germans did not require separate proofing on acceptance. The Campogiro was produced for a short time in a variety of models; small Browning-type pistols were also produced. A noteworthy contract of modern origin was the supply of the pocket Astra Cub to Colt for retail under the Colt Junior name. One interesting model was the Mauser Broomhandle copy that took the concept further in the rapid fire version by incorporating a rate reducer. Quality was as usual of very high standard.

The Astra firm has supplied the military, police and sportsman with pistols of quality for 70 years.

Right: The Beretta Model 12 is the standard submachine gun of the Italian army. It is also produced under licence by FN in Belgium as the FN-Beretta.

Berdan, Colonel H.

Hiram Berdan was a soldier who rose to the rank of colonel in the American army. He fought in the Civil War and formed his own band of sharp-shooters much to the discomfort of the enemy. During the period 1865–97 he also worked on the development of weapons and cartridges. The primer type that is named after him while not being, as is often supposed, his invention, was developed by him into a practical type. Its success may be measured by the fact that this primer type was developed in America and used in Europe instead of the British-developed Boxer type.

Beretta

Few companies in the world can claim to have been established as early as 1680 and fewer still can boast that they have been under the control of the same family for their total existence. Beretta was founded by Pietro Beretta in a remote valley of Gardone in the mountains of northern Italy. The area had been known for its weapons from the early 15th century, and the door lintel of the original Beretta forge which incorporated the present building dates from the year 1500.

The weapons supplied by the firm to the Venetian fleets soon proved so effective and of such quality that the republic of Venice took the Gardone area under its protection and control to ensure the supply of arms.

The Beretta families have always been blessed with large numbers of children and as the business grew and prospered it was handed down from father to son. When the Venetian republic came to an end in the 19th century the firm broadened its production from military weapons alone to the design and manufacture of sporting weapons as well.

The first of the modern production plants was set up in 1880 and by 1903 some 100 employees were at work. The first part of the 20th century saw sustained growth of both military and sporting weapons. It is worthy of note that the plant remained intact in World War II and never ceased production during that time.

Today the Beretta plant covers 49,000 square

metres, employs more than 16,000 people and has the very latest in production machinery, much of which is designed inside the factory. The Beretta family are proud of the fact that every part of all the weapons produced, from the smallest screw to the wooden stock, are made within the factory. Sporting weapons of all types are included in the Beretta range of shotguns, rifles and pistols. The Italian armed forces are equipped with Beretta weapons.

Bergman, T.
Theodor Bergman, an industrialist, owned a large factory that manufactured hardware. In the early 1890s he decided to venture into the field of firearms and in 1894 adopted the design of Lois Schmeisser for his first pistol. Although the name of Schmeisser does not appear on later patents his son Hugo was helped by the Bergman firm in the development of the MP18 submachine gun. The Bergman-designed pistols were manufactured by a number of other firms such as Pieper under the Bayard name.

Large numbers of models of the pistols were produced, none of which attained real quantity. A line of cartridges made for these pistols was noteworthy for the lack of means to extract them. The only success was the 9mm Bergman Bayard or 9mm Largo. The firm went on producing pistols after Bergman's death, but the name disappeared in the late 1930s. Bergman himself was active over the period 1894–1903.

Bernardelli
This family firm is based in the centre of the Italian gun manufacturing area of Gardone. It was founded in 1865 by Vincenzo Bernardelli who, not satisfied with his job in a local factory, decided to start his own business.

The first products of the small firm were barrels of the Damascus type, but after a few years it was decided to produce complete weapons. Equipment for this was not available so actions were purchased from Belgium and married to Bernardelli barrels at the factory. The family, which consisted of four brothers and their father, decided to expand. Land and a proper workshop were purchased in the early 1900s. This was a brave decision as much of the home market was, at that time, dominated by imports. The purchase was more than justified as the present company headquarters are on the same land.

World War I brought expansion which continued afterwards. The model 89 revolver was added to the range of shotguns. World War II brought the usual wartime demands and subsequent postwar problems of reorganization.

The production of a new range of pistols during the immediate postwar era was very successful and the export market continued to be the main source of revenue. The Italian market began to expand, particularly in the field of the high-quality shotgun, which continued to be manufactured by using large quantities of skilled

Below: This Bergman-Bayard pistol was manufactured by Pieper of Liège after Bergman himself had given up pistol production. These pistols were also known as 'Mars'.

labour rather than mechanized mass production. The late 1960s and early 1970s saw the construction of new premises to house both offices and machinery. The existing machinery was overhauled and new model lines planned.

The grandsons of the founder still control the factory and have seen its traditional products, the high quality shotguns, achieve an enviable reputation in addition to the success of the new products, both pistols and rifles.

Billinghurst, W.
William Billinghurst's claim to fame was in the development and production of the Billinghurst-Requa volley or battery gun. This primitive form of machine gun was produced in quantity in America. Billinghurst was born in 1807 and died in 1880.

Borchardt, H.
Hugo Borchardt, German-born, emigrated early in life to the United States. His career would seem to have been characterized by his inability to settle for any length of time with any one company. He worked for a few months with Colt before he joined the Sharps Rifle Company, where he designed the Sharps Borchardt rifle. Even though he was works superintendent he spent less than two years with the company before leaving to join Winchester. There he designed a number of swing-out frame revolvers that would undoubtedly have been successful but for the political decision by Winchester not to put them into production.

A stay of nearly 10 years at the Hungarian factory of FGGY in Budapest was followed by a return to the United States. In 1892 he joined the company of Ludwig Loewe where he designed the forerunner of the Luger. Borchardt continued to work for the DWM concern when they took over Loewe and worked on a number of designs. He died in 1921.

Boxer, Colonel E. M.
Edwin Boxer, a serving officer in the British army, soon acquired a notable reputation for his work in the development of weapons and ammunition. He was appointed superintendent of the Woolwich arsenal where he carried out development work on cartridges. The primer that bears his name was the result of this work and is in present use in the United States and many other countries.

Browning, J. M.
Born in 1855, son of Jonathan Browning, John Moses was to become the foremost modern gun designer. His father had been a gun designer in his own right and had produced revolving rifles as well as other weapons for the Mormon trek across America to set up a community in Utah

Above right: John Moses Browning. Many firearms in use today owe their design to Browning's genius. Right: The Browning Model 1900 or FN 1900. This was the first Browning design to be produced by the Belgian company. The cartridge, 7.65mm or .32acp, was specially designed by Browning for this pistol.

in the 19th century. With the founding of the Browning firm John and one of his brothers, Jonathan, started the production of a single-shot rifle that was adopted by Winchester. This was the first of a long line of successful weapons. Not only was John a brilliant innovator, he could also simplify the ideas of others into extremely practical forms. The hallmark of most Browning designs is the economy of components and simplicity of operation.

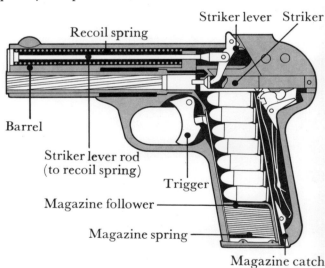

The Browning range of automatic pistols not only started trends in pocket pistol design but also brought about two designs that are still in use today. The Colt .45 and the Hi Power have armed many troops and are still standard in many countries. The range of shotguns, especially the automatic ones, were widely admired and closely copied by many companies. The machine guns, especially the renowned .30 and .50, saw service in almost every conceivable situation during World War II. The Browning automatic rifle gained a reputation for reliability and has seen use in every major conflict since 1918.

The firms of FN and Colt owe much of their success to the designs of John Browning. Perhaps his character can best be summed up by the way in which he accepted the American government's need for his designs, saying that any price that suited them suited him. His death in 1926 saw the passing of one of the greatest of all firearms designers.

BSA (Birmingham Small Arms Company)

The formation of BSA was, as with many famous manufacturers, caused by the amalgamation of a group of tradesmen. In the reign of William III there was much worry over the possibility of invasion and as many of the weapons for the army were obtained from Europe it was considered imperative to produce as many as possible in England. In 1689 the MP for Warwickshire, Sir Richard Newdegate, arranged for a group of five leading Birmingham gunsmiths to submit a trial batch of weapons for government inspection. So favourable was the reaction that weapons were provided by an ever-expanding group of gunsmiths from that area. On 7 June 1861, Birmingham Small Arms Trade Association decided to form from its 14 members the Birmingham Small Arms Company.

The company decided to mechanize the factory in order to compete with the government factory at Enfield. With the ever-present fear of war among the nations, the arms business prospered and the company expanded into the manufacture of cartridges when the name was changed to the Birmingham Small Arms and Metal Company. This was retained until the original name was revived in 1897 with the fall off in the cartridge business.

Apart from a period during the Boer War, the company's weapon production declined and the main source of income was derived from bicycle components and even cars. World War I caused expansion to fulfil huge orders for rifles and machine guns. After the war BSA Guns was formed and the business split up. The 1920s and 1930s were successfully weathered and expansion continued into other fields. The manufacture of guns was limited to small quantities of sporting rifles during this time but the onset of war once again caused the firm to return to the production of small arms of all types.

Postwar development was spectacular with the group expanding its activities. The motor cycle company, especially, prospered.

But in the 1970s the BSA empire was almost totally broken up. Holdings in many companies were sold and Manganese Bronze Holdings purchased the remaining assets. The firearms side was re-established under this company as BSA Guns Limited and is now operating profitably. It manufactures air rifles, air pistols, .22 target rifles and a line of centrefire sporting rifles.

Ceska Zbrojovka Akovia Spolecnost

The Czech Arms Factory Limited was founded in 1917–18 in Pilsen as the South Bohemian Arms Factory or Jihoceska Zbrojovka. The manager was Alois Tomiska. In 1922 the firm took over the Hubertus factory and the name was changed to Ceska Zbrojovka, with the main factory located at Strakonice. During World War II the Germans occupied the factory and kept it in production as Bohmische Waffenfabrik. In 1948 it was nationalized and the name reverted to Ceska Zbrojovka.

Ceskoslovenska Zbrojovka Akovia Spolecnost

The Czechoslovakian Arms factory was formed in an old artillery works in Brno. It was set up in 1919 under state control as the Czechoslovakian Factory for Arms Manufacture or Ceskoslovenska Zbrojovka na Vyrobu Zbrani.

Under Czech law there were problems over the export of weapons from a factory totally controlled by the government, and so the ownership was changed. The firm of Skoda took 20 per cent of the capital and a small amount went to the workforce. The name of the firm was then changed to its final form.

There is little doubt that there was close co-operation with the German firm of Mauser and that the Mauser designer Nickl worked for them. The result was a pistol that was adopted by the Czech army. The government decided that the factory should specialize in the production of rifles and machine guns and so pistol production was transferred to Ceska Zbrojovka Akovia Spolecnost.

CETME (Centro Dos Estudios Technicos de Materiales Especiales)

This is the Spanish government's weapon development agency, based in Madrid. Much of their best-known work has been carried out with the assistance of German World War II personnel. Although many experimental rifles and machine guns and ammunition have been developed one weapon has been successful above all others, and that is CETME's delayed blowback rifle.

Using the basic concept of the roller-operated two-part bolt to delay the opening of the breech the CETME engineers perfected a rifle that not only became standard as the Model C in Spain but bred the derivative, the G3.

Above: The Spanish firm of CETME made use of the design work that had been carried out by Mauser in World War II to produce this delayed blowback design. A development of this, the G3, is manufactured by Heckler and Koch and is in use in many countries.

The licence for the production of the CETME rifle was sold to the Dutch but in a complicated trade deal it was acquired by the German government who in turn passed it to the then new company of Heckler and Koch. The development of the G3 was adopted by the German forces and the company announced a range of weapons all based on the basic system. One of the better-known derivatives is the MP5 submachine gun which, because of the system, fires from a closed bolt.

Today the CETME rifle under its German alias of H & K G3 can be seen world-wide either produced by H & K or by one of the plants that have been set up in a number of countries.

Charter Arms

Charter Arms are one of the breed of modern firms that have entered the field of firearms and have, by careful analysis of the market, found a niche for themselves.

The founder of the firm was Douglas McClenahan who spent periods with other firearms manufacturers, including Ruger. The lessons learned about production methods were put to use when he opened his own factory in 1965. The basis of success for Charter Arms has been the recognition by McClenahan that there was a market for an 'Undercover' pistol for police.

The revolvers are all of the swing-out cylinder type with 2in and 3in barrels in a variety of calibres. The top of the range is the Bulldog, which combines the power of the .44 special round with a 3in (76mm) barrel and a weight of only 19oz (538g).

Chinese Pistols

Chinese weapon production has been considerable in quantity but usually lacking in originality. When the supply of pistols from other countries stopped the Chinese chose (as they did for their rifle) to adopt with little modification a Russian design. A silent pistol was developed that owed little to any other.

The standard service pistol is the Type 51 which is a locally produced version of the Soviet Tokarev TT33. It is a Browning type with the production simplified and featuring a noteworthy hammer/sear group.

The Type 64 is a silenced automatic that can have the breech locked for totally noiseless operation. By using a subsonic round, the 7.65mm × 17mm, part of the problem of silencing can be overcome. The rest of the sound and flash is contained by an integral silencer.

Churchill

The firm of Churchill was started by E. J. Churchill in 1891 in The Strand, London. Churchill had served as an apprentice at Jeffrey and Son and was well aware of the standard required for the best English shotguns. It was this ability to produce guns that the discerning shot required that brought the firm to prosperity. The Trap Pigeon gun was produced in relatively

Below: The Colt single action revolver was, even when used with cartridges, a model of simplicity. This solid-frame revolver was gate-loaded.
Below right: Samuel Colt in about 1857. A fine gun designer, he was also a showman and entrepreneur.

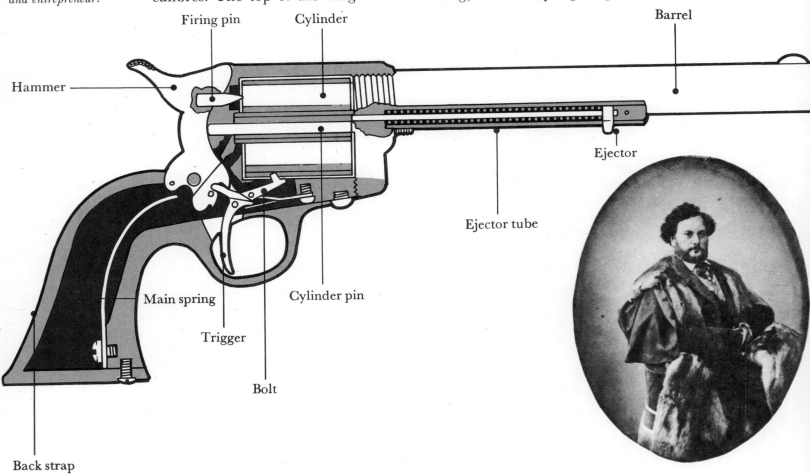

Firing pin Cylinder Barrel
Hammer
Ejector
Ejector tube
Main spring
Cylinder pin
Trigger
Bolt
Back strap

large numbers, some 750 from 1891 to 1900.

The firm began to decline as production of guns tapered off during the first part of the 20th century, and when it was sold in 1911 it was virtually bankrupt. Robert Churchill stayed with the firm and began a revival that saw the development of the famous XXV Game Gun that soon acquired an enviable reputation for excellence.

After the death of Robert Churchill in 1958 the firm was taken over by the British office of the Cummings Interarm Firm of Interarmco (UK) Limited. They decided to continue the firm under the name of Churchill (Gunmakers) Limited, under which name it trades today. The name of Churchill on an English shotgun has always meant the best.

Colt

Samuel Colt was born on 19 July 1814 and was to be instrumental in making the revolver a practical type of pistol. His first patents were taken out in the period 1835–6 and after numerous problems with the manufacture of his first designs he settled with the Patent Arms Manufacturing Company of Paterson, New Jersey. This gave the name of Paterson to the early pistols.

The American government started a trend that has never been broken of using Colt firearms for their forces when, in 1847, they asked Colt for his Dragoon model, which was produced at the Whitney factory. This prompted Colt to set up in business for himself and he did so in the same year. From this time on the development of Colt firearms was to be continuous, even after his death. A factory was opened in London in 1853 but production costs caused its closure in 1857.

Colt died in January 1862 but with the careful use of talented designers the factory went from strength to strength. The death of Colt's son, Caldwell Hart Colt, in 1894 ended the family's involvement. One of the most prominent designers used by Colt, and one who was to supply the design of the most famous automatic pistol in the world, was John Browning.

After serving its country well, not only in both world wars but also in Korea and Vietnam, the Colt company has been split into two divisions, one specifically military. Colt revolvers come in a variety of versions, some still based on the old black-powder muzzle-loading Colt. The rifles and machine guns together with the shotguns have served the military and sportsman well. All have a reputation for high quality.

Degtyarev, V.

When Vasily Degtyarev died in 1959 at the age of 69 he was a deputy of the USSR Supreme Soviet, a major general in the engineers and had won no less than four State prizes. He was born in Tula and after leaving school at the age of 11 he joined the state arsenal there. He was drafted into the army and because of his experience with armaments was sent to the Sestorets Small Arms Factory. He was later posted to the weapon test centre at Oranienbaum. Although best known for his machine gun design Degtyarev also designed a submachine gun, the PPD34/38 which was followed by the PPD1940. An anti-tank rifle was another wartime design.

Derringer, H.

Henry Derringer, born at the beginning of the 19th century, may never have managed to achieve great success with his firearms, but his name lives on as the generic term for the small pocket pistol of the single or double shot type. Derringer worked in Philadelphia where he manufactured pocket pistols. Derringer died in 1869.

John Dickson

Many famous early gunmakers were Scots and one firm that has achieved fame with their Round Action is John Dickson. The firm was first established in Edinburgh in 1820 by John Dickson. It was best known for its fine flintlock and percussion shotguns and rifles. The flintlock may well have been out of date but the company had many requests for it.

By a series of takeovers the firm absorbed some of the other famous names in Scottish gun-making. In 1934 the business of Mortimer and Son was taken over, to be followed by James MacNaughton in 1947 and in 1962 Alex Martin.

Today John Dickson is owned by a consortium of businessmen whose hobbies are shooting and fishing. The Round Action, which had not been made for a number of years, is now said to be back in production; as with all fine guns some two years elapse from the placing of an order until delivery. Considering the fact that the Round Action was originally patented before the turn of the century, it is a tribute to its excellence that it is still a much-prized gun.

Dimancea, H.

Haralamb Dimancea is known for his revolver designs which, although never produced in quantity, are of interest from a design point of view. He was born in 1855 and attained the rank of captain in the Roumanian artillery. Diman-cea's revolvers had a barrel and cylinder that were both swung sideways for loading instead of just the cylinder as in the more conventional type.

DISA (Dansk Industri Syndikat)

W. O. H. Madsen worked in conjunction with Julius Rasmussen who was director of the Royal Military Arms factory. His name has been given to both the weapons produced by DISA and more often than not to the firm itself.

The founding of Dansk Rekylriffel Syndikat in 1890 to develop and produce automatic rifles of the recoil type led in 1896 to the company being incorporated. The patents taken out by Rasmussen were transferred to the company and the result was a recoil-operated rifle. The development of a light machine gun in 1904 was to prove so successful that it was adopted by more than 25 countries. Also developed was a tripod which was to feature prominently in the future.

In 1936 the factory changed its name to Dansk Industri Syndikat and after the disruption of the war years the company resumed production of small arms, in particular a sub-machine gun, and also such items as medical equipment and petrol pumps. The technical director of the firm, an ex-Olympic rifle shot, Saetter-Iassen, developed a very good general purpose light machine gun which was judged to be a serious competitor to the FN MAG. The fact that neither this weapon nor a light rifle was developed undoubtedly contributed to the company's decision to give up the manufacture of small arms.

Today the firm is better known for its tripods, which are standard equipment for the German Army's MG1. Machine gun links are also manu-factured. The Madsen, a reliable and effective weapon, may not have been produced for some time but the gun is still seen occasionally.

Dreyse, J. N.

Although time proved the Needle gun to be in-efficient and its cartridge unsuited for development, Johann Nikolas von Dreyse's invention made the bolt action military a practical weapon. Dreyse was born in 1787. In his younger days he worked with Pauly, but by 1831 he had patented his needlefire cartridge in England and in 1835 the bolt action Zundnadelgewehr or Needle gun was in production. Despite its faults, the weapon was adopted by the Prussian army and was proved to have decided advantages over the muzzle loaders used by other European armies. Dreyse died in 1867.

DWM (Deutsche Waffen und Munitions-fabriken)

The history of the DWM enterprise also involves the firm of BKIW who, for a short time, used their own name, Berlin Karlsruher Industrie Werke, and later a combination of the names before reverting to the original. The present day company with origins in DWM is IWK, Indus-trie Werke Karlsruhe Aktiengesellschaft.

In 1883 Deutsche Metallpatronenfabrik Lorenz began to manufacture cartridges and continued to do so until Lorenz sold the firm to Ludwig Loewe and Company in 1889. Loewe dropped Lorenz from the name. In 1896 the firm was renamed DWM and acquired from Loewe its shares in the Waffenfabrik Mauser concern.

Throughout the prewar years and World War I the firm expanded with the production of ammunition and weapons for the German forces. By 1915 production from the various factories amounted to 1,400 rifles, 700 pistols (the Luger) and 200,000 cartridges. Between 1933 and 1936 the company for a short time assumed the BKIW name but then reverted to DWM. World War II saw massive production of all types of war materials but after 1945 the combine was dissolved through the confiscation or destruction of its various factories.

By 1947 production had started again in a small way and when the firm once again became properly established the name was changed, in 1949, to Industrie-Werke Aktiengesellschaft or IWK. Reorganization and rebuilding took place and by 1952 production of hunting ammunition was in progress. Today the firm, as its founders intended, still produces cartridges for both sporting and military use.

Enfield

The formation at Enfield of the Royal Small Arms Factory in England was a result of the intention to assemble parts manufactured by outside contractors. This continued from its foundation in 1804 until 1854 when the government decided that they should have a fully mechanized factory capable of supplying the army. This mechanization was brought about by the purchase of American machinery and technical know-how.

The factory's fortunes have fluctuated as the demand for weapons has ebbed and flowed. The Martini-Enfields, Lee-Enfields and SMLEs equipped the British army in its most troubled times.

Unfortunately, because of the inevitable political wrangling that surrounds the adoption of new concepts of small arms in the unified Western countries, the postwar developments, the EM1 and EM2, saw no production although they broke new ground in weapon design. The decision to adopt the FN-designed rifle led to the factory tooling up and producing a slightly modified version.

Today the Enfield-designed 4.85mm rifle and light support weapons are taking part in the NATO trials, and one can only hope for their adoption in whatever calibre is chosen. Enfield produce a number of different weapons for riot control and for sniper duty.

ERMA (Erfurter Maschinenfabrik Berthold Geipel 'Erma Werke')

The disbanding of the armament industries after World War I caused many competent specialists in this field to look for other employment. One such man was Berthold Geipel who had been director of the main arsenal at Erfurt and which had been closed in 1919. He decided to return to the industry he knew and formed Erma in 1924.

Heinrich Vollmer joined the company and, in association with Geipel, designed and patented a submachine gun that was to have the basic operating system which was retained throughout the Erma range. The Vollmer and its derivatives the EMP were used in small quantities by the German army as well as by other countries.

The German High Command did not order any submachine guns during the build-up of armaments before the Munich crisis, but in 1938 they ordered production of a design from Erma that was available almost immediately. So the German army was equipped with their standard submachine gun, the MP38 and MP40. After the war, Erma was re-established in Bavaria in 1951 resuming development of small arms and prototype submachine guns.

Federov, V. G.

Born in 1874, in St Petersburg, Vladimir Grigorevitch Federov was to become chief of the Russian small arms design office. He entered the Artillery Academy in 1897 and graduated three

Below: A design for the 1980s, the Enfield 4.85mm rifle is the British entry for the NATO trials. It is a bull-pup, that is, it lacks a butt and the magazine is behind the pistol grip.

years later. His early work on designs, while establishing his technical ability, did not lead to any weapons being adopted. He became a captain in the guards and when the small arms design office was opened at the Kovrov Small Arms Factory he became its chief. He fostered the work of other designers such as Degtyarev.

FN (Fabrique Nationale d'Armes de Guerre)

In Belgium in 1889 a number of factories and individuals decided to form a combine to produce a new rifle required by the government. Several well-known names were in the original group – Henri Pieper, August Francotte, Emile Nagant and Leon Nagant. As no mass-production facilities or machinery, far less a design, were available, and as the American firm of Pratt and Whitney could not help, FN approached Ludwig Loewe of Berlin. The order for 150,000 rifles enabled FN to purchase the necessary machinery, materials and technical assistance from the German firm. The cartridge manufacturing facility was set up in a similar manner with the help of Deutsche Metall-patronenfabrik.

FN prospered and with the payment of $2,000 to John Browning for his Model 1900 pistol, they started an association that was to be mutually very profitable. Although best known for pistols, rifles, shotguns and machine guns the FN factory also produced bicycles, motorcycles, cars and armoured vehicles.

Fosbery, G. V.

George Vincent Fosbery was born in 1834, the son of a minister. After joining the army he served in India at a time which saw the Indian Mutiny. He rose to the rank of lieutenant colonel and won a Victoria Cross for a brave attack on a fortified hill. During his time in the army he worked on a number of ideas but it was not until his retirement in 1877 that he took out several patents for pistols.

Below: Gabbett-Fairfax designs made for very powerful handguns. Mars pistols such as the 8mm version shown here, were complex weapons. Not only were such guns uncomfortable, the recoil upon firing was enormous.

Gabbett-Fairfax, H. W.

Not until the invention of the modern large magnum pistol cartridges was the power of the Mars pistol, invented by Gabbett-Fairfax, surpassed. Hugh William Gabbett-Fairfax took out a number of patents during 1895–1900 for his massive Mars hand cannon. The guns were far from successful commercially and were described in one report as being so unpleasant to fire that no soldier wanted a second shot.

Garand, John C.

When it entered service with the American army in 1936, the Garand rifle was the world's first self-loading rifle which was to see full service issue. The design survived the war and was used basically for the M14 rifle.

John Garand was born in 1888 in Quebec but 10 years later he moved to Connecticut. His first employment was with a cotton mill where he showed his mechanical aptitude by taking out his first patent at the age of 13. During World War I he became interested in gun design and submitted a design for a machine gun in 1916. The government were impressed enough to employ him and he went to the Springfield armoury in 1919. He was to remain until his retirement in 1953.

The original design concept that he worked on was the primer action of the breech mechanism. This has never proved feasible for a mass-produced weapon as the ammunition has to be produced to a very high standard. The rifles T1920, M1921 and M1924 were superseded by the T3 which was to become the M1 Garand. The M1 was developed by 1931 and entered service in 1936. Garand must have regarded with pride the gun that no one called the M1 but just simply the Garand.

Gatling, R. J.

Born in North Carolina in 1818, Richard Jordan Gatling was, like his father, originally an agricultural machinery designer and engineer. Although he started developing his hand-cranked machine gun in the 1850s and had his first patent in 1862 the weapon was not very successful because of the paper cartridges used. He launched a massive publicity campaign to show his weapon's potential to stop wars, but it had little success and few of his guns were sold. In 1867 Colt started to manufacture a modified version with a metallic cartridge. This became a success and was adopted by the American government.

A number of countries purchased guns including Armstrong of England and Paget of Austria, who manufactured the gun under licence. Gatling died in 1903 and so did not see the final use to which the Gatling gun was put. A development of the electrically driven Gatling type of machine gun has seen use in modern

Left: The Patent Model 1862 Gatling gun. Although of relatively crude construction it has all the features that made the Gatling a success. The basics are still employed in rapid-fire aircraft cannon which are fitted in many present-day military aircraft.

fighter aircraft. One of the original Colt Gatlings was the prototype for this development.

Geco (Dynamit-Nobel-Genschow)

The firm of Gustav Genschow was formed in Berlin by Karl Gustav Genschow in 1887. It is better known as Geco, and has used this name as a trade mark and as part of its trading title at various times.

The early years are noteworthy for the number of takeovers and mergers, the most important of which was the amalgamation with Badische Munitionsfabrik which had already absorbed a number of smaller firms. This merger was in 1906 and the name of the joint firm was Gustav Genschow.

Before World War I a subsidiary was opened in Austria and in the interwar years others were opened in Argentina, Brazil and Chile. An agreement to cooperate with RWS was also formed although this was terminated in 1927.

After the war, during which Genschow and Company had expanded and supplied large quantities of military munitions, the company was reformed. In 1959 the shares were taken over by Dynamit-Nobel Aktiengesellschaft. It was decided to incorporate the two companies under one heading and so in 1962 the firm of Dynamit-Nobel-Genschow GmbH was formed. This firm still supplies cartridges for both military contracts and sportsmen.

Gevelot

This company, which was to become the largest ammunition company in France, began in the back garden of a house near the Bourse in Paris. Although the firm had been manufacturing small arms for some time, it was not until 1820 that the production of mercuric percussion caps was started. Production of cartridges did not start until 1840 when a factory at Issy les Moulineaux was opened. The factory at first produced pinfire cartridges but as the centrefire priming system was perfected by then this type of ammunition was produced as well.

Gevelot, the founder, took out a number of patents on shotgun cartridges between 1855 and 1865. They incorporated the battery cup primer system into the now normal paper-based case thus finalizing the design as it is known today. In modern times this company became the first in Europe to adopt the plastic case.

Production of military cartridges was started and French government technicians spent much time at the factory before they instituted their own production of metallic cartridges. Today the company produces a range of shotgun ammunition second to none and also a line of metallic cartridges ranging from saloon cartridges to all calibres of pistol ammunition. It also has a military contract for other types.

Carl Gustafs-FFV

Although the manufacture of firearms was not begun until 1813 the Carl Gustafs factory was started when the Swedish king, Carl Gustaf X, gave his warrant to Reinhold Rademacher to set up an iron foundry at Eskilstuna in 1620.

The Gevarsfaktoreit ('weapon factory') was started in Soderhamn in 1654. The present factory dates from 1813 when the work was transferred to near Eskilstuna. Production was on a relatively large scale and the weapons produced were of the flintlock type.

By 1840 the Swedish army had adopted a percussion rifle and Carl Gustafs were contracted to produce it. The factory continued to prosper and adopted new design features as they appeared. By 1867 the adoption of a Remington rifle meant that the factory had to be changed into a mass production concern. This was emphasized by the introduction of yet another rifle, the M96. Production facilities were modelled to a large extent on that of Mauser.

World War I saw the delivery of large quantities of weapons, including rifles as well as machine guns. During this period the firm was taken over by the state-owned Forsvarets Fabrikverk (later to be Forenade Fabriksverken or FFV). After the war the firm still manufactured weapons but diversified into other products for such industries as car manufacturing. In 1969 a new factory was built at Svista near Eskilstuna which contained the most modern computer-controlled machinery. Its products include the famous Carl Gustafs antitank weapon, military weapons built under licence and internationally recognized sporting and target rifles.

Hammerli

There can be no target shot in the world who has not heard of or coveted the products of the Hammerli factory. Hammerli weapons have always been the epitome of Swiss precision engineering ability. They are always expensive but the shooter is paying for the best.

The firm was founded to produce rifle barrels for the Swiss army by the mayor of Lenzburg, Johann Ulrich Hammerli, a master locksmith. The Hammerli family were to run the factory until 1946. Johann died in 1891 and his son Jennot together with a new partner Hausch ran the factory until 1934 when Jennot's son Rudolf took over. It was Rudolf's death in 1946 which prompted the family to sell the firm.

The new company expanded into the heavy commercial vehicle trade but the target pistol and rifle side of the business was not neglected. When the Swiss won the first world championship in France it was with Hammerli target rifles. Under the new company a sales outlet was established in West Germany.

In 1971 the firm of SIG, known for its high quality of weapon production, took a majority shareholding in Hammerli. This marriage is a happy one with both contributing to the other's joint well-being. Today the joint range of pistols and rifles still display the attention to detail and reliable construction which makes them often a necessity on the firing range.

Heckler and Koch

After World War II, when the Russians insisted that the French occupation of the old Mauser factory at Oberndorf-Neckar be brought to an end, and production cease, they also stipulated that the factory be dismantled. This led to the highly skilled workforce being scattered throughout Europe. Amongst those displaced persons was Herr Volgrimmler who had been a member of the design team at work on rifle projects. He eventually went to work for the Spanish firm of CETME where he helped in the development of the roller delayed blowback system that was to characterize the weapons from that organization.

In Germany three men and a financier decided in 1948 to start a firm to manufacture sewing machines. They were all experienced in the weapon field and they wished eventually to move to that area. Edmond Heckler had been a plant manager, Theodore Koch a plant manager with Mauser, and Alex Seidel a designer with Mauser. By 1952 the firm had grown and were not only producing sewing machines but also engineering components under contract. One such contract was for components for the CETME rifle.

When the German army decided to re-equip with modern weapons the licence for the production of the CETME was granted to Heckler and Koch. Two years later, after extensive development work, the weapon was in production for the German army. The G3 has proved one of the most successful rifles of recent times and has been sold and manufactured under licence throughout the world.

The firm has continued to prosper and now produces a complete range of small arms from pistols through SMGs to rifles and LMGs. All have a family resemblance, using the roller delayed blowback system. The entry of the only non-conventional weapon, a rifle firing caseless ammunition, in NATO trials demonstrates the continual development that makes Heckler and Koch one of the world's best weapon manufacturers.

High Standard Manufacturing

One of the most popular pistols that is used in many small-bore .22LR competitions is produced by High Standard.

The company was not originally formed to manufacture firearms but to produce the special drills needed to produce gun barrels. Formed in 1926 the company purchased the Hartford Arms and Equipment company in 1932 which produced a simple blowback .22LR automatic. This formed the basis for the future High Standard pistols.

The company has developed both small-bore and full-bore revolvers as well as pump and automatic action shotguns. One of the automatic shotguns was manufactured with no stock and a torch mounted on the top for police use. If the light hit the target so did the shot.

The factory has recently moved from its original base and the production lines have been rationalized. High Standard weapons remain strong favourites because of reliable operation, accuracy and their reasonable price.

Left: The Hotchkiss Model 1914 machine gun. Although by then out-of-date it was used by the French in World War II. This was a gas-operated gun. The M14 was also built in Britain as a tank gun.

Hotchkiss, B. B.

Although Colt is given much of the credit for the revolver designs from the Colt factory, another talented designer worked there; he was Benjamin Berkeley Hotchkiss. Born in 1826 in Connecticut, Hotchkiss turned to larger weapons of the field gun type after leaving Colt. He lacked substantial backing and so went to France in 1867 where he worked with the government to produce a metallic cartridge and artillery weapons. One of the weapons produced by a French company set up by Hotchkiss was a hand-cranked machine gun of different principle from the Gatling. Although Hotchkiss died in 1885 he left behind a well tried and effective design team who expanded the line of weapons in production and had many accepted by military forces throughout the world.

Ithaca

The history of the Ithaca firm starts with a family from New York called Smith. There were two branches of the family, with three brothers forming the L. C. Smith Typewriter concern and the fourth, Leroy, being a successful businessman. A designer, W. H. Baker, asked them for capital to manufacture one of his shotguns and so the three brothers in the typewriter business, encouraged by Leroy, decided to form the L. C. Smith Gun company.

Leroy, with the help of other businessmen and Baker, set up a factory in an old mill in Ithaca, New York, and an improved model of Baker's gun was put into production. The partnership

ithacagun

was enlarged when George Livermore from the L. C. Smith concern joined him. A brief flirtation with typewriters led to a handsome profit which was promptly invested in the firearms side of the business.

With the death of Leroy, the firm came under the control of his son, Lou, and Livermore. The firm established a sound reputation with its super double-barrelled shotguns, and Wells Fargo and Annie Oakley became customers. By the mid-1930s a number of concerns, including Lefever Arms and Union Firearms, had been taken over. The adoption of a John Browning design for their repeating shotgun was an immediate success. The sales of this gun reached 1 million in 1968.

World War II caused the firm to turn to material such as the Colt .45. A Canadian subsidiary was opened in Ontario. The price of producing certain shotguns in the United States had proved to be prohibitive and so, in 1966, Ithaca combined with SKB of Japan to market the latter's product in America.

The Smith family sold the firm in 1967. Ithaca has obtained agencies from such firms as BSA, Erma and Tikka and makes new products such as the Model 51 shotgun for themselves.

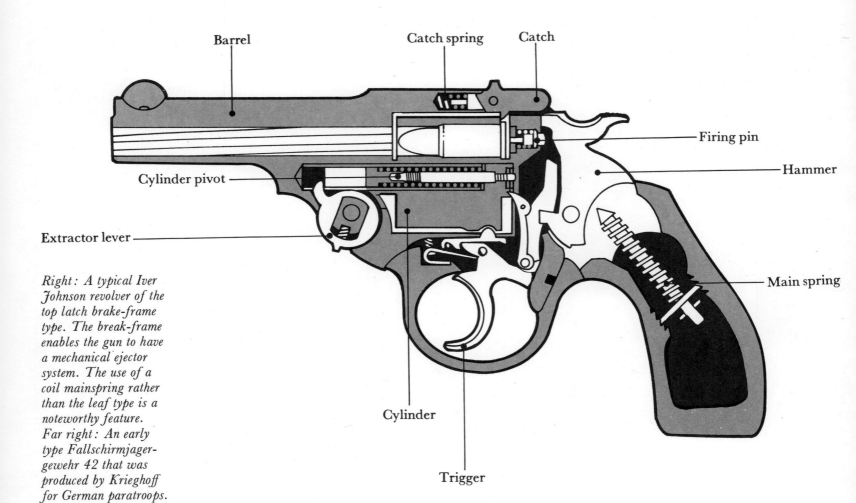

Barrel   Catch spring   Catch

Firing pin

Hammer

Cylinder pivot

Extractor lever

Main spring

Cylinder

Trigger

Right: A typical Iver Johnson revolver of the top latch brake-frame type. The break-frame enables the gun to have a mechanical ejector system. The use of a coil mainspring rather than the leaf type is a noteworthy feature. Far right: An early type Fallschirmjager-gewehr 42 that was produced by Krieghoff for German paratroops.

Iver Johnson

The slogan of the Iver Johnson Company was for many years 'Hammer the hammer'. This referred to the fact that the revolvers produced had to have the hammers pulled back before the firing pin could reach the cartridge.

The firm was founded in 1871 by a Norwegian, Iver Johnson, and Martin Bye. Their intention was to manufacture a handgun which would be reliable, safe and above all reasonably priced. The result was the 'Uncle Sam' which sold at under $1. Another revolver which started a trend that finished with many poor imitations was the 'American Bulldog'.

The firm diversified into toys, pistols and bicycles. When in 1895 Iver Johnson died, his son Fred took over as president. The family is no longer involved in the company, which specializes in what is to some an outdated design and to others a great one – the break top revolver. They concentrate on modern production methods such as investment casting and metal sintering.

Melvin M. Johnson

The Johnson rifle was unusual in that its inventor decided not on the conventional gas system but instead on recoil operation. From 1936 through the war Johnson developed his theories. The rifle, with its recoiling barrel, was adopted in small quantities by the Americans

as the M1941. Light machine guns, the 1941/1944, were also developed which were fed from the side with box magazines. The Model 1941 operated from open bolt on automatic fire and closed bolt on single shot.

As the only recoil-operated rifle to see service the Johnson perhaps deserved better, but the good gas-action weapons such as the Garand ousted it. Johnson wrote copiously not only on the advantages of his recoil-operated rifles and machine guns but also on basic infantry tactics and fire power.

Jorgensen, E.

Erik Jorgensen was the works superintendent at the Royal Norwegian Arsenal at Kongsberg. He is best known for his work on rifles with Ole Krag.

Krag, O. H. J.

Ole Herman Johannes Krag was born in Norway in 1837. He joined the army but was seconded to a number of government posts to carry out work on weapons. He became the director of the arsenal at Kongsberg in 1880 and later, in 1895, the Master of Ordnance for the Norwegian government. His rifle designs, some in cooperation with Erik Jorgensen, were adopted by Denmark, Norway, the United States and other countries. He retired in 1902 and died in 1912.

Krieghoff

The firm of Krieghoff has, since its founding in 1885 by Ludwig Krieghoff, been renowned for its high-class sporting weapons and especially for its drillings.

The family of Krieghoff managed the firm with the motto 'Built for hunters by hunters'. The firm was based in the famous German gun-making district of Suhl/Thuringia and, when Heinrich Krieghoff took over, his gun-designing talent continued the firm's prosperity. A clever development was the insert barrel for the shot-gun as well as the use of Duralamin in weapon construction.

World War II saw the firm of Heinrich Krieghoff and Sempert & Krieghoff contribute to the weapon output of Germany, producing such weapons as the Luger and the FG42. After the war the factories were dismantled but the Krieghoff family, with a number of their loyal workers, rebuilt in the Ulm district. Jagdwaffen-fabrik H. Krieghoff, a family firm, is still devoted to the production of top-quality sporting firearms.

Below: A Lahti made by the original Finnish producer. The Lahti was one of the most robust and reliable pistols ever put into service.

Lahti, A. J.

Aimo Johannes Lahti was the head of Finland's government arsenal. He was a very talented designer whose best-known weapons were a pistol and a machine gun. Production of his designs took place at the arsenal from 1926.

Lewis, I. W.

Isaac Lewis was one of the band of regular US Army officers who turned out to be a talented designer. Born in Pennsylvania in 1858, he joined the United States Military Academy at West Point and graduated in 1884. As a regular officer he spent a number of years on coastal defence then was invited by the Automatic Arms Company to develop designs for which they held the patents. In 1910 he began work and by 1911 he had produced prototypes. The weapons, although demonstrated to the government, received little attention.

A prophetic event was the firing of one of the Lewis guns from an aircraft at a ground target. This Lieutenant Colonel Lewis carried out in 1912 but received little encouragement, as the idea of 'firing guns from aircraft' seemed much too advanced for the military to consider. By 1914 the BSA company in Britain had taken up production of the Lewis gun and eventually the American Savage Company did the same.

Llama-Gabilondo y Cia

The firm was founded in 1904 by two families of cousins that gave the name the plural Gabilondos y Urresti, but when in 1909 the families split up the name became Gabilondo y Urresti. The name once more changed for family reasons to Gabilondo y Cia, based in Vittoria, Spain.

At first the firm manufactured only revolvers, but in 1914 they joined the Browning revolution by manufacturing a copy under the name of Ruby. This pistol was sold in the United States and South America; the French army adopted it as substitute standard and orders were placed in 1915. The French continued to order the pistol, at first 30,000 per month, then more. The firm could not keep up with demand and so a cooperative was formed with a number of other manufacturers in the area to produce the pistol to the same pattern and with the Ruby name. At one time five firms with a contract for 5,000 a month were in operation. This was later increased as other firms came into the group.

Other names used in the postwar production of small automatic pistols were Danton and Buffalo. The break from this early production occurred in 1931 when the Colt .45 1911 type of design was adopted. The major difference was the dropping of the grip safety. The name of this pistol was Llama. The smaller calibres retain the external shape but drop the locking mechanism. After World War II the range was rationalized and the grip safety brought back. This range is current. Pistols were also produced under two contracts from Spanish sources. These were the Mugica and the Tauler.

The present range of automatic pistols is complemented by revolvers. These are of the S & W type and are of good quality. The .357 is sold under the name Comanche. The Llama has established an enviable reputation and the modern range of handguns will add to it.

Ludwig Loewe

The Loewe company of Germany was involved in making firearms and machine tools, but tools were the main interest until a contract for the Mauser rifle was obtained. The Mauser contract lasted from 1890–6, during which time Mauser rifles were supplied to several countries. Development of the Borchardt took place during the period 1893–5 and production continued until 1896. With the transfer to DWM of the company's shares in Mauser plus some of its property and the machinery concerned with firearms, Loewe's interest in firearms ceased.

Luger, G.

George Luger was born in Austria in 1849. After a period in the army, during which he accumulated a knowledge of the practical requirements for military small arms, he joined the Nordoesterreichische Eisenbahn where he worked for a period with Ferdinand Mannlicher. Although he designed a number of rifles his work did not come to fruition until he joined the company of Ludwig Loewe in 1891. He remained with the company during its change of ownership. His work in making the Borchardt design into a practical weapon had much to do with his understanding of military needs.

The Luger pistol was only one item. He did lasting design work in connection with the 9mm Parabellum cartridge, which became (and still is) the most used submachine gun and pistol cartridge in the world. Luger died in 1923 having seen the Luger pistol become a total success and the 9mm cartridge gain massive acceptance.

Madsen, W. O. H.

Madsen, although beginning his career as a captain in the Danish army, was attached to their technical services division. Part of his work was in the government arsenal where, in cooperation with Julius Rasmussen, he carried out weapon design. One of the results was the Madsen light machine gun. This gun, said by many experts to be badly designed, nevertheless proved efficient and very reliable. Many countries purchased the weapon in quantity. Madsen rose to the rank of major general and later became minister of war.

The Dansk Industri Syndikat was formed to produce the Madsen for foreign contracts.

Manhurin (Manufacture de Machines du Haut-Rhin)

The present head of Manhurin, Paul Spengler, is the son of the founder, Jules Spengler, who started the precision engineering firm in 1920. The action that was to bring the firm into the munitions business was the purchase in 1922 of a cartridge plant from the Germans as part of the postwar treaty. This led the firm to develop its own machinery so that by 1926 it was manufacturing such equipment as well as other machinery and a range of very accurate measuring instruments for industry.

In 1928 the French government encouraged Manhurin to set up a cartridge factory at Mans. This factory was nationalized in 1936. Other factories followed such as Cusset and Montpertuis.

The war interrupted the operations of the various parts of Manhurin but soon afterwards they started to manufacture the Walther range of pistols under licence from Walther who were not allowed to manufacture firearms themselves. Today, apart from the production of machinery for ammunition construction, Manhurin produce a range of ammunition, fuses, grenades and missile components.

Mannlicher, F. von

Ferdinand (often known as Ritter) was born in 1849 and trained as an engineer. He joined Austrian railways and became chief engineer.

He later joined the Oesterreichische-Waffenfabriks-Gesellschaft at Steyr where he became not only a designer but a prolific experimenter of various methods of firearms operation. He worked with Otto Schoenauer in the development of the rotary magazine that was to become famous in the Mannlicher-Schoenauer rifle. His own work covered turnbolt, straight pull and automatic rifles as well as clip loading and rotary magazines. His rifles were adopted by Greece, the Netherlands, Roumania and Austria, and contributed to an Italian design.

His son, O. Mannlicher, took out a number of patents on behalf of his father after the latter's death.

Manufrance (Manufacture Française d'Armes et Cycles de St Etienne)

The firm of Manufrance was founded in 1885 by M. Mimard and M. Blachon. Their original intention was to provide a mail order service for firearms and at a later date to begin making firearms themselves. The first shotgun was to be of the highest quality possible and was named Ideal. A shotgun of superb quality, it is still manufactured under this name today.

The firm next branched out into the manufacture of bicycles and produced the Hirondelle range that is still produced today. The next diversification was the manufacture of sewing machines under the trade name of Omnia which continues today. Mail order business is now substantial and a number of stores are also owned by the company.

One of the best known of the early products was the Le Français pistol, announced in 1914. Other trade names used are Robust, Rapid, Perfex, Rival, Reina, Populaire and Buffalo. At present the firm manufactures the Robust side-by-side shotgun, the Simplex shotgun, the Rapid-Perfex self-loading shotgun, the Reina .22LR self-loading rifle, and the Vera range of shotgun cartridges and reloading components.

Marlin Firearms

On State Street in the famous firearms town of New Haven, Connecticut, John Mahlon Marlin set up a gunshop. At first, Marlin concentrated on the production of Derringers and then on revolvers. In the late 1800s Marlin took out a number of patents on rifles as well as producing Ballard single-shot rifles.

What was to become a bitter feud with Winchester started in 1881 when the first Marlin lever action rifle was announced. The top ejection, similar to the Winchester, was abandoned and a side ejection standardized. This has been

Below: A Mannlicher-Schoenauer double set trigger sporting rifle. It uses a rotary magazine (a detail of which is shown separately).

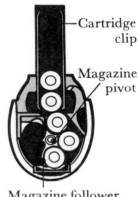

Cartridge clip

Magazine pivot

Magazine follower

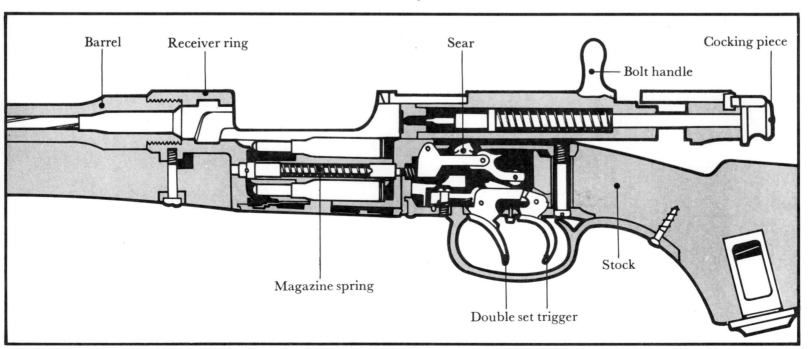

Barrel   Receiver ring   Sear   Cocking piece

Bolt handle

Magazine spring

Double set trigger

Stock

Marlin ®

a feature of the Marlin lever action and is continued today.

John Marlin died in 1901 and his sons ran the company until 1915 when it was sold to a syndicate and renamed the Marlin-Rockwell Corporation. The new company management had little or no interest in sporting weapons and during World War I concentrated on military production. By 1923 the company was on the market again and for a nominal sum Frank Kenna became the new owner.

The Kenna family has directed the fortunes of the Marlin company ever since and has brought in such innovations as Micro-groove rifling. A massive modern factory with sophisticated machinery still turns out side ejector lever action rifles as well as automatic and bolt action .22 rifles. Shotguns were manufactured under the well-known name of L. C. Smith.

MAS (Manufacture Nationale d'Armes de St Etienne)

The present firm of MAS is part of the Groupement Industriel des Armements Terrestres or GIAT, a French government combine for the manufacture and sale of weapons for the French armed forces and for export.

As with many manufacturing firms that have an extensive history, the original reason for forming a factory in the St Etienne region was the existence of water power from Mount Pilat, reserves of coal and nearby iron ore. In the 8th century crossbows and bladed weapons were made. In 1535 the king decided that military production should be centred on the area and, as a result, started to organize it himself. This was carried on in 1666 by Louis XIV who also incorporated the areas of Charleville and Mauberge.

The competitive testing of weapons in France was well advanced and in 1717 the new French army musket, the Fusil Modele 1717, was chosen from the Mauberge area. By 1764 nine companies existed under the banner of Manufacture Royale and produced both muskets and pistols as well as edged weapons. Even before a new factory was completed in 1868, the group were producing some 700,000 firearms per year.

With world war facilities simultaneously expanded, but postwar development under GIAT has brought into use numerically controlled machines and an IBM computer to produce the best in French small arms. The present French service rifle, which has been developed at MAS, is the Fusil Automatique MAS 5.56mm. It has performed creditably.

Below: The Fusil Automatique MAS is the new rifle adopted by the French army. It is of bull-pup design. The FA MAS uses a delayed blowback system that is much favoured by MAS.

Mauser

Originally the firm of Mauser was formed by the Mauser brothers, Paul and Wilhelm, to produce parts for the rifle which had been adopted by the German government in 1871. The government took an interest in the factory in that the state bank stood guarantor for the money required for expansion, and the brothers acquired the state armaments factory. The firm was prospering when, in 1882, Wilhelm died. The firm then became a public company known as Waffenfabrik Mauser.

The fortunes of the firm continued with the production of the modified versions of the rifle and licence agreements with other companies. The Mauser C96 pistol was added to the production line in 1896. The coming of war in 1914, which was to bring the company's products so much prominence, was preceded by the death of Paul Mauser. In 1922 the company was reformed as Mauser Werk and contributed much to the German war effort in the 1940s with all types of weapons and weapon development.

The postwar company was reformed as Mauser Jagdwaffen and began manufacturing sporting weapons. In 1976 production of the Luger pistol was undertaken. An abortive flirtation with a submachine gun was the company's first venture back into the military market. The latest venture is a very advanced rifle firing caseless ammunition.

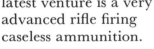

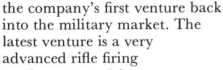

Top left: Wilhelm Mauser who with his brother, Paul, developed the basic bolt action rifle into a shotgun that was to be used all over the world.
Left: An early M89 Mauser rifle that was produced in Belgium. The Mauser rifle was adopted as standard by many armies in two world wars.

Maxim, H. S.

Hiram Stevens Maxim was an outstanding inventor and engineer. His work ranged over a vast field and included a self-setting mouse trap and one of the world's most successful machine guns.

He was born on 5 February 1840 in Massachusetts; his family had originated in France. Maxim early dabbled with different projects and always managed to make improvements on the original article. The first was as a carriage maker, then a miller and finally a wood turner. Two of his brothers fought in the Civil War but Maxim, owing to the 'not more than two per family' rule, moved to Canada.

After working for his uncle on gas lighting, he moved back to Boston and established his own

the Maxim company was born.

In 1888 the company bought out the Nordenfelt company and became Maxim Nordenfelt. The adoption of the Maxim gun by Britain in 1891 was followed by the purchase of the company by Vickers. This was logical as Vickers were manufacturing the weapons in any case. The resulting company was known as Vickers, Son and Maxim.

Maxim was knighted in 1901 for the design and manufacture of his weapons. He died in 1915 before the full impact of the German Maxim guns were felt by the world. The Vickers derivative of his gun was to equip the British army throughout World War II and became a firm favourite with the soldiers who used it.

Morris, R.

The name of Richard Morris will always be associated with the training of soldiers before and after World War I. Morris specialized in the development of sub-calibre adapters for all types of weapons, large and small. His main work was carried out between 1880 and 1910. The two conversions best known are for the .455 revolver and for the .303 rifle.

Mosin, S.

The Russian service rifle Pattern 1891, used in large quantities during World War I, was the Mosin Nagant. Colonel Sergei Mosin of the Russian army played a leading part in the design of this rifle.

MOSSBERG

Oscar F. Mossberg, founder of the Mossberg firm, trained with a number of well-known firms. He had been born in Sweden in 1866 and went to the United States when he was 20 years old. One of his early jobs was with the Iver Johnson Arms firm where he contributed to the design of some products. A short stay with Shattuck Arms, where he was works superintendent producing shotguns, was followed by a 13-year period with J. Stevens.

In 1919 Oscar Mossberg started a full-time business in conjunction with his two sons, Iver and Harold. By 1926 the firm of O. F. Mossberg and Sons was well established with two plants manufacturing rifles and pistols. After their father's death in 1934, the sons embarked on a course of expansion, adding another production facility and numerous producer lines.

During World War II many different weapons and components were produced. Today the company makes high-quality .22 rifles, sporting rifles and pump action shotguns for their customers.

company, the Maxim Gas Company. His next move was to England where he set up a machine shop in Hatton Garden, London. During the period 1882–5 his fertile brain devised a number of methods of operating self-loading guns. These were patented and, in 1884, he decided to set up an armaments company. So, with Albert Vickers of the Vickers company as chairman,

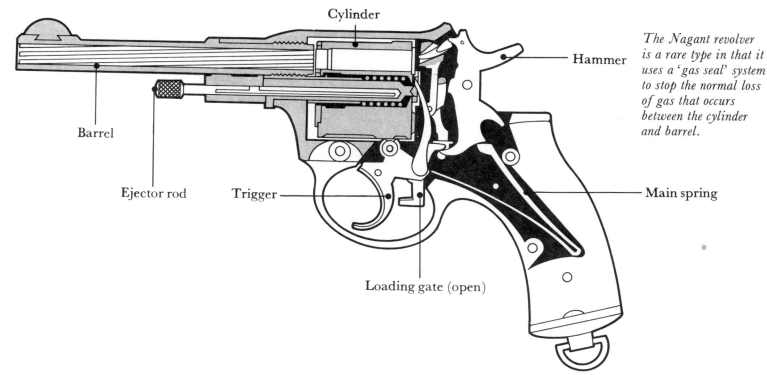

Cylinder

Hammer

Barrel

Ejector rod

Trigger

Main spring

Loading gate (open)

The Nagant revolver is a rare type in that it uses a 'gas seal' system to stop the normal loss of gas that occurs between the cylinder and barrel.

Nagant, L. and Nagant, E.

The exact relationship between the two Nagants has yet to be accurately established. They were blood relations but whether they actively worked together to any great degree is unknown. Leon was the designer of the gas seal revolver that was adopted by the Russian forces in 1894, while Emile would seem to have developed the ejector mechanism used on the non gas seal Nagant revolvers used by Belgium and other countries. Leon was certainly the owner of a gun firm in his own name and was involved in the development of the Mosin Nagant rifle.

Nambu, K.

Kijiro Nambu was an army officer who became a gun designer. His first design was produced by the Kayoba factory in 1904 and was followed by a thinly disguised copy of the Hotchkiss machine gun. This and other weapons by Nambu were adopted by the Japanese army. In 1927 he set up the Nambu firm which in 1937 amalgamated with Chuokogyo Kaisha. The Model 1925 pistol became the standard service pistol. Nambu rose to the rank of general in the Japanese army.

Parker-Hale

Founded in 1880 by A. G. Parker the firm has grown steadily until today it stands as one of the prime manufacturers of sporting firearms and accessories. The firm has achieved an admirable reputation for conversion of military actions to superb target weapons. A hammer rifling plant has enabled the production of fine barrels. The PH sporting rifles which are of the Mauser action type are very popular, especially

in America and Canada. A very successful venture has been the recreation, with the help of the original gauges, of the early percussion Enfield rifles and carbines.

Pieper, H.

Henri Pieper was not only a talented designer of firearms but also did much to ensure mechanization of their production. By 1866 he had his own firm that produced weapons on a mass-production basis with extensive use of machinery. He had amongst his patents one for a gas seal revolver which predated that of Nagant. After his death in 1898 Nicolas Pieper continued production and design work at the family factory and by 1900 it was turning out automatic pistols in quantity. Many weapons were produced under the company's trade mark, Bayard.

Prideaux, W.

William de Courcy Prideaux was one of the designers who, while not producing any weapon of note, contributed to the general design of firearms. Rapid loading of the revolver with its six separate chambers in the heat of combat had always proved a problem and the rapid loader designed by Prideaux provided a solution. After producing a number of partly successful prototypes dating from 1893 onwards he managed to have the final version adopted by the British army for use with the Webley .455 revolver. Another invention was the disintegrating link-belt for a machine gun that he patented in 1915. This was a very early use of a system which is now almost universal.

Radway Green

The Royal Ordnance Factory at Radway Green, England, has achieved prominence in a relatively short time. Its main claim to fame is the production of target class ammunition which has won a reputation for accuracy that is the envy of any factory in the world. Almost as important is that this reputation has been built by the target shots themselves.

The factory grew out of the wartime need for the manufacture of components for .303 and 20mm ammunition. Construction started in the winter of 1939 and the factory was in production by the summer of 1940. In 1942 the production of completed rounds was started when a filling plant was built for .303 rounds. Production at the peak was an incredible 15 million rounds of .303 and 1 million 20mm empty cases per week.

With the end of the war, arms production was run down and the manufacture of much-needed domestic goods and brass strip was begun. The factory returned to production of ammunition on a large scale in 1948 when first the Korean War and then the conversion of the British army to a new calibre 7.62mm NATO ammunition kept output at a high level.

To ensure that a run down of skilled personnel and plant did not occur again on such a large scale, the factory diversified and in the 1950s it pioneered a number of processes for the nuclear industry. The early 1960s saw diversification in the development of explosive forming of components and the production of coin blanks for the Royal Mint's change to decimal coinage. The production of press work such as ammunition boxes and machine gun links is carried on so that they can service their own and other factories' products.

At present the factory has developed the British entry for the NATO trial, the 4.85mm small arms cartridge. Whether this is adopted or not, the factory will be in the forefront of production of high quality ammunition to produce the new calibre when it is decided upon.

Remington®

The Remington company is one of the oldest gun manufacturers in America. The firm was founded by Eliphalet Remington in 1816 at a place that is now Illion, New York. Although originally a blacksmith, Remington was soon making rifles, and as his reputation for excellence spread so his business grew.

He early purchased a farm that was later to provide an area for expansion of the plant in 1828. The Civil War saw further expansion but in 1861, mainly through over work, Eliphalet died. His sons took over the business and changed it into a corporation with the name of Remington.

In 1888 Marcellus Hartley became associated with Remington. He had a wide experience in the field of sporting firearms and ammunition, and in 1854 had opened a sporting goods store in New York City. Seeing the chance to move into cartridges he managed to purchase two companies which he moved to Bridgeport, Connecticut. The resulting company he named Union Metallic Cartridge Company. This led to the purchase of a major share in Remington in 1888. In 1912 the two firms combined as Remington Arms-Union Metallic Cartridge Company and in 1921 a full merger took place. An innovation was the first of the non-corrosive priming compounds that led to the Kleanbore name on cartridge boxes.

In 1933 E. I. du Pont de Nemours and Company purchased a controlling interest in the company. Du Pont had for many years been a supplier of propellants to the cartridge side of the business. The Peters Cartridge Company was purchased in 1934. The war saw the vast expansion of the manufacturing side and also the running of a number of plants for the American government. The company successfully changed to sporting weapon production and ammunition after the war.

Rheinmetall Wehrtechnik

Rheinische Metallwaaren und Maschinenfabrik was founded in 1883 by Heinrich Ehrhadt, a specialist in metal working techniques, who named the company after the great river Rhine. Before World War I the firm built up production to include artillery and ammunition and opened the proving ground at Unterluss that is still in use today. During the war production was expanded to include small arms. This was helped by the purchase of the firm of Dreyse in 1901.

The interwar years saw the gradual build up of the combine with the acquisition of Waffenfabrik Solthurn in 1929 and Borsig in 1933, after which the name was changed to Rheinmetall-Borsig. With the outbreak of war again the firm expanded and acquired a number of other concerns such as Maget. By the end of the war production included everything from pistols and ammunition through AA guns, field guns and their ammunition, tanks and even at the end guided missiles.

In about 1956 the company was permitted to resume the production of military goods and one of the first was the MG42 machine gun. The Bundeswehr needed a number of heavier calibre weapons and arranged for the firm to build them under licence. Rheinmetall also entered into subcontracts for projects such as the Leopard tank.

The present Rheinmetall Wehrtechnik group includes 28 companies, all but two in Europe. Production includes small arms, antiaircraft guns, howitzers and their ammunition.

Ross, C. H. A. F.

Sir Charles Henry Augustus Frederick Ross, the ninth baronet of Balnagown, was born in 1872 in the family castle, which stands in 350,000 acres in Rosshire, Scotland. At Eton he showed an aptitude for mechanical design. His first patent, taken out in 1893, was for a most complex rifle that was never manufactured. In 1896 he designed and had manufactured by an English gunsmith the first of his practical designs. All the Ross rifles were to be based on the straight pull type of action. Externally they showed the influence of the Mannlicher designs.

In 1897 he emigrated to Canada, where he designed and helped build a hydroelectric power station. In 1902 the Canadian authorities decided that they needed a new rifle, but they would only adopt one manufactured in Canada. Against much pressure from Britain, which wanted to have Canada adopt a British rifle, they opted for the Ross. Two points influenced this decision. First, the British were short of rifles for their own use and could not have supplied sufficient even if their weapon was acceptable; secondly, Ross had an admirer in the Canadian government.

The Ross Rifle Company, set up in 1903, was in production by 1905. Initial rifles were made through purchasing components from outside concerns, some of which were in the United States, which led to political wrangles. Further trouble was caused when some of the rifles were found to be not of very high quality.

After World War I the company was wound up and became the property of the Canadian government, which paid Ross a relatively large sum of money and intended to manufacture a British rifle after all. Ross settled in America but spent a lot of time travelling about the world. He died in Florida in 1942.

A belated compliment for the much maligned Ross rifle came in 1954 when the Russian team won the Running Deer event in the world championships with, of all things, a Ross rifle.

Roth, G.

Georges Roth, a designer, worked during the period 1898–1913. He designed both pistols and rifles as well as cartridges for them. One of his designs, the Roth-Steyr pistol, was adopted for service use by the Austro-Hungarian cavalry in 1907. This pistol fired an 8mm cartridge that was peculiar to the design. Roth's designs all exhibited clever if overcomplicated engineering.

Sako

The history of the Sako company is unique amongst firearms manufacturers in that, for a number of years, the firm was owned by the Red Cross. The company owes its existence to the National Guard of Finland which was formed in 1917–18. The need to equip this body with arms led to the acquisition of a large number of rifles which were war salvage. These were mainly of Russian and Japanese manufacture and had seen hard use. The National Guard therefore set up an ordnance department to recondition the weapons and in 1919 and 1923 this was carried out under the control of the National Guard. In 1921 the factory was given financial autonomy.

The gradual wearing out of much of the original equipment led to the purchase of Swiss barrels to fit the Japanese and Russian rifles. This proved a success and the order was increased for those to fit the Nagant. This rifle, an odd mixture of Russo-Swiss and Finnish work, was named the M24. A change took place with the purchase of worn barrel-making equipment from Germany which was totally reconditioned by Sako. This led to the fitting of Finnish manufactured barrels and the beginning of a reputation for superb accuracy on target ranges. Equipment for the manufacture of bullets was ordered and obtained from Germany in 1928 and within a year production had started. The manufacture of complete ammunition did not begin until a contract was obtained for 9mm in 1937. Machinery for the manufacture of am-

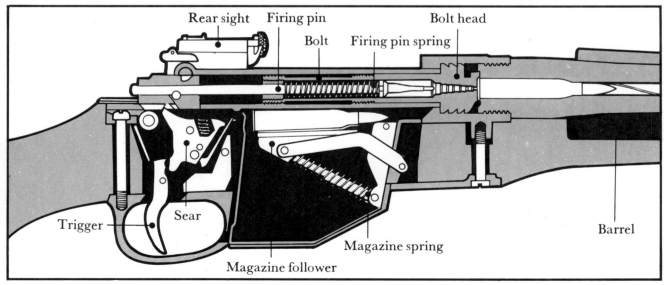

Left: The Ross rifle proved to be unsuited to the rigours of military service. A straight pull action with a multiple lug bolt, the rifle made a brief comeback to win a medal in the 1954 world championships.

Rear sight · Firing pin · Bolt head · Bolt · Firing pin spring · Trigger · Sear · Magazine follower · Magazine spring · Barrel

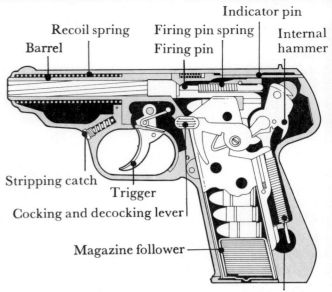

Right: The Sauer Model 38 was a design that deserved more recognition than it in fact received. It embodied features that were well in advance of the time. The trigger was of the double action type and the lever on the left side could cock or uncock the pistol.

munition was made at the plant.

In the 1930s the name was changed to Oy Sako Ab. World War II caused expansion of the factory which managed to produce 275 million cartridges and nearly 71,000 rifles.

On the conclusion of peace with Russia the National Guard was dissolved and the Sako factory was saved by gifting it to the Finnish Red Cross. The firm turned to production of textile machinery and the profits went to the Red Cross. When the market for machinery disappeared, disagreement surfaced. The firm returned to the manufacture of firearms, but the Red Cross demanded such securities for the necessary loan that they were unacceptable. The company was taken over in 1962 by the Finnish Cable Works. A later merger was with Oy Nokia Ab.

Today the company manufactures rifles of all types and also target pistols.

Sauer und Sohn

The firm of Sauer started in the Thuringa district of Germany in 1751. Its founder was J. P. Sauer who worked until the 1800s. The firm flourished and, as with other German firms, witnessed expansion in World War I, the depression which followed and the massive build-up to World War II. After 1945 the factory found itself in the Russian zone and the firm ceased to exist under the name of Sauer. The new name, which included other appropriated firms, was Ernst Thalmann Werk.

The Sauer family had escaped to the West, and the son of the wartime owner, in partnership with a financier, set up a factory under the old name. The place chosen was Eckernforde and the year was 1951. Ownership changed several times during the 1950s and 1960s.

In 1974 a modern factory was built and the latest machinery and technology employed. Production today is centred on traditional German sporting firearms. Over and under shotguns and drillings are also manufactured, as well as bolt action rifles. The rifle, a turn bolt design with locking lugs that cam out into the receiver, has been adopted by Colt, FFV, and FN. An agreement to coproduce pistols with the famous firm of SIG has led to the production of pistols that have been accepted by the Swiss army and the German police.

Schoenauer, O.

Otto Schoenauer was an employee and later manager of the Oesterreichische-Waffenfabriks-Gesellschaft at Steyr. Also working at this factory was F. von Mannlicher who combined with Schoenauer in the development of the rotary magazine that was typical of the Mannlicher-Schoenauer sporting rifle.

Sharps, Christian

The vanishing herds of buffalo can be attributed in large part to the superb rifle developed by Christian Sharps. The Sharps rifle, patented in 1848, was a breech loader using paper cartridges but the action was so successful that it easily accepted metallic ones as well. It was basically a falling block type.

The other successful weapon designed by Sharps was far removed from his powerful rifle. It was a small rimfire, four-barrelled pocket pistol that used a rotary firing pin to fire each barrel in turn. Although Sharps produced a number of other designs there is little doubt that he will be best remembered for his Buffalo gun.

Shpagin, G. S.

The designer of the Russian PPSh41 and its Chinese copy, the type-50 submachine gun, George Shpagin worked in collaboration with Degtyarev. He became a lieutenant general in the army and was awarded the honour of Hero of the Socialist Labour.

SIG (Schweizerische Industrie Gesellschaft)

The fact that one of the main items produced today by the SIG firm is railway engines and carriages may seem at first odd. The explanation lies in the formation of the Swiss Railway Carriage Factory near Schaffhausen in 1853. This company was formed by three Swiss businessmen, Frieddrich Peyer im Hof, Heinrich Moser and Colonel Conrad Neher. It was not until 10 years later that the firm changed its name to that of SIG. Today it continues the railway work and also packaging machinery as well as a line of machine tools and equipment.

One of the first people to work under the factory director, Colonel Burnard, was a gunsmith by the name of Prelaz who had developed a system of rifling barrels. Between them they produced the Prelaz-Burnard muzzle loading rifle. When in 1864 Friedrich Vetterelli took over the directorship the days of the muzzle loader were almost over. By 1869 the Vetterelli turnbolt weapon with a tube magazine had been adopted by the Swiss government as their standard service weapon. Although the next Swiss weapon was the Schmidt-Rubins the factory still produced parts for this and in 1908 took up the manufacture of one of the earliest self-loading rifles. This was the Mondragon which had been designed by a Mexican general of that name. This weapon, while not proving a great success, was used by the Germans during World War I.

During the interwar years sales and production of the machinery necessary for making weapons was developed along with prototypes of self-loading weapons. It was after World War II that the factory started volume production of the new standard weapon for the Swiss army, the StGw57. Today SIG are world renowned for the quality of their weapons which are, if expensive, second to none in construction.

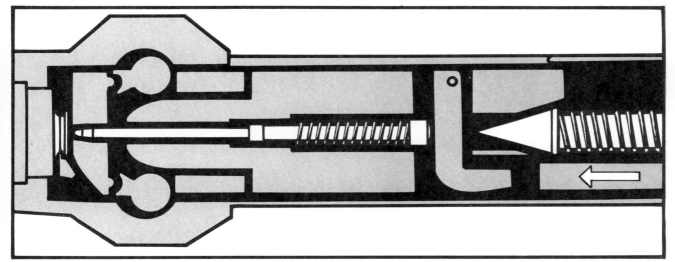

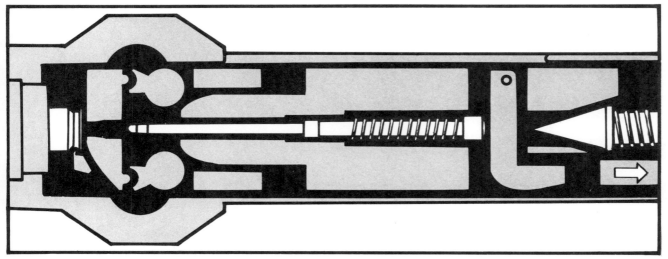

Top: The SIG factory in Switzerland. The company started out as the Swiss Railway Carriage Factory in the 1850s.
Left: The bolt of the SIG 7.5mm assault rifle, in the locked position (top) and unlocked (below).

Right: Horace Smith (left) and Daniel B. Wesson, founders of Smith and Wesson. The company was formed in the 1850s and still produces pistols today.

Smith and Wesson

Although Horace Smith and D. B. Wesson formed a partnership in 1852 the company was not formed until 1854. The first pistols produced used the Volcanic ammunition. In 1855 Smith and Wesson sold their interest in the company to the Volcanic Repeating Arms Company and though Smith and Wesson worked for the new company Smith soon left. Wesson followed and the two men decided to form a new company in 1856.

This prospered and a variety of pistols of modern design emerged. Although, as with many firms, they went through hard times they managed by producing what is probably the best double-action revolver in the world. Although the Smith and Wesson families may no longer have any interest (Dan Wesson left the company to set up his own firearms business) the guns are produced to the highest standards.

Springfield Armoury

When in 1968 the arsenal at Springfield, Massachusetts, closed after 191 years of continual service to the American armed forces, many lamented the passing of an era. The founding of a manufacturing unit at Springfield in 1777 was the beginning of the armoury. Paper cartridges were early produced and by 1794 the newly established Congress passed an act designating the factory as a National Armoury. The first weapons produced were flintlock rifles, but by 1818 pistols of the same type were being manufactured. The introduction of percussion saw the armoury in production of weapons of that type by 1842.

A weapon that has survived time to be reproduced as a collector's piece is the Trap Door Springfield. This famous weapon went into production as the Model 1866 rifle but because of the method of operation the breech loader soon acquired its nickname. Although the first bolt action rifle was the 1892 Springfield, better known as the Krag, this was not a success and the government ordered the armoury to develop a better design. The result was the famous M1903 Springfield, a Mauser development. It was to remain in use as standard issue and then as a precision sniper weapon until the Korean War.

The era of the self-loading rifle was well under way during World War I although general use lay in the future. The great John Garand was an employee of the Springfield armoury and after many developments his .30 M1 rifle was adopted in 1936. This rifle was soon to be known by most as the Garand; it served the soldiers of America as the first general issue self-loading rifle.

The adoption of the NATO 7.62mm cartridge to replace the 30-06 and the need for an updated weapon led the armoury to develop numerous prototype weapons. In 1957 the M14 was adopted as standard. This modified Garand design was not as successful in numbers produced as its illustrious predecessors; the 5.56mm cartridge became the norm and the AR15/M16 was adopted as standard. The M16 has proved to be superbly accurate and is used as a sniper weapon and for target use as well as a reserve weapon. It is perhaps appropriate that with this weapon of quality the armoury closed its doors.

Starr

The Starr Arms Company of Binghamton, New York, was once the third largest manufacturer of percussion revolvers. The Starr revolvers that enjoyed the greatest success were first sold in the 1850s to the United States army. With the coming of the Civil War numbers produced exceeded 45,000. After the Civil War the firm went bankrupt in 1867, the surplus stocks ending up in the arsenals of the French for use in the Franco-Prussian War.

Sterling Armament Company

When G. H. Lanchester of the Sterling Engineering Company adapted the German MP28:11 and manufactured it in 1939–40, it started a trend for the firm in submachine guns. G. W. Patchett, working for Sterling, designed the Patchett submachine gun that saw limited service before the end of World War II. Extensive development saw the adoption of a new version, the L2A3, in 1954.

The Sterling, as the submachine gun became known, has been sold to over 60 countries and is still in full production. A development, the L34 or Sterling-Patchett, is totally effective as a silenced weapon.

Today the company, under new ownership, still produces submachine guns but has added the production of the AR18 rifle to the range. The design department has produced an automatic rifle.

Steyr-Daimler-Puch

With the discovery of iron ore in the Austrian Alps near the rivers of Enns and Steyr, the area began to acquire a reputation for iron work. This soon turned from the production of bladed weapons to that of firearms.

In 1834 Leopold Werndl set up a factory in which he manufactured, with the help of hydraulic power, both blades and gun barrels. His son Joseph Werndl, born in 1831, was apprenticed in Vienna with Fruhwirth. When he visited the government arsenal at Prague he was impressed with the American-made machinery and decided to visit the United States to look at production more closely. While there he visited the Remington and Colt plants. When his father died in 1855 Joseph took over the factory and began to develop it. A further trip to America provided not only machinery but ideas. With his foreman, Karl Holub, he designed and produced a new breech-loading rifle. The Werndl-Holub rifle was adopted by the Austrians in 1867. It achieved the highest production rate of any weapon in Europe.

The production of other people's design proved a lucrative endeavour and an early success was the Mannlicher straight pull bolt rifle, as was the Schwarzlose machine gun. After World War I there was a sudden decline and the Steyr company, as it was then known, diversified into cars and aircraft engines. In 1934 Steyr merged with the firm of Daimler-

Left: The Steyr Model 1912 pistol was clip loaded with an internal magazine. The rotating barrel locking system is very strong and the original 9mm Steyr cartridge is powerful.

Puch to form the present company.

Wartime production gave way to peace time and the production of rifles for the Austrian army and a range of superb hunting rifles. The Mannlicher-Shoenauer which dated from the prewar years continued to be a much sought after weapon as was the Steyr Mannlicher.

Stoner, Eugene

Stoner is one of the great weapon designers of modern times. He came to prominence with the designs that he developed while working for the firm of Armalite.

The most famous weapon was the M16 rifle which has achieved a production of some 4.5 million units by various producers, primarily Colt. His own weapon system did not achieve great sales but a design that he helped with before he left Armalite, the AR18 (developed from his earlier work), is in production with Sterling Armament in England. Stoner has worked on a number of projects not just in the small arms field but also on cannon.

Sturm, Ruger

Born on 21 June 1916 in Brooklyn, New York, William B. Ruger was the son of a lawyer. He was brought up to value the use and appreciation of fine firearms and was soon avidly learning

all he could about them.

Ruger worked in an engineering shop making knitting machinery parts, then came an offer from the government's Springfield arsenal to work for them, but he left after less than a year. A light-machine gun design which he had worked on interested Auto-Ordnance and he moved to them. Although no orders for the machine gun resulted, Ruger learned much about the production of guns, and when he left in 1946 he decided to set up in business for himself. Although guns were never far from his mind he decided to manufacture high class hand tools. It was a disaster and he went out of business in 1948. Providentially, Ruger met Alex Sturm who was impressed with his talent and enthusiasm and they decided to embark on a joint venture with the necessary finance coming from Sturm. So Sturm, Ruger and Company was formed in January 1949.

The initial product, a simple .22LR pistol, was soon a success after receiving glowing reports. It was so reliable that the factory jokingly said that spares for it were kept in a cigar box. The factory prospered but Alex Sturm died suddenly in 1951 at the age of 29. Today the company produces a line of pistols, rifles and a shotgun – all successful – and show an appreciation of the shooter's wants.

Below: The Ruger company have done more to revive the single action revolver than any other company. The single six revolver, however, owes little to the early types and features all that is best in modern weapons.

Sudarev, A. I.

The designer of the much-maligned submachine gun received such awards as the Order of Lenin and the Red Star, for during the German siege of Stalingrad the Russian army was in need of such a weapon and Alexei Sudarev was able to provide it.

Born in 1912, at Alatyr in central Russia, Sudarev was trained as a fitter before he became a technician on heavy machines. During the early 1930s he took out a number of patents on plant and equipment before enrolling at the Gorky Industrial Institute in 1936. In 1939 his work turned towards military lines and he joined the Artillery Academy where he achieved the rank of lieutenant.

In World War II his famous PPS-42 and PPS-43 submachine guns were produced in very large quantities. These weapons survived the war and saw use in China as well as Poland and other Russian satellites. Sudarev died in 1946 while still in his 30s.

Thompson, J. T.

Born in 1860 in Newport, Kentucky, John Taliaferro Thompson was destined for a military career. He graduated from West Point in 1882 and joined the artillery at first and then, in 1890, the Ordnance Department.

In 1914 he retired from the army and joined the Remington factory as a consulting engineer. There he met Commander John Blish who had a method of delayed blowback that Thompson thought worthy of development. These two, along with a financier, formed the Auto-Ordnance Corporation in 1916.

Thompson rejoined the army in 1917 as a colonel and retired with the rank of brigadier general in 1918. The design of the Thompson submachine gun was finalized soon after and in 1920 the production version was ready. Thompson died in 1940 without seeing his gun receive its greatest use in World War II.

Thompson-Center Arms

The Thompson-Center single shot pistol that has made the company's name is the result of an amalgamation of the talents of the much travelled Warren Center and the K. W. Thompson company.

The K. W. Thompson Tool Company was formed in 1947 on Long Island and specialized in the production of parts by the investment casting method. These parts were supplied to other companies. In the 1960s the firm moved to New Hampshire and after Ken Thompson had met with Warren Center it was decided to produce the latter's pistol. The decision was primarily a commercial one as the factory had been running at less than full capacity.

Center started in the gun trade in a gunsmith's workshop of his own in the 1930s. Before he met Thompson he had interspersed working on his own account with stints with a number of major companies. He was general manager of Iver Johnson from 1954 to 1959. After another period on his own he joined Harrington and Richardson for two years, where he ended his time as head of research and development.

During this time he was developing his own single-shot interchangeable-barrelled pistol, and after leaving H & R he decided to produce the pistol himself. One of the original concepts was that it would be produced with investment castings and he obtained quotations from a company. Although he never did go into production, these quotations were to have far reaching effects, as one of the company's salesmen left and went to work with Thompson. At his suggestion Center was approached, and so the partnership was established.

The results of this combination of talent have been not only the Contender single shot but a number of black powder rifles and pistols. Center has a number of ideas on the drawing board and any that are produced are sure to be up to the company's standards of sound design and quality production.

Tokarev, F. V.

Born at Egorlikskaya in 1871, Fedor Vasilevitch Tokarev designed the service pistol which would remain standard until the late 1960s with the Soviet forces and many of their allies, sometimes in modified forms.

Tokarev's parents were Cossacks and it was to the 12th Cossack Regiment that he was eventually posted. He received his initial training with the village blacksmith. He later became a gunmaker and then went to the Novocherlassk Military Trade School. After his four-year attachment to the Cossacks he rejoined the school as an instructor. He attended the officers' training school at Oranienbaum and after graduation he served at the Sestorets factory before joining the famous arsenal at Tula. His pistol may have been based on the well-tried Browning designs, but it exhibited careful attention to ease of production and featured a removable hammer group. His rifles, the M1938 and M1940 were also standard Russian equipment.

Voere

The firm which formed a basis for Voere was founded by Krieghoff of Germany in 1940 to produce components for weapons. After World War II the firm came to an end but Georg Gatterer restarted it under the name of Tiroler Maschinenbau und Holzindustrie. Using the old machinery from the original factory he began to manufacture tools for industry.

In 1950 the firm once more began to produce weapons, under the name Tyrol Luftdrukgewehre, and by 1958 there was a barrel manufacturing plant and a number of air weapons under development. In 1964 the factory went bankrupt and was purchased by Voere, and a year later the factory was back in business. Production lines have been increased and sales built up in many countries.

Walther

The area of Thuringia, with its mountains and forests, had from the latter part of the 16th century been a centre of firearms construction. The twin towns of Zella and Mehlis formed a centre of this area and it was in Zella that Carl Walther opened a gunshop. In 1866 it catered

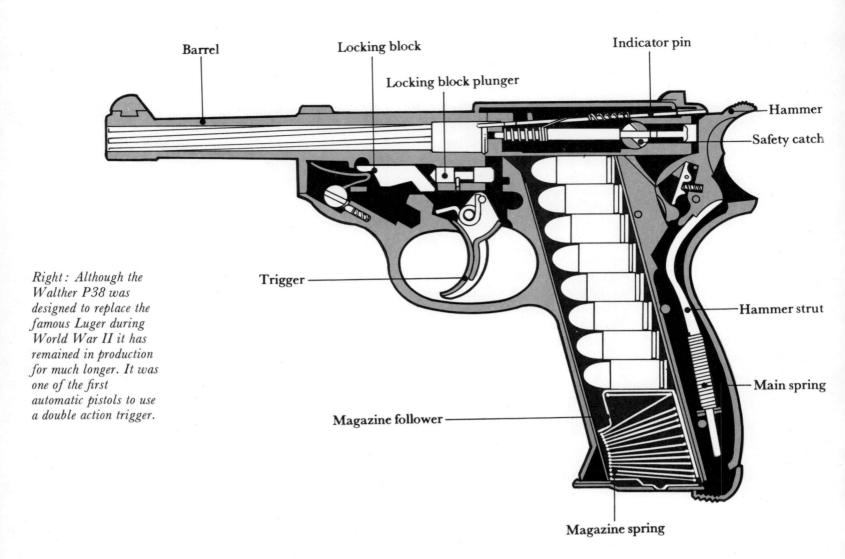

Barrel — Locking block — Indicator pin
Locking block plunger — Hammer
Safety catch
Trigger
Hammer strut
Main spring
Magazine follower
Magazine spring

Right: Although the Walther P38 was designed to replace the famous Luger during World War II it has remained in production for much longer. It was one of the first automatic pistols to use a double action trigger.

for the precision target shot, a tradition that the factory has continued to this day.

Although Carl Walther tried to develop a reliable small-calibre automatic pistol it was not until his son Fritz designed the Walther Model 1 in 6.35mm calibre that the firm started production of a line that was to extend to the present day. The Model 1 was announced in 1907 and did much to establish the company's early reputation.

In the mid-1920s after the dramatic upheavals of the war, the company under George Walther diversified into calculators. Little did they know at the time that this move would be important in the company's survival. In World War II the company had upwards of 2,000 employees producing the famous Walther pistols and a number of rifles. After the war the factories at Zella-Mehlis were destroyed and much of the machinery confiscated by the Allies.

Two factors enabled the firm to rebuild in a new location in Wurtemberg. The first was the flow of royalties from the production of pistols made under licence by the French company of Manhurin, and the second was the rapid development of business in calculating machines. The calculating machine proved a success and from small premises in Wurtemberg factories at Niederstotzingen and Gerstatten were opened.

When the restrictions on weapon production were lifted the firm once more went into a field that they were famous for, the target weapon. This was first in air weapons but soon covered all types of rifles and pistols. Many Olympic and other medals have been won with Walther weapons. A further factory at Konigsbronn has brought the organization to one of prominence in small arms once more.

Weatherby
Roy E. Weatherby entered the world of firearms design advocating a premise that has been the basis of many arguments: 'Small calibre light weight bullets at high velocity are more effective than the large calibre, heavy weight ones at low velocity.' During the 1940s and early 1950s Weatherby developed a number of cartridges based on his beliefs. After World War II he used surplus military actions for his custom rifles, rechambered for his cartridges. Later he adopted the FN-manufactured Mauser action.

In 1958 Weatherby announced the Mk V rifle and produced it at his modern factory at South Gate, California. The Mk V is an advanced turnbolt rifle using a front-locking multilug bolt. The rifle was developed into a number of variants chambered for both Weatherby and commercial cartridges.

Webley, and Webley and Scott

The name of Webley has been synonymous with the British service revolver. In use through both world wars and numerous other conflicts, the revolvers were supplemented by a range of automatic pistols, the largest of which also saw service.

The firm was first formed by two brothers, James and Philip Webley, in the 1830s. A contract for revolvers from the Irish constabulary resulted in the RIC model revolver. This was a great success and before its production was stopped at the turn of the century it had been adopted by many military and police units. A series of models followed which used patents of individuals. The major ones are Webley-Pryse, Webley-Wilkinson and Webley-Green.

The British army adopted their first Webley in 1887 and this was developed into the Mk6 in 1915 which fired the .455in cartridge. The .38in Webley revolver was used during World War II and remained in service until superseded in the 1950s by the Browning Hi Power.

The Webley-Fosbery was an automatic revolver produced in small quantities. The true automatic pistols ranged in calibre and size from the massive .455 Webley, which was a locked breech design, downwards through the blowback calibres of 9mm, .32 acp, .25 acp and .22LR.

Webley still make revolvers as well as shotguns, air pistols and rifles.

Dan Wesson Arms

Daniel B. Wesson was the cofounder of Smith and Wesson and the present Daniel B. Wesson is his great grandson. After working in the Smith and Wesson empire (as had all his family), Dan Wesson left soon after the firm had been taken over by the Bangor Punta organization. His first business after this, in 1967, was the Daniel B. Wesson Company, which manufactured screw machines. His love of guns was paramount, however, and he soon put his ideas on paper. The firm's engineers had a working prototype revolver ready in 1968 and, as this showed great promise, Wesson decided to go ahead and start production. A new company was formed called Dan Wesson Arms which not only was designed to manufacture the revolver but also to sell a complete range of firearms, many of which were manufactured by Brno.

White, R.

Rollin White was a Colt employee who patented one of the basic patents that led to the modern revolver. Unfortunately he made little in the way of money from the patent, so assiduous was he in protecting his patent regardless of cost. Because the patent was so crucial the legal wrangling became very expensive.

The patent was for the boring through of the revolver cylinder. As all but the oddest cartridges rely on being loaded from the rear of the cylinder, unlike the percussion type, it followed that without the use of this patent cartridge revolvers were almost impossible to manufacture.

Colt did not take up the patent but their great rival Smith and Wesson did so for their rimfire revolvers. It was not until the expiry of the Rollin White patent that other manufacturers were able to use the bored-through cylinder.

Williams, D. M.

When, in 1952, MGM released a film called *Carbine Williams* starring James Stewart, they brought to the public's attention one of the most incredible stories in the history of firearms. David Marshall Williams was born in 1900 in North Carolina. His early jobs included a spell in the US Navy and a time working on the railroads. In common with many people he took part in the supply of illicit alcohol during the Prohibition era and as a result became involved

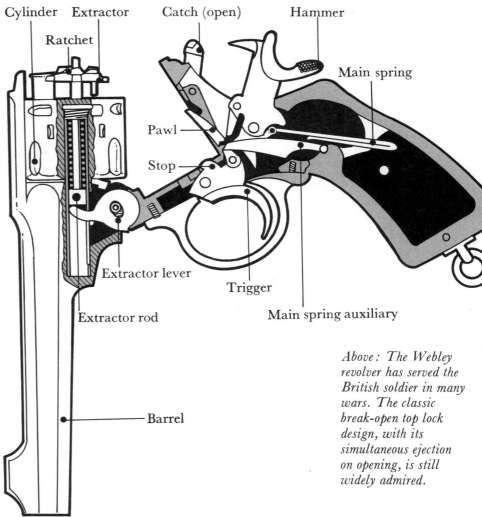

Above: The Webley revolver has served the British soldier in many wars. The classic break-open top lock design, with its simultaneous ejection on opening, is still widely admired.

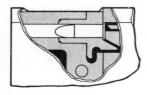

Above: The Williams floating chamber, before firing (top) and after firing.
Below: An 1876 Winchester, one of the 'thousand' that the company said would be produced in 1876. In fact the total number of these selected rifles fell short of the projected 1,000.
Opposite: The Smith and Wesson .44 Magnum, a gun that has become a legend. It is the most powerful production hand gun in the world.

in a gunfight with the law. An officer was killed and at the trial Williams was sentenced to 30 years in prison for manslaughter. His work on firearms while in prison may have seemed extraordinary, but the prison governor was a man who recognized genius and did all in his power to help.

An early release in 1930, together with a number of prototype guns constructed in prison, started him on a career in gun design. He took out the first of some 70 patents in 1931 and designed two valuable training aids. The first was a unit that allowed the army .30 machine gun to fire .22 rimfire ammunition, and the second was a similar device for the .45 automatic pistol. Although Williams produced a successful rifle for Remington it was not until Winchester produced his classic M1 carbine of 1941 that fame came his way. The little M1 carbine became a firm favourite of both the American army and civilian customers. More than 6 million military weapons alone were built. Williams died in 1975 and the world lost one of the truly original designers of weapons of the 20th century.

Winchester

It was the enthusiasm of a shirt manufacturer, Oliver Fisher Winchester, that led to the formation of the Winchester company. When he sold the shirt business and set up shop in New Haven, Connecticut, Winchester took with him Benjamin Tyler Henry who was already a brilliant gunsmith with a rifle design to his credit. Henry had been working for Winchester at his New Haven Arms Company factory before the decision to concentrate on guns, not shirts, was taken. The new concern was called the Win-

chester Repeating Arms Company, and their ability to make reliable repeating rifles led to rapid expansion. The Model 66 was followed by the 73, which has often been called the gun that won the West. The company then announced the 76, which proved every bit as successful as its predecessors. The addition of the designs of the great John Browning to the firm's line led to more success, and by the time Winchester died in 1890 the company was a multi-million dollar enterprise.

World War I brought expansion and its termination the problem of too large a labour force and too many machines to be supported by the depressed home market for sporting goods. Valiant efforts to diversify were made but only led to further losses.

The Western Cartridge Company was, however, set on expansion and had at its head John Olin who, in 1931, bought Winchester and renamed the concern the Winchester-Western Company. War work again saw the company expand and the reputation for sporting ammunition and firearms was maintained. The Winchester-Western Company later became a division of the Olin Mathieson Corporation. The company still produces sporting ammunition and guns that are considered amongst the best.

Zbrojovka Praga

Czechoslovakia was formed at the conclusion of World War I and the factory of Zbrojovka Praga was formed by A. Nowotny in 1918, the same year. The company was located in the capital, Prague, and was to specialize in the manufacture of pistols. Bankruptcy in 1926 forced it to become the property of a bank and eventually to close. In its short life it not only produced pistols but employed very talented designers. A pistol designed by Vaclav Holek, later of Bren gun fame, became standard issue for the police. Both Karel Kranka and Frantisek Myska also were employed at the factory for short periods.

Revolvers

The *Oxford Dictionary* defines a revolver thus: 'A pistol provided with mechanism by which a set of loaded barrels, or (more usually) of cartridge-chambers, is revolved and presented successively before the hammer, so as to admit of the rapid discharge of several shots without reloading.'

While this does not include the revolving rifle or the closely-related revolving feed weapons, it embodies the basic requirements.

Although the revolver is normally, as a type, identified as a handgun, a number of long guns of all types have used the system. The desire to fire more than one shot at reasonable speed led, in the first instance, to the loading of more than one barrel. An early relation to the revolver was the so-called Holy Water Sprinkler, manufactured in the late 15th or early 16th century. This weapon was a combination of a club and a multi-barrelled longarm. The three barrels were of the matchlock type and were rotated by means of the staff on which the whole assembly was mounted.

A document dated about 1400 shows another form of revolver, one that resembles a wheel mounted on a vertical axle. The wheel incorporates four barrels, one pointing to each of the points of the compass. The four barrels are little bigger than a large

Above and opposite: A percussion sporting rifle using turnover barrels. This rifle has a set trigger for more accurate shooting and is beautifully stocked and engraved. The catch for the barrel rotation is at the front of the trigger guard. The problems associated with this system – size and weight – are well illustrated.

Below: This very early form of revolving rifle uses a matchlock. The use of multiple barrels which were muzzle loaded makes this weapon heavy but this was presumably felt to be of little consequence when considered against the ability to fire more than one shot. How reliable this system was must be open to doubt when the primitive construction is considered.

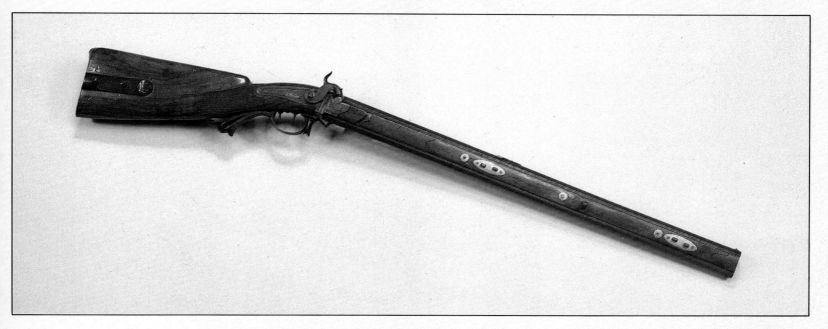

pistol and are of cannon ignition. This use of a barrel arranged like spokes on a wheel was revived at a later date with the wheel either in a vertical or horizontal mode. There is little to prove that such a weapon was made at this early date, but perhaps this was due to the lack of success, as was certainly so with later derivatives.

Both of these weapon types pointed the way to the development of the real revolving firearm. The history of the revolver seems to cover a number of phases. Initial interest was maintained for some time but, probably because of the problem with the cannon or flintlock ignition systems, it languished until the advent of percussion. The rush of development which then took place brought the revolver to the forefront and the invention of the cartridge emphasized the trend. Development again slowed with the evolution of the self-loading weapon, which designers hurried to produce. The 20th century has seen a revival of the revolver, which has now taken its place alongside the automatic with much work still being done to improve the breed.

The first known handgun to use a revolving system was an Italian three-barrelled pistol, dating from about 1550. The ignition was matchlock. A pistol of similar date was a three-barrelled wheellock of German origin. Both of these employed hand rotated barrels and because of the almost total dependence on hand operation the advantages were not very great. Development of the first longarm was somewhat later. The first can be dated from the late 1500s or early 1600s; they were more in the shape of large wall gun-types than shoulder portable. The problem of having a longarm with multiple barrels was that the weight became prohibitive. Such weapons were produced in small quantities.

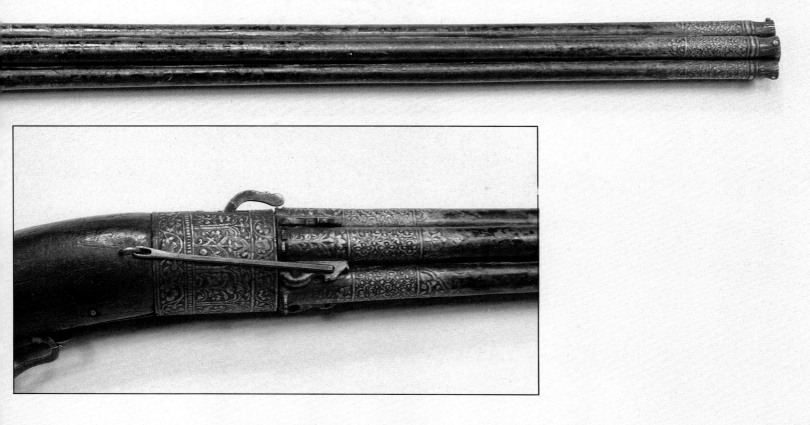

Right: The lock of a hand-rotated flintlock long arm. This is a true revolver in that the powder charges and projectiles are contained in a cylinder and fired through one barrel. One problem with the single lock was that it had to be primed for each shot.

Below: The relatively compact configuration would have made this a practical repeating weapon. The intricate inlays of metal in both the action and the stock and fore-end would indicate a most highly prized weapon almost certainly manufactured to special order.

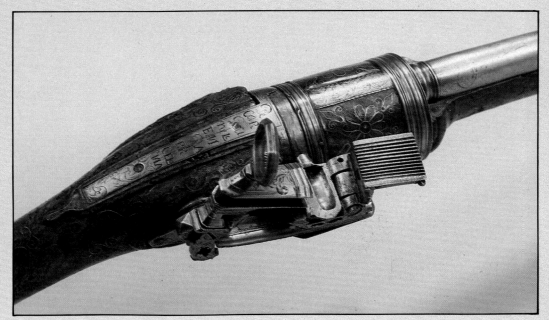

A basic form of the revolver that came into vogue in the early to middle 17th century was the turnover barrel type. This had two barrels set vertically and pivoted so that they could be turned when one was fired. The fact that there were only two barrels and that they both carried their own flint-lock made the pistols somewhat cumbersome and only marginally better than a single barrel. They became very popular weapons in Europe, especially in France and Holland. The longarm version was developed but was relatively heavy and bulky.

A much needed development was the use of a single lock for multiple barrels. A typical example is one manufactured by Lorenzoni in about 1680. This had three barrels but only a single lock. The rotation of the barrels by a system other than the hand received attention and a five barrelled pistol by Kolbe in the 1730s had the barrels rotated when the lock was cocked. This did not, however, overcome the problem of priming, which had to be carried out each time the weapon was fired.

The use of the multiple barrel in pistols has led to the generic term pepperbox or pepperpot, because of their similarity to the domestic item. The multiple-barrelled longarm soon became almost obsolete with the adop-tion of the revolving cylinder system. Even the invention of the percussion system brought it little popularity. The pistol, on the other hand, experienced a revival and there are numerous examples of percussion pepperboxes.

The use of a cylinder to hold the load and thus the ability to use a single barrel brought about the beginning of the revolver as it is now known. An early example was a German wheel-lock that had to be primed for every shot. The barrels were hand rotated and a tube or tunnel connected the lock to a hole at the rear of the barrel. This dates from 1600. Use of the flint-lock with a very similar operation appears a little later with a Russian example dated in the first quarter of the 17th century.

Much work was done to develop this type of pistol in order to refine the principle and although most remained hand-rotated, many employed forms of automatic priming. Far from being a short lived type, some were manu-factured well into the 19th century. One typical example was the Collier which was made in London as late as 1820.

The longarm grasped the advantage of the deletion of the heavy barrel cluster, and from the beginning of the 17th century the matchlock longarm was produced. The French produced five- and eight-chambered types with primer pan covers that were pushed back by hand. As the cylinder was hand-turned this was not as incon-venient as it first seems. The Germans, with their preference for the wheel-lock, developed a hand-rotated six-chambered longarm in the same period. This had to be primed for each shot. It is interesting to note that, as with the single-shot weapon, the Indians were still manufacturing matchlock revolv-ing longarms as late as the 18th century and presumably using them much later.

Both the pistol and the longarm show the lock development with Snaphance, Miquelet and true flint-locks. The Wheeler Flintlock Long-arm with its four chambers and a magazine primer system was produced in England as late as the 1820s. A form of automatic rotation was developed with the action of the hammer, which either rotated or caused the rotating of the chambers. This was used, albeit rarely, on some of the later pistols. Typical was the Collier development which used a spring as the means of rotation. The automatic rotation and magazine primer systems represented a high point in the development of the revolver before the percussion era.

The percussion system brought a resurgence of interest in multiple-

The main photograph (far left) shows a true revolving rifle with a hand-rotated cylinder and a single lock. The lock is a wheellock and is shown with the hammer in the loading position. At left is the London-manufactured Collier flintlock revolving pistol. Superbly finished pistols had a relatively long life and they were still in production in the first quarter of the 19th century. The Collier marked the high point in early revolver design.

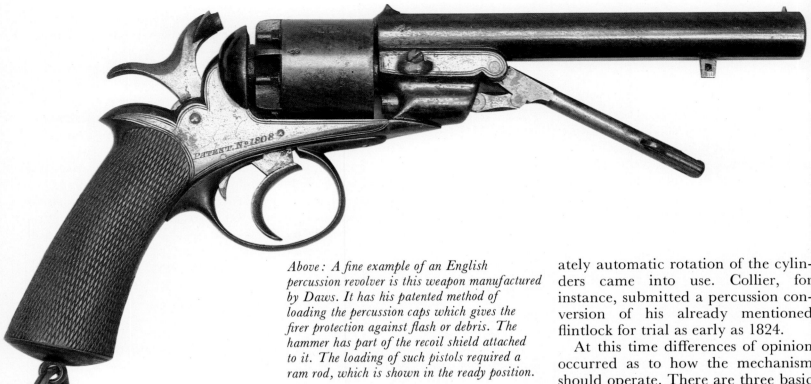

Above: A fine example of an English percussion revolver is this weapon manufactured by Daws. It has his patented method of loading the percussion caps which gives the firer protection against flash or debris. The hammer has part of the recoil shield attached to it. The loading of such pistols required a ram rod, which is shown in the ready position.

Above: The simplest form of revolver is probably the 'turnover barrel' type. This example is a percussion-fired pocket pistol that features a sliding safety catch behind the hammer. This system for giving more than one shot was quite popular in pocket pistol size but because of the bulk and weight of the barrels it was little used in longarms.

ately automatic rotation of the cylinders came into use. Collier, for instance, submitted a percussion conversion of his already mentioned flintlock for trial as early as 1824.

At this time differences of opinion occurred as to how the mechanism should operate. There are three basic methods of operation used in revolvers. The first is the single action. In this the hammer is cocked and at the same time provides the rotation of the cylinder or barrels. The second is the self-cocking, where the trigger actuates both the hammer and the rotation of the cylinder or barrels as it is operated. The final type gives the firer the option of either hand-cocking or pulling the trigger and accomplishing the whole operation in one. A further group of systems, used only during the evolution of these methods, used a separate mechanism to rotate the barrels or cylinder, but as this forced the firer to operate two separate systems before he could fire they were short lived.

The first use of the single-action and self-cocking on the pepperbox has been claimed by a number of inventors, but the date can be set in the early 1830s. A single-action pepperbox was in production by its patentees, the brothers Darling, in the United States in 1836. By the 1840s the self-cocking type was popular in England and many were produced.

Perhaps the classic form of the pepperbox pistol to be evolved was the Ethan Allan type, which had a self-cocking mechanism. The action of the trigger raised a bar hammer (a long bar that struck the percussion cap almost vertically) and rotated the cylinder via a separate lever that engaged in teeth on the rear of the

barrelled pepperbox firearms. It also brought about the final development of the self-rotating mechanism. The pepperbox seems to have pre-dated the cylinder revolver by only a few years. The use of the percussion system on longarms of the multi-barrel type did give rise to some development but the problems of weight and size once again discouraged wide use.

The first pepperbox percussion pistols were the hand-rotated type and date from the early 1820s. While they were definitely a vast improvement on what had gone before, almost immedi-

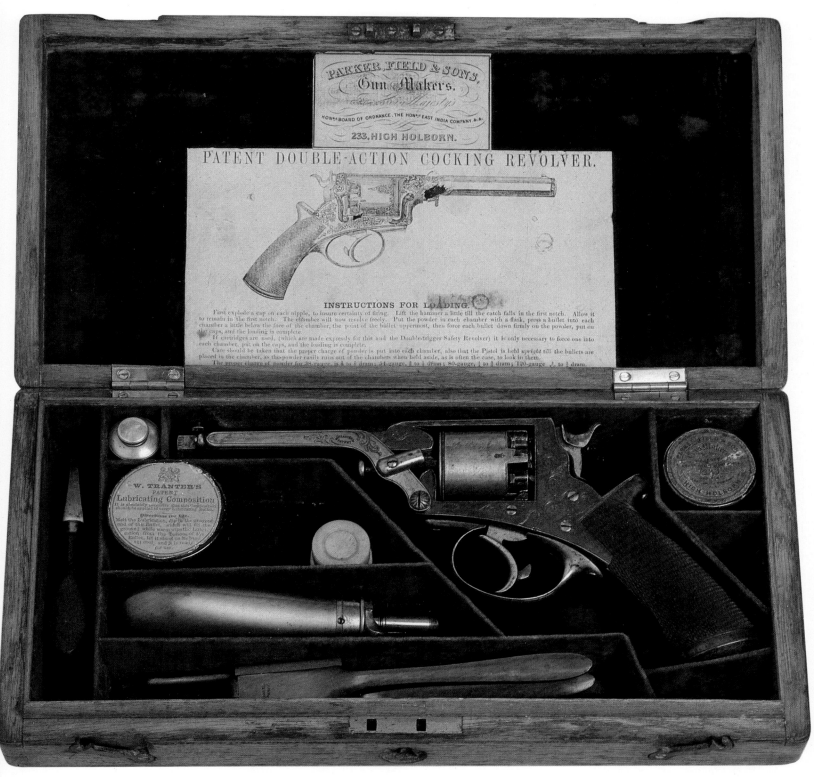

cylinder. The other popular type was the Mariette, which used an under hammer (on the underside of the pistol). The feature of this type later to be copied was that the nipples were in line with the bore as opposed to the Allan type, which were at right angles.

The pepperbox pistol lasted longer than its longarm equivalent but the compactness and lighter weight of the revolving cylinder type caused its eclipse. The adoption of the cartridge saw a brief surge of interest but production had almost stopped by the early 1870s.

Sam Colt's revolver

The inventor of the first percussion revolver to have a cylinder rather than a pepperbox will always be debated. There were, without doubt, a number of self-cocking cylinder revolvers at the beginning of the 19th century, many based on the flintlock revolver such as the Collier. But the first practical revolver capable of being produced in quantity and which worked with reasonable reliability must be attributed to Samuel Colt. Colt took out his patent in Europe before the master one was taken out in America.

A Tranter double-action percussion revolver. This English-manufactured revolver was very popular because of its high quality of production. This particular Tranter is cased as sold originally by Parker Field and Sons of High Holborn, London. The case contains not only the revolver, which is engraved in the traditional English style, but also the accessories needed for firing. With a bullet mould, powder flask, bullet lubricant and percussion caps, the owner had only to melt some lead and he could then start firing.

The English patent was taken out in 1835 as No. 6909 and covered the rotation mechanism, the cylinder lock and the fact that the percussion nipples were in line with the bore of the chamber it fired. The lock was of the single-action type and the frame of the weapon of the open type. Loading had to be carried out chamber by chamber from the front of the pistol.

Before the patents, Colt had made a number of weapons to develop his ideas. The first were revolving rifles manufactured by such gunmakers as Chase and Rowe. These had the cylinder rotated by a lever rather than the hammer or trigger, and thus harked back to earlier weapons. They date from 1832. The first pistols followed two years later, being manufactured by Pearson, Chase and others. With no production facilities of his own, Colt had all his early pistols and rifles manufactured by others.

Colt was not only a talented inventor, he was also a very persuasive salesman. With little or no money of his own to produce his pistol, he managed to persuade others to fund the Patent Arms Manufacturing Company, based at Paterson, New Jersey.

The first production pistol was a five-shot, open frame with a folding trigger. There was no trigger guard and the trigger came into the firing position when the weapon was cocked. To load the weapon the barrel was removed by driving out a wedge. The chambers could then be loaded with powder either individually or, with a specially designed loader, all five at once. The ball could then be forced in and the barrel refitted. The percussion caps were then fitted to the nipples and the weapon was ready to fire.

The first Colt production rifles still used a lever or ring to operate the cylinder and it was not until 1851 that the rifles dropped this feature. Fortunately for Colt, the courts declared that the pawl cylinder revolving patent covered not only a pawl system but any mechanical rotation system. This, with the addition of a patent extension until 1857, effectively stopped the development of the revolver in America until that date.

The English-made percussion revolver was the only challenge to the Colt. The well-known Birmingham gunsmith Robert Adams was in the fore-

front. The firm of Deane, Adams and Deane produced self-cocking revolvers, the patent model of which had been seen at the Great Exhibition in London in 1851. In Europe the Belgians were the most active but the majority of their designs owed more to Colt and Adams than to Belgian designers.

By the time of Colt's death in 1862 the percussion revolver was being manufactured by a number of well-known gunsmiths both in England and America. Typical of these were the English makers Tranter, Beaumont-Adams and Webley, and in America, Remington (Beal's patents of 1856–7) and Starr Arms (Starr patents of 1856 and 1861). The expiry of the patents led to great activity. The percussion era closed with numerous developments in the trigger mechanism and the adoption of the solid frame, in which the top of the barrel was joined

to the breech by a top strap which allowed the use of more powerful loads than the inherently weaker open frame designs. The double-action trigger incorporating the advantages of both the self-cocking and single-action types was used by such developers as John Adams in 1867 and had been patented as early as 1855 by Lieutenant Beaumont.

One brave and successful revolver design came at the close of the percussion era. This was the two barrelled 'grape shot' revolver of the New Orleans doctor Jean Le Mat. He produced a nine-chambered percussion revolver in 1856 which had a shot barrel as the pivot for the bullet-firing cylinder. The hammer could be made to fire the standard cylinder under normal conditions but when the enemy were especially numerous the shot barrel could be selected and fired.

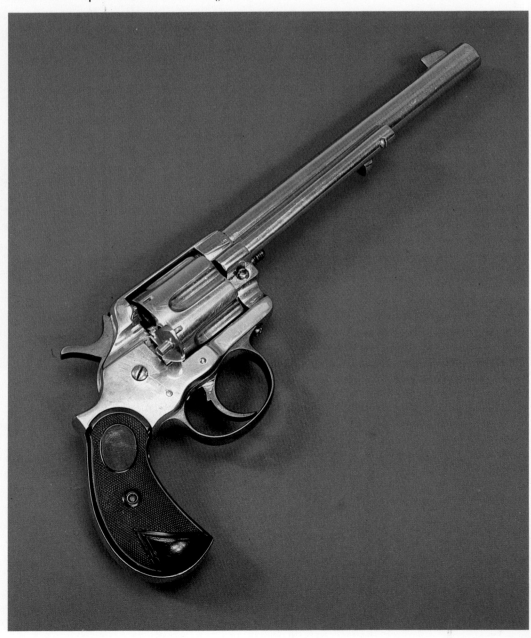

Pinfire and rimfire cartridges

The development of the cartridge was the start of the last era in the evolution of the revolver. The pinfire cartridge, although made almost obsolete by the invention of the rimfire and centrefire types, enjoyed popularity in Europe and lasted until just before World War I. The first cartridge revolver to be developed and put into production was of the pinfire type. The son of the patentee of the cartridge itself, Eugene Lefaucheux, took out a British patent in April 1854, No. 0955, for a single-action gateloaded pistol with an open frame in 11mm calibre.

The pinfire revolver received its first military use by the French navy after extensive tests against British and American revolvers of the non-cartridge type, including the Colt. The pistol was produced at the St Etienne arsenal from 1858. In 1863 Spain followed with purchases of the basic type and Norway and Sweden with a double-action version.

It is perhaps unfortunate, and in some respects undeserved, that the pinfire as a type has been condemned as a cheap and badly made weapon. This reputation arose from the popularity of the pistol which caused production to spread into the hands of the less professional gunsmiths and rank amateurs. Such people produced very second-rate weapons that often show signs of hand fitting in the shape of rough file marks. Makers such as Mangeot-Comblain, however, made pistols that show the highest quality of craftsmanship. Even today, if they have been carefully looked after, they are capable of being fired with safety.

The pinfire was not produced in the United States, as the rimfire was already available, although some were imported during the Civil War. Britain manufactured a number of pinfires and imported many more. The similarity between some of the continental pinfires and those alleged to have been manufactured in Britain have led experts to suspect that the weapons were merely assembled and finished in Britain and not totally manufactured in the country.

The next development was to have far reaching results. This was the patent of Horace Smith and Daniel Wesson for the rimfire cartridge in America in 1854 with the Flobert type and then in 1860 with the definitive type. The patent was important, but both men realized that when the Colt patent on the mechanically-rotated cylinder expired the use of a breech-loaded cartridge would be a great advance. So they contacted Rollin White who worked in New Haven and who had taken out a patent which they thought would help them. White, an eccentric, had patented a revolver that was loaded from the rear of the cylinder with a cartridge backed up by a leather wad. The system employed

by him was not satisfactory and Smith and Wesson had no interest in it, but they realized the importance of the other part of the patent which dealt with the boring through of the cylinder for the purpose of loading the cartridge. It was obvious that this would be the only practical means of loading a cartridge.

The agreement worked out between Smith, Wesson and White was that the former should have the patent assigned to them solely and that White would be paid a fee on every pistol produced. Another important clause which, like the Colt patent, was to block development, was the provision that White should pursue anyone who infringed the patent. The patent was bitterly contested on a number of occasions but held fast until it expired in 1869. The Smith and Wesson concern were fair in their dealings, however, and anyone who would meet the necessary licence criteria were granted licences to produce pistols with the bored-through cylinder.

The methods adopted by other makers to load the cylinder from the front led to all types of weird and wonderful inventions, the best of them probably being the 'teat' fire of Williams and the 'cup' fire of Ellis. In Britain, where the master patent did not apply, there was a rush to produce rimfire revolvers. William Tranter in particular and others such as Deane and Webley all manufactured single or double action revolvers.

Once again Europe was the first to develop a different system when they adopted the centrefire cartridge for the revolver as early as 1860. The White patent blocked its practical use in the United States, but with its demise the market was open and the centrefire revolver became the standard for all calibres of any consequence. The rimfire, however, remained and is still in use today.

Opposite: An early Smith and Wesson 'tip up' .22 rimfire revolver. First produced in 1857 this revolver used the famous Rollin White patent for a bored-through cylinder.
Right: A Smith and Wesson Highway Patrolman revolver. This is a typical high-quality, modern .357 magnum revolver with a solid frame and a swingout cylinder. The model has proved very popular with American policemen.

Loading and unloading

With the basic design of the revolver stabilized with its bored-through cylinder and, for the main part, the solid frame (that is, not open topped), diversification in the mechanics of loading and unloading became the main area of development. The two systems that were the basis for much experiment were the hinged frame and the solid frame. A number of pistols were made with pivoting frames of one sort or another but none achieved any real production volume.

The hinged frame revolver divides into two sub-types. First the tip-up which was exemplified by the original Smith and Wesson rimfire, where the hinge was on the top strap and the catch at the bottom. This system was not used in many types and with the adoption of the ejection mechanism it would only have been a problem. Secondly, there was the tip-down revolver where the catch was at the joint of the top strap and the breech face with the pivot at the front bottom. This was to become the standard in Britain where the Webley in particular was developed in many forms.

The solid frame had been the basic weapon and the method of loading had started with a gate at the rear on one side of the frame through which the cylinder could be loaded and unloaded. This was limited in that only one round

at a time could be unloaded or loaded. A simple solution was to make the cylinder itself removable by the use of a cylinder pin that was able to be drawn out. The final combination of the strength of the solid frame and the convenience of the break frame was found in the swing-out cylinder. This system, which has achieved acceptance in the vast bulk of modern pistols, pivoted the cylinder on a crane that, when released, allowed it to be swung out of the frame normally to the left. This allowed easy loading and unloading.

The ejection of the empty or unfired round from the cylinder became a matter of importance. The hinged frame revolver allowed the development of an automatic ejector that worked by the action of the barrel being swung down. On other designs the cases were pulled out horizontally by the extractor. The solid frame soon settled on the swing-out cylinder with its centre rod operating the ejector.

Although the adoption of the cartridge could have led to the most efficient of revolving rifles, the very fact that it was a self-contained unit led to development in other areas. As a result, few revolving rifles were made. Smith and Wesson manufactured one, but this was little more than a permanently fitted shoulder stock on a pistol. A successful use of the revolver

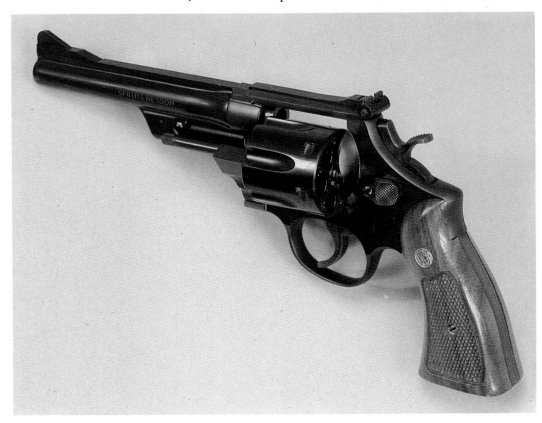

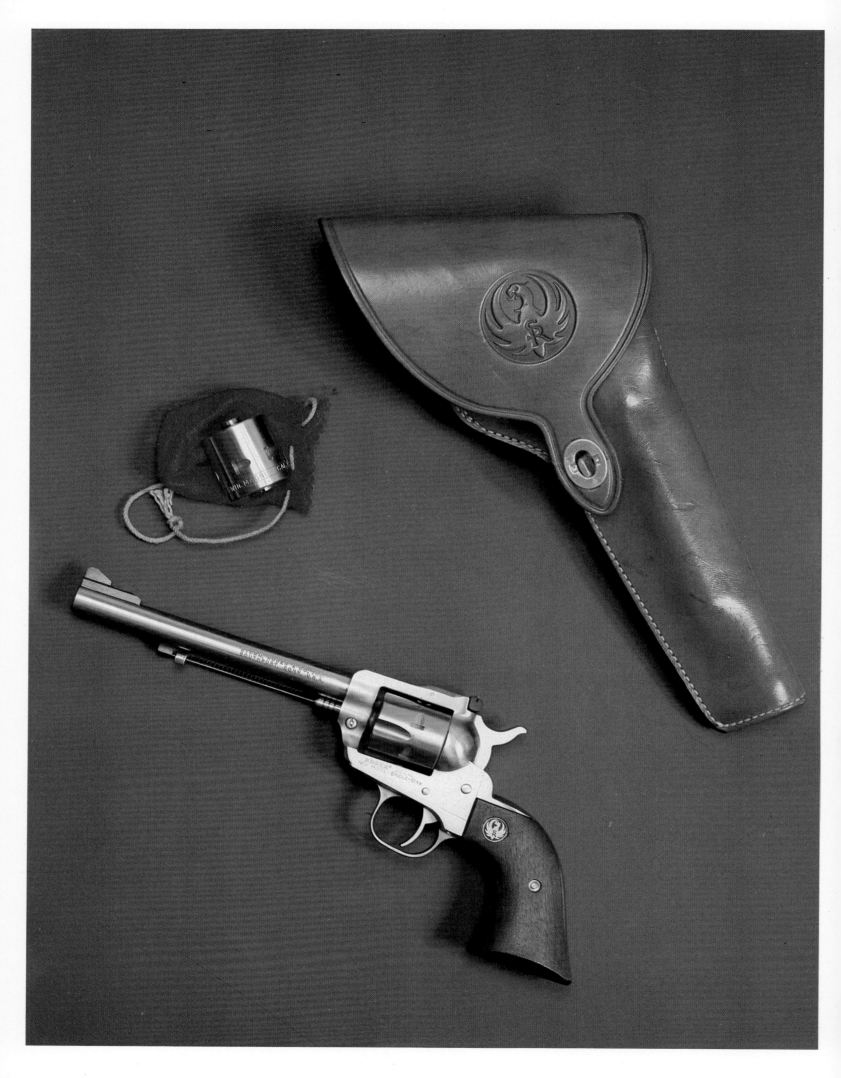

other than in the pistol was the revolving barrelled machine gun. The combination of the pepperbox barrel configuration and the cartridge led to a most efficient system that has lasted until today.

The first Gatling had been designed during the percussion era. But with the rimfire then the centrefire cartridges the weapon became fully effective and saw service with many armies including those of Britain, America, France, Russia and China. From its original patent in 1865 through its adoption as a rimfire in 1866 and centrefire in 1868 development continued, but the standard design was the 10-barrelled version. As the handle was turned the bolts were moved back and forward as the barrels rotated. The cartridges thus would first be fed into the chamber then fired at the five o'clock position, then extracted and ejected before the cycle started again.

Another revolving machine gun was the French Hotchkiss that fired a cannon-type shell. This saw service with the French navy in the early 1880s.

The final part of the story of the revolving cannon was the American development of the electric-driven version of the Gatling. Gatling had in his early days achieved 3,000 rounds per minute, and with the emergence of high-speed aircraft and the need to have the maximum amount of destructive material on its way in the minimum time the Gatling has found favour. It has also been developed as a short range antiaircraft weapon both from the ground and from armoured vehicles and ships. One such weapon, with its massive ammunition storage, is larger than a small family car.

One mechanical defect of the standard revolver is the gap between the barrel and the cylinder. This allows a certain amount of the propellant gases to be lost, although tests have shown

that the loss is not significant. A group of inventors held that any loss should be avoided and so the gas seal revolver was developed. The system of locking the barrel against a chamber had been used in flintlock weapons and therefore the idea was far from new. The percussion revolver had also seen attempts to produce a practical design. The use of metallic cartridges was to bring the only successful production of the gas seal revolver. Experiments by Pieper in 1886 led to the production of a revolver by his own company and by Steyr in Austria.

The pistol that is best known and has been used most recently as a target weapon was patented in 1894 by L. Nagant of Liège. This pistol was adopted by the Russians in 1896 and served them until World War II. The basis is a cartridge case that has the bullet seated some way down. As the weapon is about to fire the cylinder is cammed forward and the case mouth seals the barrel cylinder joint. At the point of firing the cylinder is wedged firmly forward. The added complications of operation have caused modern designers to ignore any form of gas seal as the advantages of a marginal gain in velocity do not outweigh the disadvantages.

As with the gas seal so the automatic revolver did not achieve popularity. Only one design has survived to any

extent, and even it is rare. There had been a number of weapons in which the feed mechanism was of the revolving type but the mechanism was either gas or mechanical. These are not true revolvers and come into the category of revolving feed.

The G. V. Fosbery patent of 1895 established the principle of using the recoil energy to cock the hammer and rotate the cylinder. The pistol was improved by successive patents by Fosbery himself and then after he had started to work with Webley and Scott, in conjunction with them. The basis of the weapon is the standard Webley hinged frame with the 'zig-zag' cylinder with a rotation groove on the cylinder. This gave rise to a weapon that was not only capable of extremely rapid fire but also great accuracy. While never achieving official adoption the Fosbery was carried by many officers in World War I but suffered in the mud of the trenches. No other automatic revolvers of any note have been produced in quantity.

Revolving feed systems

The use of a revolver-type mechanism to feed a weapon while not producing a true revolver is sufficiently closely related to be worthy of a brief study. The box magazine has become the universally popular way to feed ammunition into a weapon, but there have

Opposite: The Ruger new model super single-six revolver. This model brings the traditional design up to date and provides the single-action enthusiast with modern design and technology at its best. This particular pistol is chambered for both the popular .22LR and the more powerful .22WMR. It is manufactured in stainless steel.
Right: A Webley hinged-frame revolver for the .455 cartridge. This is the WG model.

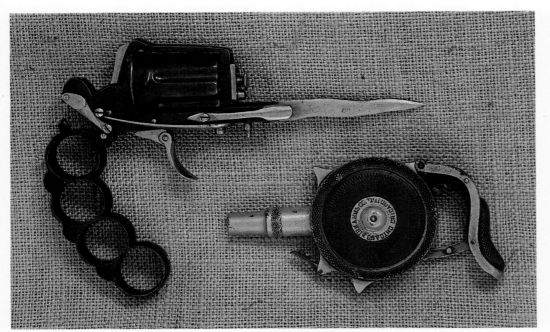

was in line with the barrel for firing and the third was open for the empty to be ejected. The trigger had to move the cylinder 120 degrees each shot. This potentially good idea did not become a success although it was revived in various forms.

The revolver today is still the basic weapon of many police forces although it has largely been superseded by the self-loader for military use. The single action has seen a revival of interest with manufacturers such as Ruger and Colt producing pistols in calibres from .22 to .44 magnum. The double-action swing-out cylinder of the Smith and Wesson design is now the standard revolver type although Webley and Harrington and Richardson still produce the break-frame type. Developments such as the interchangeable barrel for the Dan Wesson revolver have met with success.

The one area in which the revolver has undisputed superiority over the self-loader is that of power. It can use cartridges of immense size. The development of the so-called magnum cartridge, first in .357 calibre, then in .44, has given the shooter a gun that is the closest possible relation of a hand cannon. The fact that many shooters just cannot handle the recoil energy of the .44 magnum round does not deter those who like to have the most powerful handgun in the world.

been a number of successful (and many more unsuccessful) revolving types of feeds or magazines.

The use of a rotary magazine was patented in 1884 by Schoenhauer on behalf of the firm that was to become Steyr in Austria. This magazine is one of the few to be still in use today. The manufacturers of the Mannlicher-Schoenhauer sporting rifles still prefer it to the box type. Other modern manufacturers such as Ruger have used the rotary magazine, but examples are few.

The detachable rotary magazine which uses the rotary concept for the

success, but for reluctance on the part of the public to move from the 'tested and true'. It was made by the Dardick Corporation of Hamden, Connecticut. This pistol was based on a new ammunition concept, the basis of which was the 'tround'. The 'tround' was a plastic case shaped in a triangular section with the sides curved so that they corresponded to the diameter of the outside of the cylinder. The three-chambered cylinder did not totally enclose the 'tround' but left the outside of the three sides open. The 'trounds' were fed from a magazine below. The first of the chambers was filled, the second

carriage of large quantities of ammunition has been seen on two well-known weapons. The first patented in 1911 was the 'Trommelmagazin' for the Luger pistol, better known as the 'Snail' drum. This fed 32 rounds of 9mm or, in an abortive experimental version, 100 rounds. The Thompson submachine gun used a drum magazine of either 50 or, on rare occasions, 100 rounds. Many other examples are known but the concept has never proved popular mainly because of the loading problems and the overall weight of the loaded magazine.

A modern version of the revolver feed mechanism could have been a

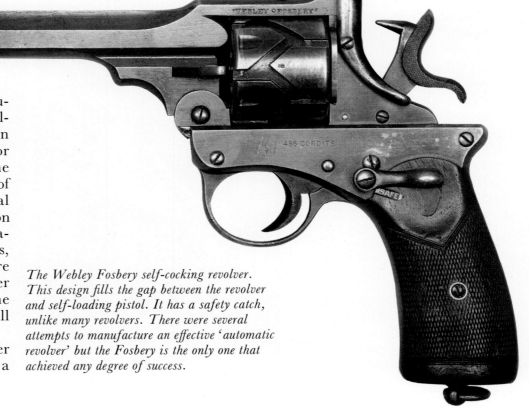

The Webley Fosbery self-cocking revolver. This design fills the gap between the revolver and self-loading pistol. It has a safety catch, unlike many revolvers. There were several attempts to manufacture an effective 'automatic revolver' but the Fosbery is the only one that achieved any degree of success.

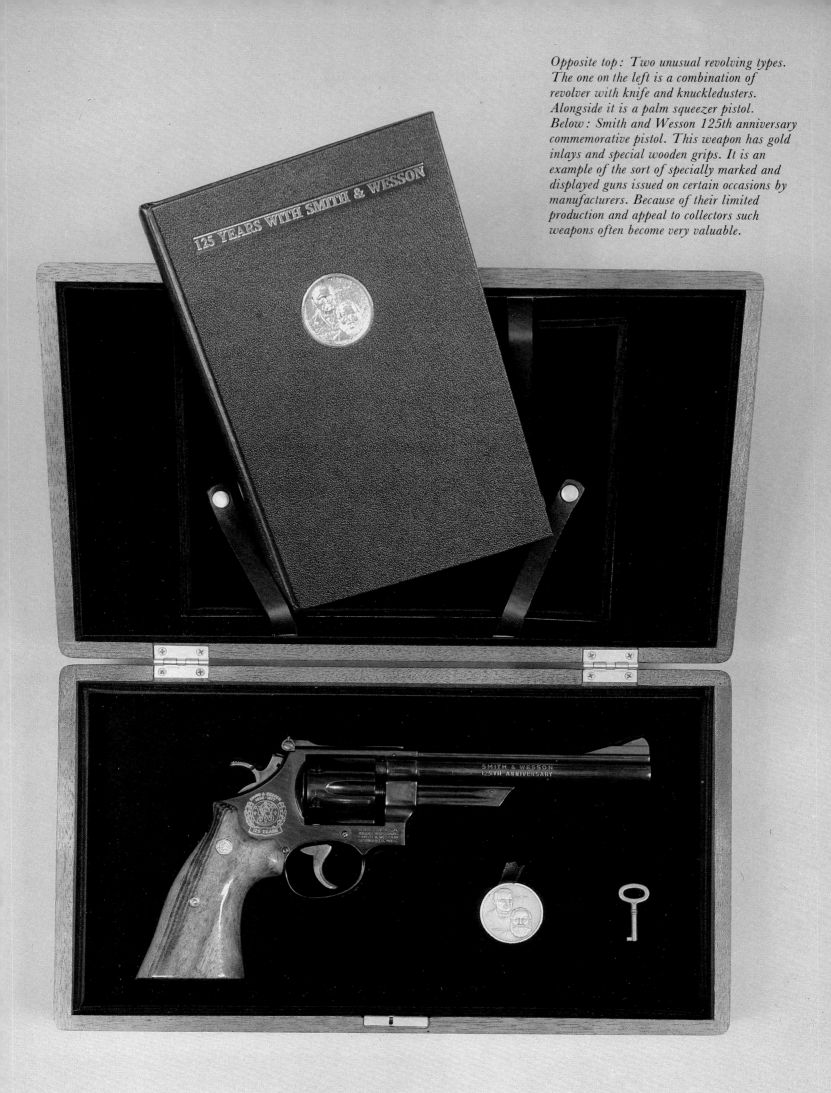

Opposite top: Two unusual revolving types. The one on the left is a combination of revolver with knife and knuckledusters. Alongside it is a palm squeezer pistol. Below: Smith and Wesson 125th anniversary commemorative pistol. This weapon has gold inlays and special wooden grips. It is an example of the sort of specially marked and displayed guns issued on certain occasions by manufacturers. Because of their limited production and appeal to collectors such weapons often become very valuable.

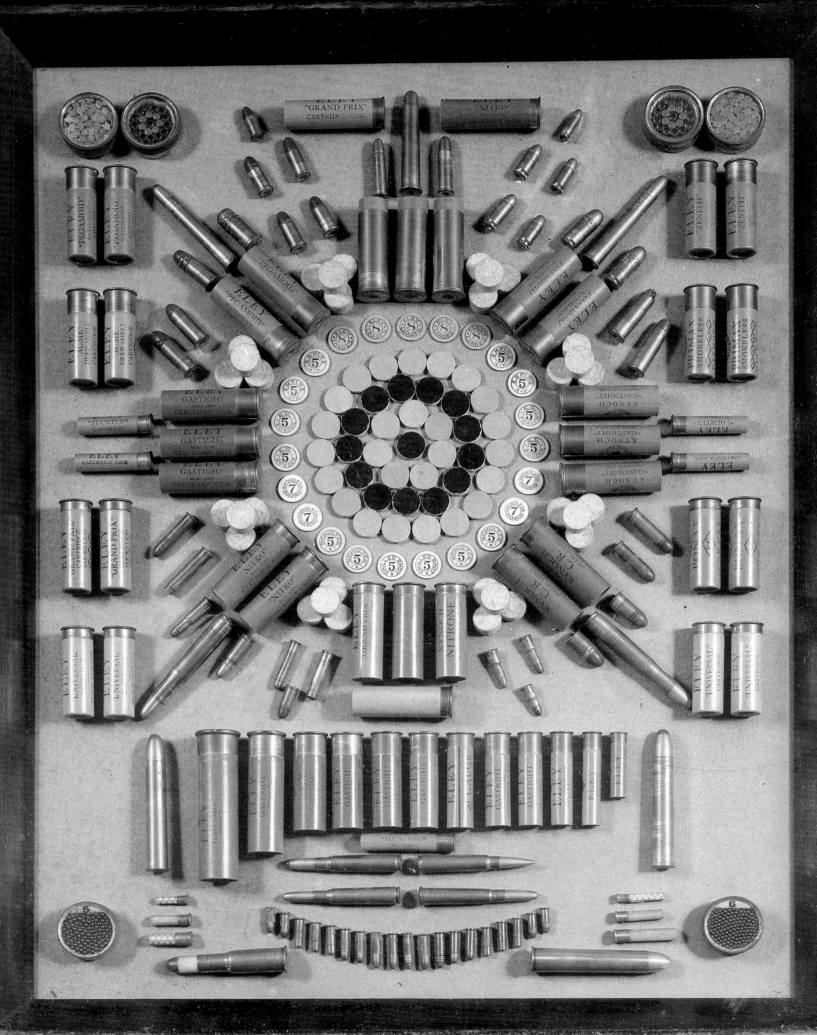

Towards Accuracy
Ammunition & Gunsights

The development of sights and sighting systems has been governed largely by the accuracy of the weapon itself. There was little point in sights that were usable at long range if the weapon itself was inaccurate. Not that this has ever stopped the optimistic claims of the gunmaker as to the efficiency of his product. Sights on many weapons show wildly optimistic belief in the long-range ability of weapons that are quite unsuitable. Pistols, not noted for long range shooting ability, have had sights marked with 1,000m (3,280ft).

In the first instance all types of firearms were aimed at the target rather than sighted. The dangers inherent in the firing did not encourage the firer to spend extra time taking a careful look at his intended target. The weapons themselves were, in any case, totally incapable of any real accuracy. The general maxim was 'point and fire in the general direction of a preferably massed target'.

The addition of a small aiming mark at the end of the barrel was the first form of sight and has lasted to this day as the bead on the shotgun. A rib, often raised and patterned, has been added to the shotgun to give a better aiming mark.

To provide a simple sighting system a second mark was soon fixed to the breech end of the weapon enabling the firer to line up the target and barrel accurately. The use of sights of this type on longarms was prevalent in the mid-15th century but not until the late 17th century were they incorporated in a pistol. Indeed, only in the late 18th century were sights on pistols a common fitting. The second mark took the form of a notch in the shape of a V or U. It has become the standard sighting system that is still used throughout the world.

Today many refinements have been added for both pistol and rifle. The front sight has had

the bead replaced by a blade or post. This can, in certain weapons, be illuminated in poor conditions by a Beta light. The rear notch has changed little, but now coloured or luminous outlines are used. The U backsight is known as the Patridge type.

At first no thought was given to the adjustment of the sights because of the inaccuracy of the weapon, but as this improved, the use of some form of adjustment was demanded by those who wanted to adjust or zero the weapon to their particular needs. The first system relied on a sharp tap with a hammer or some similar instrument. The rear or front sight was fitted into a dovetail that enabled it to be driven from side to side. This allowed for an adjustment in windage but not in elevation. The judicious use of a file on the front sight or in the rear notch had to suffice to lower or raise the point of aim.

The adjustable sight on a handgun as opposed to a rifle is less used and is normally reserved for the target range. Exceptions to this

Opposite: A case of Eley ammunition.
Below: Types of sight. Foresights: A Patridge blade with coloured post added; B McGovern gold bead insert; C Patridge blade on ramp; D Baughman quick draw sight with coloured insert; E Baughman quick draw. F is an adjustable rear sight with a white outline blade. The separate blade shown alongside, G, is of the plain type.

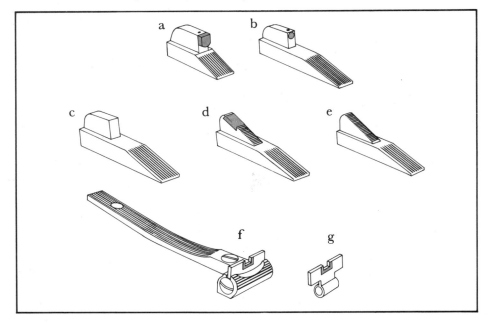

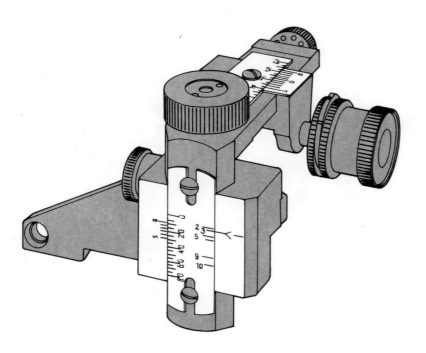

Above: Parker-Hale are world famous for their range of target rifles and sights. The Model 5 illustrated is designed for the 1200TX 7.62mm NATO rifle. A complex sight is needed to allow for wind variations at distances of 1,000 yards.

Below: A Zeiss 21.5-6 magnification variable telescopic sight. This type enables the firer to adjust the magnification to suit the target range and type.

include the Luger and Mauser, both of which have in some models complex and effective adjustments.

The simplest form of adjustment was to provide a series of flip-up or even replaceable rear sight blades, each of a different height. This system has been used on sporting rifles. Some pistols and rifles use interchangeable front sights of different heights, a system that is used extensively in a modified form today. The front sight is in the form of a post and is threaded into a mount. By screwing it up or down the zero for elevation can be achieved.

The rear sight developed and a small hole was used instead of the notch. This is called an aperture sight. Combined with a variety of types of foresight, it has proved almost universal on target rifles and is much used on military ones. The adjustment of the aperture sight ranges from the simple flip-over blade of military rifles that gives a choice of two ranges, to the very complex micrometer adjustable sight of the target rifle. The foresight for the target rifle is often of the 'tunnel' type with replaceable insert.

A telescope on a rifle was first used in the 18th century. The target shot, game shot and military sharpshooter all found that the optical aid in a variety of magnifications improved their

shooting to the limit of the rifle's accuracy. During the American War of Independence the sniper, able to hit his target from a place of concealment, brought danger to anyone who was foolish enough to raise his head from shelter. This often frowned-on branch of shooting had developed as far as the available equipment allowed. The sportsman had an array of scopes depending on his requirements. The low powered 4 × to the ultra high-powered 20 × were ideal, respectively, for general usage and the long range target shot. The stalker and game hunter, whether they are hunting the humble rabbit, the noble stag or more dangerous game rely on the scoped rifle.

Today the military have, because of the problems of adequate training, increased the use of telescopic sights. Indeed, such weapons as the new British 4.85mm rifle have a scope integral with the weapon. These scopes have such advanced features as illuminated aiming marks for use in low light conditions.

Another development is the sight which can 'see' in the dark. At first this used an infrared illuminator and a scope that could pick up the resultant image. This so-called Active principle was in general use until the Image Intensifier became an expensive but better solution. The Image Intensifier takes the available light and amplifies it to give the firer an accurate picture. Because of the high cost of these units they are restricted to special purposes within the armed forces.

Another type of sight that has seen some use is the Single Point type where the firer keeps both eyes open and the sight projects a dot into the firer's sight plane. This dot is laid on to the target and the weapon is aimed. The dot can be replaced by a variety of aiming marks in different systems. It has seen limited success fitted to the shotgun, pistol and rifle.

Regardless of the complex and expensive developments that have taken place the basic blade and notch, or its derivative the post and aperture, are the most popular sights after 500 years.

Evolution of rifling

The use of rifling to impart a twist to the projectile can be accurately dated but the true in-

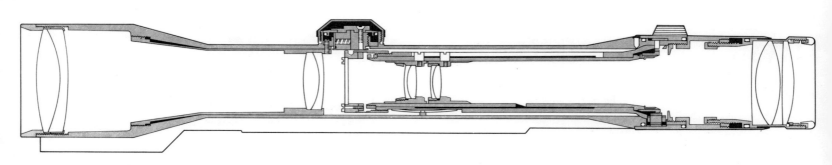

ventor is unknown. Grooves in the barrel may well have been introduced as a means of collecting the powder residue for early weapons show grooves with no twist. It is possible that once the effect of twisting projectiles in the form of arrows was known it was applied to the firearm.

A longarm of German origin and dated 1542 is rifled, as is a pistol of similar origin dated 1594. Both weapons use the wheellock form of ignition. The use of rifling was limited initially because of the problems of production and in the case of longarms did not come into military use for some considerable time. It was not generally adopted in the pistol until the 19th century. In this, as in other cases, the sporting weapon was often much superior to the military issue type.

One of the much quoted reasons for the effect of rifling concerns the devils that are naturally attracted to shooting. These evil spirits are very partial to taking a ride on the bullet as it flies towards the target. Needless to say the devil makes the shot inaccurate. When the barrels were rifled the spinning projectile was very difficult to sit on and the devils fell off and the bullet went on to hit its intended target. Conversely another tale said that the good spirits liked sitting on a rotating projectile for they found the non-rotating one something of a bore.

The rifling did nothing to stop fouling and weapons that were rifled had to cope with an additional problem than those with a simple smooth bore. The bullet had to grip the rifling to be effective and yet had to be loose enough to be loaded down the barrel when the latter had a good measure of fouling. An undersize bullet was needed for loading and an oversize bullet for shooting. The shooter of game could clean the bore of the weapon between shots and then force an oversized bullet down the barrel with the ramrod, but the soldier in the heat of combat had to be able to load and fire quickly. So a variety of systems were used to try and aid the expansion of the ball or bullet into the rifling.

A piece of paper or cloth to take up the difference in the respective sizes of the bullet and the bore was an early solution that has proved effective, and is still used by the modern devotees of the muzzle loader. The common use of the Patch, as it is named, dates from the 16th century when weapons had inlet patch boxes in their stocks.

A simple and effective solution was used in the English turn-off barrel, Queen Anne-type pistol. The barrel could be removed by unscrewing it at the breech. Powder and an oversized ball could then be loaded into the breech and the barrel screwed back on.

The idea of using an undersize ball then hammering it out of shape into the rifling was tried in a number of different ways. As the ball rested on the powder at the breech end the use of a

Left: the rifling of the barrel was attempted in all manner of ways. Top row, from left: Typical Kentucky, Whitworth hexagonal, Lancaster oval; centre row: Brunswick, Metford segmented, ratchet; bottom row: three-groove Springfield, four-groove, multi-groove. Below: The percussion system at its simplest required the firer to carry powder, ball and cap.

hammer on the rod was not particularly effective, but Captain Gustav Delvigne invented a system in 1826 whereby the powder was contained in a counterbore or chamber in the centre of the breech area. This enabled the ball to rest on a solid surround and thus be deformed efficiently by the ramming rod. It was not particularly effective as fouling soon filled up the recess and the very fact that the ball was deformed did not increase the accuracy. But in good conditions results improved greatly and it was used by the French army in 1842.

In 1821 Colonel Thouvenin invented the Pillar system. This was in effect the opposite of the Delvigne system in that there was a pillar in the centre of the breech with the powder chamber surrounding it. The ball, seated on the pillar, was expanded when it was driven on to

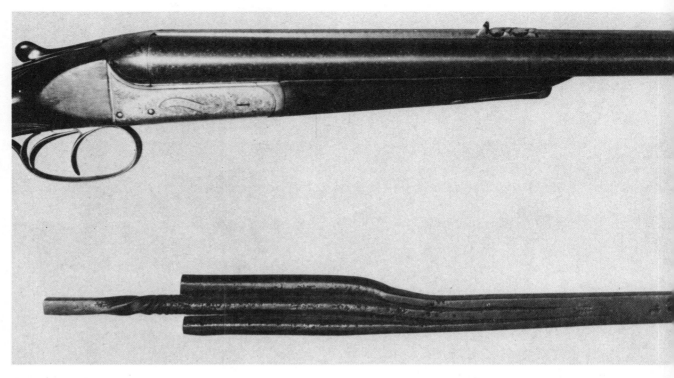

the pillar. This system was tested by France in 1846 and taken into service where it was known as the Tige system.

Ammunition at first consisted of any projectile, probably of stone, that roughly fitted the barrel, and a handful of propellant and some priming powder. The barrel itself was far from cylindrical, as was the bullet, so the result was very inefficient. More gas probably escaped round the projectile than was used to drive it. The barrels were made of cast iron and in the early days were extremely crudely cast. Accurate boring out of the barrel was difficult and smooth bores were rare. Furthermore, fouling built up in the barrel. This was caused by the remains of the combustion of the powder. It was a problem that lasted as long as black powder was used.

The use of lead as a material for projectiles could date from the 14th century as records show that lead was stocked in arsenals at that time. Certainly the Italians attributed their defeat by the French in the 16th century to the dastardly use of iron cannon shot instead of stone.

The bullet developed from its spherical shape at a very early date according to drawings by people such as Leonardo da Vinci in 1508. As early as 1742 Robins reported on the problems of air resistance on the projectile. Although he did not know it, this was a start to the science known as 'exterior ballistics'. By the early 18th century a conical bullet was in use. Not only did this give a better shape, it also helped to create an efficient loading system. As sometimes happens, however, the ultimate answer was tried earlier and discarded for want of efficiency.

The base of the bullet was hollow and thus the skirt of the bullet could expand under the pressure of the gas and seal the bore, or in the case of a rifled weapon fill the grooves. It was not totally successful, but in 1849 Captain Minie patented a combination of the hollow base with a cup made of a variety of materials. The result was that on the weapon being fired, the cup was driven up into the hollow base forcing the bullet skirt to expand. This system was to be developed and used by many countries in a number of different ways. The composition of the base was not vital. Britain used iron cups but these were later replaced by those made of clay.

A mechanical system of rifling led into a blind alley for the rifle and pistol. One type used two deep grooves in the barrel that fitted with corresponding grooves round the bullet. This got rid of the problem of making the bullet fit the rifling but still led to problems when the bore became fouled. The Brunswick rifle is a typical example which was developed in Britain during the reign of William IV. It had a two-groove barrel and a belted ball projectile. It proved very accurate as did other systems of this type, but they were not yet totally suited to the requirements of soldiers.

The Whitworth system of 1854 was, as befitted the inventor of a thread system, an efficient if complicated answer. Both the projectile and the barrel were of hexagonal shape and this resulted in the efficient use of the rifling.

The rate of the twist of the rifling in the bore is normally expressed as one turn in the distance that it takes to make that turn. The required twist is a function of the bullet weight and its diameter-to-length ratio, and must be sufficiently fast to ensure that the bullet is stable.

One deviation from this is the gain twist rifling which increases the rate of twist towards the muzzle. The object of this is to ensure that the bullet grips the rifling firmly before the

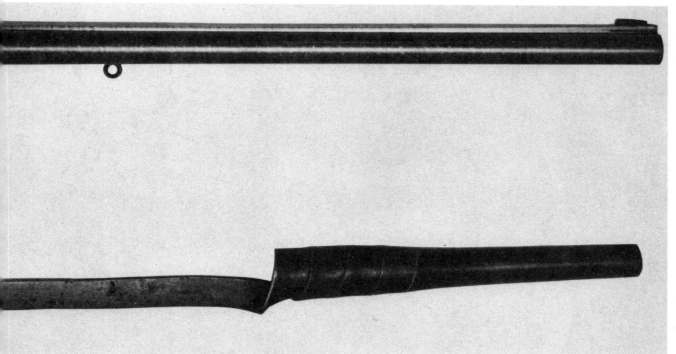

Left: The Damascus method of barrel manufacture consisted of the hammer welding of a number of strips of iron around a mandril. The use of an acid etching solution gave an attractive and characteristic pattern on the outside.

maximum acceleration of twist occurs. Some extremely large bore rifles had the initial part of the barrel smooth and the last few inches at the muzzle rifled. These are known as Paradox guns.

The taper of the barrel can vary. A lot of barrels during manufacture have a very small taper due to the manufacturing process, but some were manufactured with a deliberate taper from breech to muzzle. The Enfield rifling in the long Snider was of this type.

The construction of the rifling varied from the effective to the fanciful. The basic type which had lands and grooves of varying number, depth and width remains in general use today. The elliptical rifling, which uses the shape of an ellipse rotating down the bore, was used by Lancaster. The short Snider also had barrels of this type. Polygonal rifling is seen in the Henry rifle and this system has been, in a modified form, revived by the German company of Heckler and Koch in their P9 pistol. They claim that the reduced resistance to the bullet leads to greater muzzle velocity and that the barrel is easier to clean. A form of rifling that has not seen much use is the ratchet type, in which the groove tapers from nothing to its full depth with a relatively sharp edge.

The manufacture of the barrel itself, whether for a shotgun or for a rifle, requires considerable expertise if it is to be of reasonable quality. For many years the shotgun used a barrel that was built up from rods of iron twisted and hammer-welded round a mandril. When etched with acid the surface of the barrel became marked with intricate patterns. These barrels are known as Damascus. Although the best of them are suitable for the modern high pressure cartridge, the cheaper sort are not, because of the possi-

bility of impurities being included during the welding. The manufacture of barrels for long-arms was carried out in a similar fashion and as late as the 1850s the American Springfield armoury was turning out musket barrels by the wrap-round and hammer method. This type of construction was favoured because of the inability to 'deep hole' drill, that is to drill a hole with reasonable accuracy through a blank of two, three or four feet in length.

By the late 1800s, engineers such as Sir Joseph Whitworth were producing barrels from the solid. This, coupled with the better quality of material available, brought a rapid improvement in the barrel when mass produced for both the shotgun and the musket or rifle. Certain makers artificially marked the outside of their solid barrels to simulate the Damascus type as the public believed that this was still the best, and mistrusted the solid type.

There has been continual striving for the twin aims of quality and speed in the mechanics of rifling the barrel. The first barrels were rifled by pulling through a single cutter that was indexed in position where the grooves were required. The metal that was removed with each cut was extremely small and the cutter had to be packed up between each pass so that the cutting of even a four-groove barrel took a considerable time. The results of this hand-cut rifling were often very good, but the bore was not smooth and had to be polished to give the best results. The typical depth of cut in a .30 barrel is in the order of 0.004 to 0.006in. Although a variety of methods of speeding up the process were used it was not until the early part of the 20th century that use was made of the gang broach method, whereby a broach with all the groove cutters on it was pushed or pulled through the barrel. This

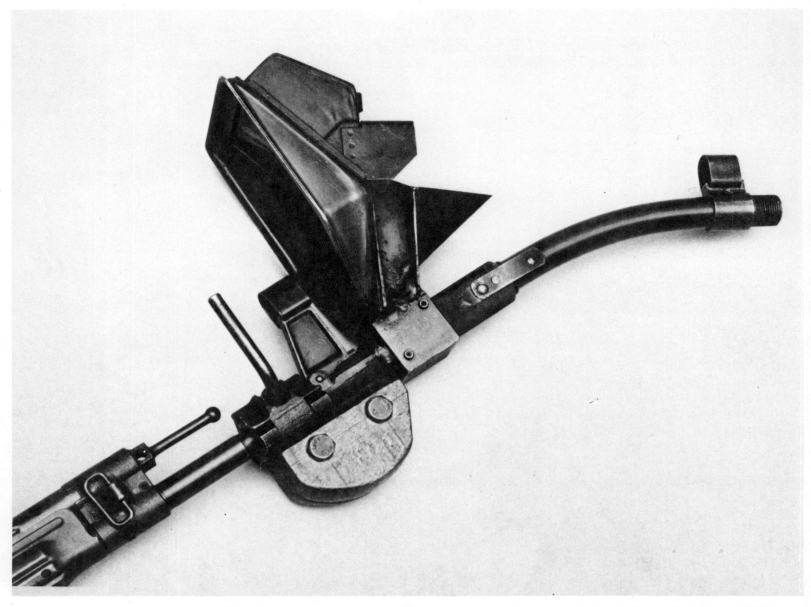

Above: An MP43 automatic rifle fitted with a Krummlauf device. This was an attempt to enable a firer to shoot around corners. The Krummlauf was used both as an infantry weapon and on armoured vehicles during World War II.

made possible the mass production of barrels of a reasonable quality.

Another development was button rifling, in which a hard carbide button with the shape of the rifling on it is forced through the bore. The metal in this system is not cut but forced out of the way as the button moves through. Movement of the metal mass gives a smooth, and more importantly, a work-hardened bore surface.

The final method, which is finding many adherents, is almost a reversion to the original barrel-making technique. A reverse impression of the rifling is manufactured on a hard steel mandril. This mandril is put through a steel tube which is hammered until the rifling is impressed along with the chamber at the same time. It thus cuts out the drilling and reaming that is normally required. As with the button rifling, the bore is work-hardened.

Throughout the history of firearms there has been a strange fascination for weapons that are able to shoot round corners. The practical use of such weapons seems often to be more illusory than real. The solution appears simple: just bend

the barrel and the bullet will follow. While this system did work, problems arose in aiming the weapon. There seemed little point in keeping oneself under cover and not being able to aim, or for that matter using the curved barrel. Yet by looking round the obstacle a shooter presented a good target.

The curved barrel was therefore dropped for a time, but particularly during World War I in trench warfare various weird and wonderful devices were used to fire over the parapet while remaining in the trench below. Some of these devices proved relatively efficient and entered service with one army or another. A similar device for a machine gun was developed during World War II by the Germans whereby a soldier could lie down behind cover and, thanks to a periscope-aiming device, fire at the enemy. To the Germans must go the credit for perseverance in making the curved barrel a practical weapon. They made a device that could be fired from either an armoured vehicle or an infantry weapon. The Krummlauf bent the bullet's path by 30 degrees and with its complex aiming device allowed a precise aim to be taken.

Importance of pattern

In the shotgun the accuracy of one projectile is not important, but it is important to have a 'pattern' of shot that is even and has no large gaps through which the game can escape. While the barrel that is of parallel or cylinder bore gives a reasonable pattern at short ranges, it was soon found that the pattern broke up when fired at distant targets. The answer was the choke bore. The choke is a constriction in the bore normally at the muzzle end. The inventor of the choke is not known, but a patent was taken out in 1886 by an American called Roper, and by William Pope May in Britain. Early attempts showed little appreciation of the mechanics of the choke.

The problem of deviation, whether of the recess type or the true choke type, was finally overcome by the famous English gunsmith, W. W. Greener, in 1874. With the choke, the shotgun became effective at much greater ranges. The degree of choke, and the resultant increase in effective range, goes from cylinder, modified cylinder to quarter, half and full choke. With a double-barrelled shotgun it is normal to have the first barrel more open or less choked to take the game in close and the second barrel tighter to take a shot at a more distant target missed with the first barrel.

The barrel of a pistol or rifle or single-barrelled shotgun has a basic problem in mounting, and this can be engineered in the manufacture. For the traditional double-barrelled shotgun or the over-and-under the two barrels have to be joined together at least at the breech end. The methods of joining the breech end range from the very expensive chopper lump barrels that have the breech end as part of the barrel and thus can be joined into a single unit with the maximum of strength, to the barrels that are fitted into a forging. The barrels must be joined together at the barrel end and preferably taper all the way down so that they converge and both shoot to the same point of aim. This is typically 60ft (18.2m). Joining the barrels is normally by the soldering on of the ribs that fit between the barrels on each side, or top and bottom.

The ever-recurring problem which occurs when dating an invention is that, at best, patent records give the date when the supposed inventor put his ideas into an officially recorded form. The original inventor often took little trouble to make this move and competitors could, in a different country, often be working in an almost identical area and be equally lax. Some applications were made by employees or agents either on behalf of the originator or perhaps stolen from him. Short of money, inventors often sold the idea and thus may not appear as a name on the patent papers.

The need for some convenient form of carrying the muzzle-loading components is obvious when the average equipment of an infantryman is considered. He carried one pound of propellant powder, a quarter of a pound of priming powder and a bag of musket balls. Measuring the ingredients during battle must have been difficult and the variance in the powder charge that resulted added to the inaccuracy of the weapon. It was the inventive genius of Leonardo da Vinci who showed the way. He detailed the wrapping of the powder and ball together in one unit, although this did not form the complete cartridge as no primer was included but it supplied the basis for further developments. In the late 16th century this type of container was used as a holder for the measured amount of powder and was torn open to load the weapon. Improved powder composition allowed a small amount of the propellant to be used for priming. Soon the container was being loaded as a complete entity, and with the advent of percussion this became a normal way of loading a weapon.

Cartridge design

The cartridge at first glance would seem to be just a convenient method of carrying the constituents of the ammunition, the bullet, the powder and the priming system, yet it carries out other very important functions. One of the main problems with the early breech loaders was the leakage of gas from the breech area. Various methods of sealing were tried but most relied on a near perfect mechanical fit and thus as wear occurred and gas erosion took its toll, the breech became far from gas tight. Rubber seals and leather washers all failed when the hot gases made them brittle. What was needed was a flexible seal to withstand both the temperature and pressure of the gas at the time of firing, and which would not wear out. This sealing is known as obturation.

The use of paper or card cases did little to help as they burnt through before the job was done. However, a Frenchman, Samuel Jean Pauly, managed to solve the problem although initially his vital invention was given little heed. Pauly decided that if the cartridge case base could be made of a ductile metal, this would flow under the gas pressure and seal the breech

Above: An extract from The Gun Digest *of 1957 showing a range of English cartridges available in the United States at that time.*

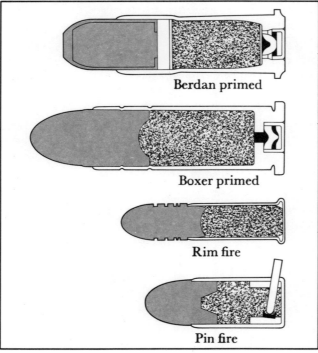

Berdan primed

Boxer primed

Rim fire

Pin fire

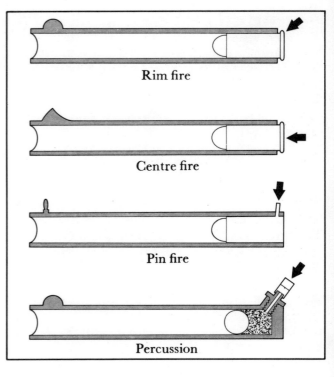

Rim fire

Centre fire

Pin fire

Percussion

Right: Types of cartridge. Far right: Types of firing. Below: The action of the Prussian Needle gun. The name comes from the fact that a long needle firing pin is used to fire the primer that is in front of the powder. This bolt action rifle opened the way for further development.

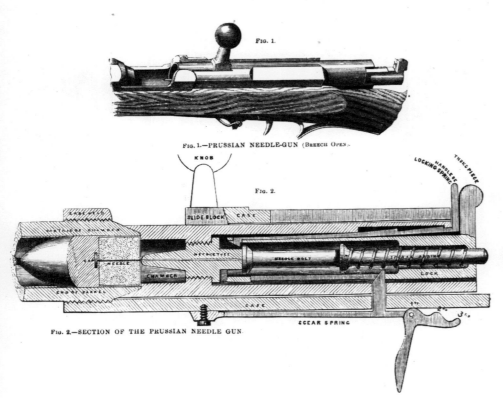

FIG. 1.—PRUSSIAN NEEDLE-GUN (BREECH OPEN).

FIG. 2.—SECTION OF THE PRUSSIAN NEEDLE GUN.

when the pressure was at its highest. All the criteria were met, the breech was sealed and as the cartridge case was removed after firing it meant in effect a new seal with every shot. Pauly's patent was taken out in France in 1812. He took out two related British patents in 1814 and 1816. The Pauly cartridges used a cardboard case attached to the brass expanding base. The ball cartridge was green and the shot cartridge yellow.

Pauly was ahead of the times. He also developed a centrefire primer that had all the requirements needed for success. It was reliable, simple and self contained. He demonstrated the weapon and the cartridge to various French officials including Napoleon. They were impressed with the perfection of the breech seal but did not seem to notice the primer system. One person who did take notice was a co-worker of Pauly who was to develop his own system. His name was Dreyse, and he was destined to become more famous than his mentor.

Other French patents such as that of Pottet in 1829 show centrefire priming, and in this one there was a built-in firing pin and rechargeable primer chamber. It is one of the earlier attempts to provide the reloader with an easily reloaded cartridge. This was vital as at that time cartridges were not available for purchase and the shooter in most cases would have to reload his own.

The pinfire that used a pin protruding from the case, normally at right angles, had many developers. The Pottet patent was in effect a type of pinfire. In 1832 Lefauchaux took out his first patent on a pinfire. He followed this with a series of patents in 1835 and 1849. These patents detailed various types including a removable base similar to the Pottet type. Houllier took out a patent in 1846 for a pinfire as did Chaudin in 1847. This pinfire cartridge in its final fully developed form was most effective but had certain disadvantages. Because of the pin, the cartridge had to be carefully positioned on loading and prevented any form of self-loading development. Storage and the safe carrying of the cartridge also presented difficulties. Nevertheless, large quantities of pinfire weapons were manufactured especially in Europe. This particularly applied to the revolver. The system was still in use long after the centrefire and rimfire had made it obsolete.

Needlefire, where the primer was held between the projectile and the propellant, reached its ultimate development with Dreyse who patented it originally in 1827 and in Britain with his agent Adolphe Mose in December 1831. This basic form was used to good effect by the Prussian army. The fact that the breech sealing relied on a metal-to-metal joint that became inefficient and made the weapon unpleasant to fire did nothing to detract from the use of the needle gun as a cartridge breech loader. Furthermore, the primer soon became eroded and brittle with the action of the hot gases. Other needle gun patents show the priming compound in the normal place at the rear of the propellant.

Samuel Pauly's patent, discussed earlier, showed a form of centrefire ignition that went almost unnoticed. Other types of centrefire primer came in profusion, many using similar types of operation. Cazalat in 1826 showed a centrefire primer system with a cartridge case. Boucier in 1847 invented a centrefire primer system that was in effect a percussion nipple on the rear of a solid cartridge case. This was also an early use of the centre single flash hole primer. Both Pauly and Pottet took out patents in 1855 for primer systems as did Morse in 1858.

The primer system divided naturally into two types. One group of patents used the cartridge case as the anvil on which the priming compound was struck, and the other group used a primer containing the anvil as an integral part. Who in fact invented the systems is very much in doubt, but the two people normally associated with them, and gave the system their names, are Boxer and Berdan.

Colonel Hiram Berdan, an American army colonel, took out a patent on a cartridge with a built-in anvil, and E. M. Boxer, who worked for the British government in the Woolwich Laboratory as superintendent, used the combined primer and anvil. The patents appear in both Britain and America at various dates around 1866. The advantage of the Berdan system, which has seen use in Europe for both military and sporting cartridges, is that the primer is cheaper to manufacture and the case little more expensive. The problem comes if there is a wish to reload the case. The primer flash hole or holes are offset and because of the anvil they present a problem of location in automatic machinery. The Boxer system, which is in universal use in the United States, has a flash hole in the centre of the primer pocket and the anvil in the primer and thus is easy to work with.

Experiments have been carried out to make the Berdan system easier to produce by modifying the primer pocket design. The Chinese have used a small ball bearing as the anvil and the French a U-shape punched into the base to form the flash holes and the anvil at once. The Chinese system does not seem to offer much in the way of a saving, but once again the French have shown originality.

The shotgun primer has to have one addition, caused by the fact that the shotgun shell is, unless of solid brass, manufactured with a rein-

Left: Colonel Berdan developed the priming system used in Europe. He led a band of sharpshooters and is shown here with one of his men, 'California Joe'.

forced card or plastic base. This is not strong enough to support a primer pocket of the type used in metallic cartridges. To support the primer a 'battery cup' is used. This is a cup that is pressed into the base and in effect acts as the primer pocket. The anvil and primer are pressed into the cup.

The amount of energy that is contained in a cartridge is considerable and the pressure of the gas is very high. The early black powder weapons worked at reasonably low pressures in the 10,000 psi to 20,000 psi range, but modern propellants can generate pressure in the region of 50,000 psi to 55,000 psi.

The most popular cartridge on the civilian market other than the shotgun type is the humble rimfire. It has in its time been used to good effect by the military, the cowboy and the gambler. One of the first to detail the application of the priming compound to the rim of the cartridge case internally was Robert in 1834, although the patent of Flobet for a cartridge in which the annuler priming compound was also used as the propellant in a small saloon-type weapon is often cited as the first practical rimfire. The rimfire was used by the Swiss in their rifle cartridge and was used in the Colt line of revolvers and the Derringer. The Spencer rifle armed many cowboys and some Indians. The larger calibre rimfire soon died with the introduction of the reliable centrefire but today remains almost universally as the .22 in a variety of types in target and game shooting.

Caseless ammunition enjoyed success early on but it has, in small arms, proved problem-atical. In the early days the question of rapid fire and the resultant heat in the weapon did not arise, but with the modern self-loading weapon that can fire at rates of 1,100 rpm another advantage of the cartridge case has become very evident. The case not only protects the propellant from physical damage but also protects it from the heat of the chamber. The empty case also removes from the weapon a not inconsiderable amount of the heat of combustion.

The external design of the cartridge case is controlled to a large degree, apart from the mechanical considerations of the weapon, by the need to achieve a correct 'head space'. The head space is the correct fit of the cartridge into the chamber so that it is neither too deep nor too shallow. The head space can be achieved by the use of the case mouth edge, the neck if the case is bottle-necked, or by the use of a belt or a rim on the head of the cartridge.

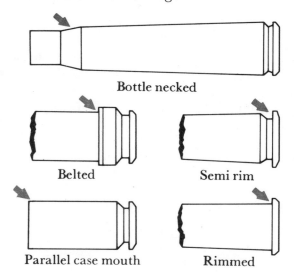

Bottle necked

Belted

Semi rim

Parallel case mouth

Rimmed

Right : Headspace is the correct seating of the cartridge in the chamber of a firearm. If a case is not correctly supported by the chamber and breech face the high pressure gas could split or burst the case and allow gas into the weapon. The arrows indicate the part of the case that is in contact with the chamber to ensure the correct position of the case. Below : Sporting rifle cartridges from The Gun Digest *of 1957.*

Pitfalls in calibration

The calibre of a weapon has often confused the expert as much as the amateur. The statement that the calibre is .38 S&W so it must fit a .38 S&W Special chamber sounds logical as both are .38, but the Special's true size is .357, the S&W .359 and the case diameters of the two are different, as are the lengths. The British .303 actually has a true diameter of .312 but on the other hand the .308 Winchester turns out to be just that. The American 30-06 turns out to be a .308 in diameter and was adopted in 1906.

The continental designation tends to provide more information and be more correct. The 7.62 × 51mm is the same as the .308 Winchester but does give the correct case length as 51mm. The 7.9 × 57mm German service round is, however, often known as the 8mm Mauser. The most accurate method is the metric bullet diameter followed by the metric case length.

There is unfortunately no way out of the maze for the pistol and rifle shooter but the shotgun enthusiast knows that the 12 bore or gauge is the same wherever it is bought – well almost, for the shooter has to be careful about the case length, as a 3in case in a 2½in chamber will do the shooter and gun no good at all.

The first of the caseless rounds were bullets which were hollowed out at the rear to contain the propellant and the primer mechanism. The Volcanic repeating pistol operated with a bullet of this type. The patents were taken out in America by Walter Hunt in 1848 and it is believed by D. Stephen Taylor acting as his agent in England the year before. The original idea was to ignite the charge by percussion nipple but this was dropped in favour of the self-contained type. Smith and Wesson took out a patent in 1856 that detailed a similar type of cartridge. This basic idea has been revived by Chirnecker and in these weapons the cartridge case is part of the projectile and on firing swages down into the bore diameter and exits as the projectile. The pure caseless round which has the propellant attached to the rear of the bullet underwent much development during World War II by the Germans and afterwards by many of the Allies.

A practical weapon that did not have too much commercial success was the Daisy caseless rifle that reverted to the Pauly hot air ignition system to ignite the propellant attached to the rear of the .22 bullet. Smith and Wesson have experimented with electrically ignited primers seated in the propellant block with little success. Today Germany has two companies developing a round and attendant weapon. Indeed, Heckler and Koch entered a caseless round and weapon for the NATO trials that will result in a weapon for the 1980s. It was not a complete success because of 'cook-off' (the propellant igniting in the chamber before the weapon is fired because of residual heat). Mauser have also taken out patents on their version of a rifle. Needless to say the experiments have by no means been confined to Germany.

Other forms of experimental round that have been developed in recent years include the folded cartridge, where the case is in effect folded round to lie parallel to the projectile. The advantage of this system is that the length of the round is very short and so the action of the weapon has only to reciprocate through this short length. The Hughes Lockless round has a plastic case with the propellant on either side of the projectile, thus giving a thin rectangular case.

A field which has interested many but failed to prove practical is the true rocket bullet. The firm of Gyrojet manufactured both a weapon and ammunition. This was a rocket using the

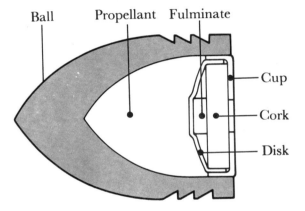

Left: Smith and Wesson cartridge of 1856.

bullet jacket as the motor casing. To give accuracy the jet exhaust at the rear was angled so as to spin the projectile. The accuracy, however, was very poor and one very severe disadvantage became evident. The round was still accelerating on exit from the barrel, unlike the conventional bullet, and at the muzzle it had not reached an effective energy level. It was a gun which was safest at point blank range rather than at any distance. (Point blank range, or *point blanc*, comes from the French designation for the bull's eye or centre of a target. Any weapon at ultra-close range will naturally shoot into the bull's eye or *point blanc*.)

The original projectiles were either of lead or a lead alloy. As velocities rose and the bore sizes became smaller, lead proved unsuitable as it could not stand up to the friction and heat in the bore. It resulted in a film of lead attached to the bore surface that rapidly destroyed accuracy. The solution was to cover the lead with a jacket made of a harder metal. This jacket prevented the bullet from expanding and producing a very severe wound. The Geneva Convention ruled that the only type of bullet that should be used in war had to be of the fully jacketed type.

The Dum-Dum bullet, so-named from the

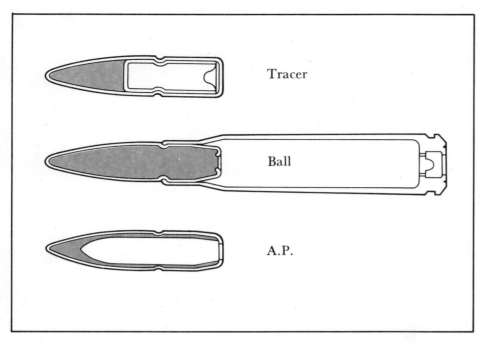

Above: Bullet types.

rounds, a number of types have been developed. The main ones used in small arms are Tracer bullets, which provide a visible indication of the bullet's flight. A cavity at the rear of the bullet is filled with a phosphoretic compound that ignites when the bullet is fired. To penetrate a target that has some form of protection the Armour Piercing bullet has been developed. This consists of the replacement of part of the lead core with a penetrator of hard material such as steel or tungsten. The development of this type of ammunition has given rise to proposals that the tip of the bullet inside the jacket should be of steel so as to provide better penetration than the standard ball round.

A military development that has now come into use in the sporting field is the DS or Discarding Sabot round. The sabot is, in effect, a filling ring that brings an undersized projectile up to the full bore size. It is discarded as the projectile leaves the muzzle. The advantage is that a lightweight projectile can be fired from a large bore and higher capacity cartridge, thus giving high initial velocity and better exterior ballistics than for the full weight and calibre round. This had been a standard round in tanks where the high velocity leads to better armour-piercing qualities. In the sporting field the 'accelerator' round has enabled the .30-06 to become an efficient small-calibre weapon with a high muzzle velocity.

Problems of accuracy

The projectile itself has seen experiments, including reversion to the firing of small arrows or flechettes. The project has encompassed many types firing one, three or even salvoes of these small darts. An insurmountable drawback has been the lack of accuracy. Another salvo project has been the old multi-bullet technique. The American version used a standard type of barrel with an internally tapered extension at the end. The 9mm, .45 acp and .50 mg rounds had a number of wedge-shaped projectiles that separated as they entered the taper at the end of the barrel. This led to a spread of three or five projectiles that, in close range or jungle conditions, gave a better chance of hitting the target. A Duplex round used two lighter projectiles in a standard case and was fired from a standard weapon. Both these projects have had limited success and application. A somewhat simpler solution has been the addition of burst control devices that limit the weapon to three or four rounds with each pull of the trigger. The muzzle rise of the weapon when fired on fully automatic meant that the third round was high and successive rounds probably missed their target.

Shotgun ammunition has seen little basic development since its invention. The primer used in the shotgun with its primer cup was one

arsenal in India that produced one of the many open point bullets, used a hole in the nose to expose the lead core and thus promote bullet expansion. The sporting ammunition used today for most types of game is of the exposed nose or hollow point type. The French used a solid bronze bullet in the Lebel Balle D'ammunition. The American Chrysler company tried a similar type by sintering the bullet during World War II. Another solid metal bullet was the sintered iron type developed by the Germans in the same period. This was a wartime expedient to conserve vital material as the bore wear over a period would have been unacceptable.

The manufacture of the first bullets was carried out by melting lead, possibly with a little tin to harden it, and pouring it into bullet moulds. The mould could be made of anything that would resist the hot lead and yet be easy enough to shape. Stone, bronze and iron moulds, either producing one or in so-called gang moulds many bullets simultaneously, were used. If lubricant was to be used on the bullets, bees wax or tallow would be melted. Patches were cut with specially shaped patch cutters.

When the jacketed bullet became necessary, the bullet making became more complex. The jacket was first pressed into shape from an alloy – cupro-nickel, copper and nickel, or gilding metal which is 90 per cent copper with amounts of tin and zinc. The use of a steel jacket with a thin coating of gilding metal has also been used.

A lead 'slug' is put into the jacket and the two swaged together. For military use the bullet always has a full jacket but when the sportsman wants the best result an exposed lead nose or even hollow point are used. The big-game hunter, when faced with an elephant, often uses a steel jacket to ensure that the bullet does not disintegrate against the heavy hide and bone.

For other than anti-personnel bullets, or ball

of the early developments and credit is usually given to Pauly who used it in 1855. Concentrated work has been done in controlling the spread of the shot – the pattern – on its exit from the muzzle.

Design of the barrel plays an important part but so does the construction of the cartridge. The shot is pushed up the barrel by a wad that seals the bore against the gases and provides for a measure of protection to the shot from the initial violent acceleration. The design of the wad has much to do with the pattern, and modern wads are sometimes made of one piece of plastic that gives almost total protection to the shot. Spreaders have been used to open up the pattern in a tight choke gun. Under certain short-range applications the shotgun can do the duty of the rifle. A solid shot can be fired consisting of one ball or a shaped slug. This is a very powerful weapon as the slug can weigh upwards of 1oz (28g).

The manufacture of lead shot is far from simple if the end result is to be a perfectly spherical shot of uniform weight. If the shot contains non-spherical or damaged shot, the pattern will have gaps in it.

The first manufacture of shot was carried out by the same method as early bullet production. The large gang moulds, however, were slow and more importantly they were unable to produce high-quality shot in small sizes. The typical

size ran from 250 to 300 per pound which today would be classed as buckshot.

The inventor of the dropped shot process is unknown but the date was probably during the early to mid 18th century. The first system was to pour molten lead through a sieve and let the drops fall a short distance into water. This did not allow the drop to become perfectly spherical but a reasonable quality of shot was obtained.

The shot tower, when the molten lead was allowed to fall for anything up to 200ft (60m) before hitting the water, led to the perfect shot of today. Material for the shot, a mixture of lead with additions of tin, antimony and arsenic to impart hardness, was melted in large vats at the top of the tower. Typical of this was the tower used by Remington in the 1960s which had two vats each containing up to 10 tons (10 tonnes) of alloy. The liquid, at a temperature of 750°F (381°C), falls from the collanders some 130ft (40m) to a tank of water 10ft (3m) deep. After the shot has been recovered it is polished and sorted. Many imperfect balls are discarded. A coating of nickel or copper is given to the shot by some manufacturers.

Because of the environmental problems of large quantities of lead being used, steel shot has seen much experimental work. So far this has not been widely adopted, although shotgun shells with steel shells are not uncommon in the USA.

An interesting reversion to earlier concepts is an Italian shotgun cartridge that fires a number of large pellets attached to each other by wires. This gives a very similar effect to the Chain shot fired by the early cannon.

Another interesting field of development has been the non-lethal round. The projectiles range from the drug carrying devices used to tranquillize animals through many employed to try to incapacitate humans without injuring them unduly. A small bag of shot similar to the child's 'bean bag' has been fired from pistols and riot-control weapons. This spreads out on firing and does not penetrate on impact. A very successful round has been the rubber bullet. This is a 1½in (38mm) diameter projectile fired from a modified flare pistol with reasonable accuracy and produces a stunning blow that is non-fatal.

The purpose of the development of sights, barrels and ammunition was to aid the efficiency and accuracy of the weapon, and it is worthwhile comparing accuracy through the ages.

The longbow was a very accurate weapon in the hands of an experienced bowman. There is no doubt that the advantage would have been with the side that had bowmen and not musketeers.

The longbow in the hands of an expert could fire 12 aimed shots in a minute and expect to hit a reasonably sized target at 600ft (182m) 90 per

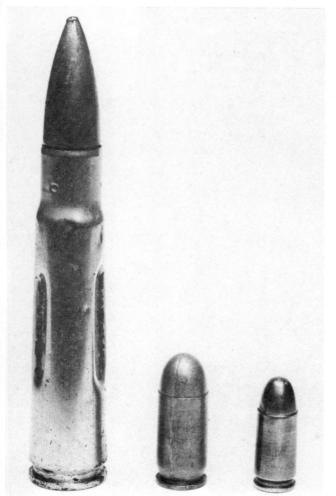

Left: Typical small-arms cartridges. At left is the .50in Browning machine gun round in dummy form. A .45 acp and a 9mm Parabellum are also shown, and these are used in pistols and submachine guns.

Far right, top row: A clip or charger for the .30-06 cartridge as used in the Springfield rifle (left), and a charger for the .303in round for the Lee-Enfield rifles.
Far right, centre row: A typical pistol magazine (left). This is normally known as a box magazine. Note the butt extension on the right. Alongside is a Garand clip, an integral part of the feed mechanism and which is ejected with the last shot. On the right is a Swiss charger.
Below: A Brown Bess musket made in 1810.
Below right: The box magazine can be loaded by hand round-by-round, or by means of clips such as this. An adapter is built into the clip so that it fits the magazine.

cent of the time. The ballistics may not seem too good in this day of the magnum, but the arrow flew at approximately 135ft (41m) per second and had an energy of 25ft/lb. It could penetrate 1in (25mm) of hard wood at 600ft (182m) and was not to be trifled with. The firearm must be measured against these abilities during its development.

It is fortunate for the historian that the American Civil War saw the use of most of the weapons available at that time by one side or the other. Records were kept and tests carried out to assess efficiency.

The Brown Bess musket used by the British between the end of the 18th and beginning of the 19th centuries was hard put to hit a 3ft (1m) diameter target at 300ft (91m) with every sixth shot. The vertical dispersion or variance was in the region of 5ft (1.5m) and the horizontal worse than that! The dispersion at a distance of 600ft (182m) was 9ft (2.7m) by an almost indeterminate horizontal area. The rate of fire was very poor, so the longbow was considerably more effective.

The French smooth-bore weapons provide an interesting study as France was probably the first country to launch a programme to study the ballistics of their military small arms. The infantry musket managed a meagre 30 per cent hits on a 6ft × 6ft target (1.8m × 1.8m) at 500ft (152m). The Musketoon managed an impressive

90 per cent efficiency but at only 330ft (100m) and at a target nearly 10ft (3m) square! A pistol fired at 65ft (20m) managed to hit a target of 6ft × 4ft (1.8m × 1.2m) only 68 per cent of the time when fired from the ground; on horseback this dropped to something nearer 7 per cent. The target was stationary on the ground, so this low hit achievement from horseback must be considered in relation to the apparent expertise of the cowboy, who with both rifle and pistol achieved remarkable hits at incredible ranges from his horse against other mounted adversaries.

The Americans proved more efficient. In 1837 a test gave $2\frac{1}{2}$ shots per minute with ball and 3 with buck and ball. (The buck and ball cartridge contained one ball and a number of small pellets of buckshot.) The ball penetrated 1in (25mm) at 30ft (9m) with the buckshot penetrating less than $\frac{1}{2}$in (12.7mm).

By the 1840s accuracy had improved with the rifling of the barrel. A typical example was a group 9in × 6in (228mm × 152mm) at 600ft (182m) with the 1842 Model Rifled Musket. A rifled barrel pistol managed $6\frac{1}{2}$ft × $4\frac{1}{2}$ft (2m × 1.3m) at 300ft (90m). This was a dramatic improvement and at last the bow and arrow were surpassed. An interesting test was that of the Whitworth rifle with its mechanical rifling in 1857. It shot better at 3,000ft (914m) than the rifled Enfield service weapon did at 500ft (152m).

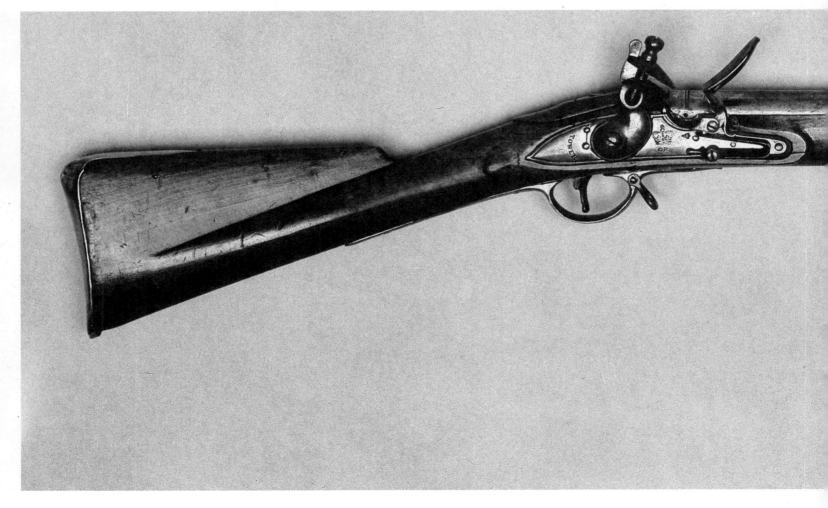

At 3,300ft (1,005m) carefully loaded and aimed the Whitworth grouped in a circle of less than 5ft (1.5m) while the Enfield managed only 16ft (4.8m). Accuracy had at last arrived.

Today the practical range for the infantryman has shrunk from the 3,000ft (914m) of World War I to a mere 1,200ft–1,500ft (365m–457m) and weapons are designed to achieve this. At longer ranges the specialist sniper with his weapon can regularly shoot at 3,300ft (1,005m). The hunter can hit game with the correct weapon at ranges that are governed not by the weapon and its ammunition but by the firer's ability. The pistol has proved that in expert hands it can group consistently at distances of 600ft (182m). Today it is not the weapon that governs accuracy so much as the person using it.

With the development of the bolt action and the self-loading weapons came the need for the storage and loading of more than one round of ammunition. Storage of the ammunition is in a magazine which can either be integral with the weapon or detachable. The integral magazine comes in three basic types. The box type has the

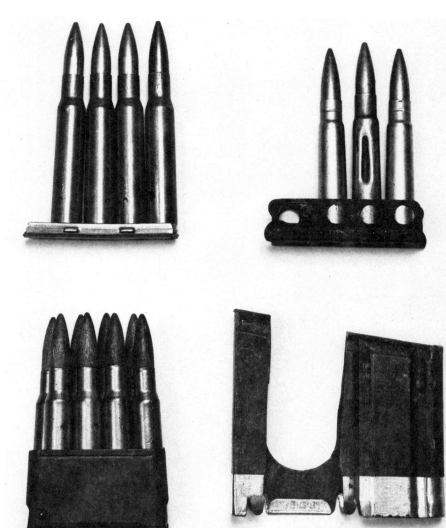

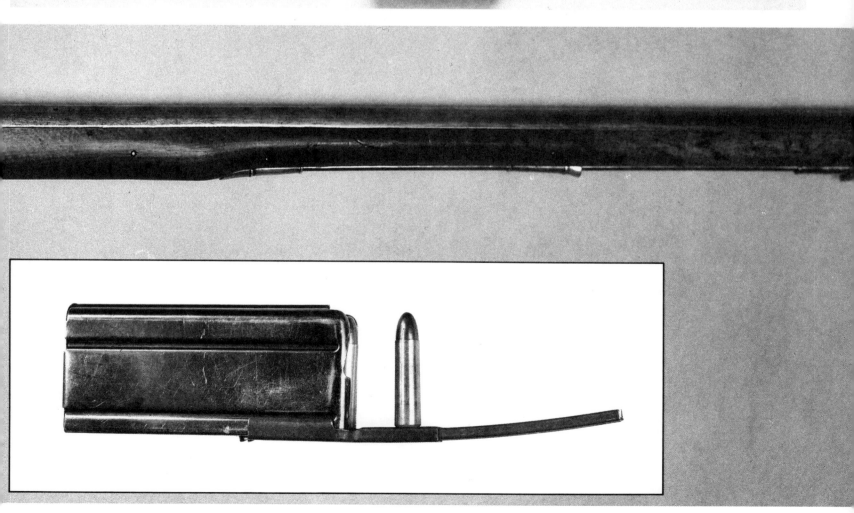

Right: A 'half moon' clip (top) which enables the rimless .45acp cartridge to be fired in a revolver designed for a .45 rimmed cartridge. A 'quick loader' (below) is designed to enable the revolver to be loaded rapidly. Bottom, from top: A disintegrating link belt; a metal non-disintegrating belt; and a fabric non-disintegrating belt. To the right is a metal articulated tray feed. Opposite: 'Over the Top', a 1917 painting from World War I by John Nash.

rounds contained in either one or two columns; in the rotary type they are carried in a spool which rotates a fresh round to the loading position; and in the tube type the cartridges are contained nose to tail in a tube usually under the barrel. The tube type has one disadvantage in that the nose of one bullet rests on the primer of the one in front, and if too sharp a point is used an accident can result. This system is almost universally used now in shotguns. The detachable magazine is produced in the first two types, and for the rotary type it has been extended to a drum that has extra capacity.

A variety of clips or chargers have been developed to hold loose cartridges. Some, such as the first Mausers and the Garand, were designed to remain in the weapon but for the most part they serve as a container for the cartridge and an aid to reloading. The clips can often be used to load the weapon directly as in the Enfield and Mauser bolt-action types, but with the detachable box magazine they are often issued with an adaptor either integral or separate to enable direct loading.

The revolver with its integral cartridge storage can be loaded by means of the quick loader pioneered by Prideaux. Another form is the use of the half-moon clip to enable the rimless Colt .45 round to be used. The machine gun uses either a box magazine, as in the Bren, or a belt as in the Maxim.

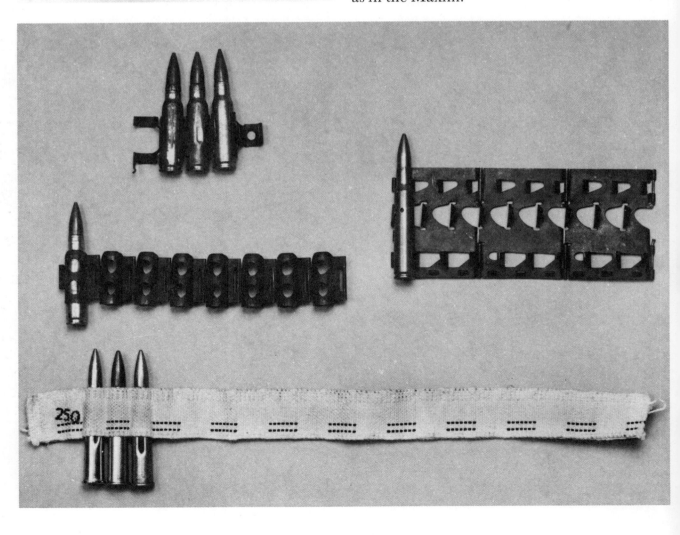

Military & Sporting Rifles

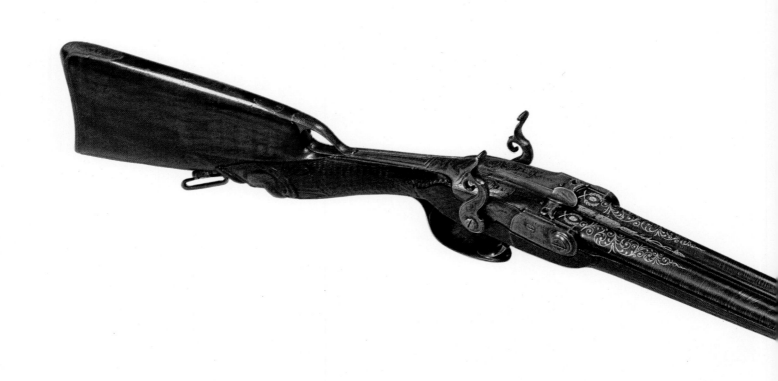

Once the cartridge and the rifled barrel had been established the development of the cartridge breech-loader rifle could begin in earnest. From the middle of the 19th century certain characteristics could be distinguished and divided into four basic types: the single shot action, which had all kinds of hinged, sliding and turning breech systems; the bolt action, which evolved primarily as a magazine rifle with different types of bolt locking; the lever action that provided the American West with its weapons; and finally the little-used pump or slide action rifle.

The basic forms of mechanically operated breech mechanism used in the single-shot weapon are the pattern for many of those used in self-loading types. Although today the single shot is used only as a sporting weapon for both target and, to a small extent, game shooting there have really only been one or two basic types; its history is not so simple. The breech mechanism has gone through innumerable permutations and the patents taken out would fill many files. However, there are only a few types and even fewer weapons that have become successful in both the military and the sporting fields.

Let us look at the mechanism itself and then consider its application to the various rifles as they evolved. The hinged frame with a standing breech is typified by many of the 'big game' rifles, and of course the standard shotgun action. The barrel is hinged so that it can be pivoted away from the breech face for the ejection of the fired case and the loading of a new round. Normally this is accomplished by downward hinging but this has been unsuccessfully challenged by a weapon in which the barrels hinge in every possible direction. This type has seen little military application although the American grenade-launching M72 has a hinged breech system which hinges down and fires its projectile through a rifled barrel.

The falling block action (with its rare brother, the rising block) uses a breech block that is hinged at the rear. When the breech is opened the block moves down, or up in the case of the rising type, to expose the breech face. The action is often combined with a lever acting on the block. The most famous example is the Martini type that is still very popular.

The dropping block uses a breech block which moves at right angles to the breech face, normally in a vertical plane. This system has seen much use in the field artillery type of weapon but, because of its inherent strength, has also been used in small arms. The Browning/Winchester single shot used this system as does the Winchester lever action. A small divergence in the design has the designation 'high' or 'low' wall. This refers to the fact that in the Winchesters the slots for the breech block either carry to the top of the receiver (the high wall) or are only as high as the bore centreline (low wall). The high wall, the stronger, is used for the higher-powered cartridges.

Perhaps one of the neatest and certainly the simplest of the actions is the rolling block. This action was used with great success by Remington and consists of two major components, the hammer and the breech block. The breech block is pivoted in much the same way as the hammer and is spring-loaded to swing forward and close the breech. As the rifle is fired the hammer swings forward and acts as the locking piece itself.

A group of weapons that have seen much use as sporting guns and even more as military weapons have hinged breech blocks. This type of system was popular for it meant that the muzzle loader could often be converted to a

Opposite: An early breech-loading type, the Pauly. It was used on sporting guns and military pistols. This double-barrelled sporting gun is in the Tower of London collection. The decoration of the stock (inset) features a mask. The metal work, in particular the hammer and trigger guard, are worthy of note.

breech loader by fitting this type of breech. The actual position of the hinge varied according to the particular designer's fancy. A typical example was the Snider conversion of the Enfield muzzle loader for the British army in which Snider substituted a block that was hinged on the left side of the breech. The American Springfield often named the Trapdoor Springfield used a breech block that was hinged at the front. None of these systems has survived except in sporting-type replicas.

The bolt action developed along three separate lines of locking systems. The first two employ the classic turn bolt that was used by Dreyse. They operate in the manner of the standard door bolt in that the lever is lifted to unlock and then drawn to the rear to load and unload the cartridge. Opinion differed over whether the locking surfaces should be at the front of the bolt at the breech itself, or at the rear. The question as to which is best has been argued by many top designers, target shots and soldiers. Both types, used in conjunction with safety, good design and construction, produce a weapon with plenty of capacity to shoot well.

The Mauser action has been the classic front-locking type and has been used in battle and copied and manufactured by many companies as a sporting rifle. Its advantages include the short distance that the stresses of firing have to travel as the lugs lock at the rear of the breech face.

The Enfield type has the locking lugs at the rear of the body which leads to a long stress path, and theoretically to the stretching of the body on firing. History has shown that both Mauser and Enfield types provide excellent rifles. There is a tendency to favour the Mauser action as a sporting weapon although many target shots still use the Enfield.

The third type of bolt action is the straight-pull. The motion to operate the bolt is not one of turning but merely a pull to the rear and then a push to the front. This action has been little favoured as it was found to be unsuited to the rigours of war. One country that has stayed with the straight-pull type of rifle is Switzerland with its well-manufactured Schmidt-Rubins, which has proved to be extremely accurate and very reliable.

Much of the opposition to the system arose from the disastrous problems experienced in the trenches in World War I with the Ross rifles.

A turn bolt with other than the lug lock system where the lugs turn with the bolt has been revived in the Colt Sauer rifle, which uses locking lugs cammed in and out by the action of the turn bolt. This has proved very effective and uses many high-powered cartridges in a fine sporting rifle.

The American West has made famous the lever action rifle and the type is still in production today. The classic Winchester type was developed not only by Winchester themselves but by others, and different types of locking systems evolved. One of the latest to be used is the combination of the lever action and the turning bolt. The action of the lever unlocks the bolt by turning it, and as the bolt is pulled to the rear the upward action of the lever reverses the action. In one the traditional coupling of the lever to the action components has been dropped and a rack and pinion system

adopted. To some the old lever action cannot be seen to have any advantages but many would not use any other type.

Use of the pump action, or as it is sometimes known, the slide or trombone action, has been limited on rifles but those that have been produced, such as the famous Winchester .22, have been manufactured in great quantity. Today there are a number of .22 rifles but the days of the Colt Lightning are over.

Single-shot breech weapons

Breech loading single-shot weapons fall into two categories. The first involves conversion of the vast stocks of muzzle loading weapons already available, and the second the adoption of a weapon from scratch. Although both categories contain innumerable variations and patents, relatively few managed to survive to equip armies or satisfy the sportsman's needs.

In Austria the great factory of Steyr, under their director Joseph Werndl, developed a breech loader using a system which, to say the least,

was unusual. The development was started in 1868 and used a combination of a bolt-turning action with a solid breech block. The rotation of the handle caused the block, contained in the receiver, to rotate and uncover the barrel allowing it to be loaded and unloaded. The block was then rotated back to seal the breech. There was no rearward motion as in the normal bolt action; the system is perhaps best described as a turning block. This rifle was adopted by the Austrian army in 1873 in 11.2mm calibre. No sporting use is known, although surplus weapons were no doubt used for that purpose.

The Belgians in 1867 adopted the Albini-Braendlin. This rifle had a very chequered career. It was designed by an Italian officer, Albini, and manufactured in Birmingham, England. It used a very similar action to the American Springfield. The breech block could, when the hammer was cocked, be swung up and over the breech. In this system it was relatively easy to adapt the muzzle loaders as the barrel could be screwed into the new breech, which could be fitted with the minimum modification into the original stock. Although they kept this as the standard rifle in 1871 the Belgians did adopt a more modern type, the Comblain, for limited use. This was an American design and used the lever-operated falling block. It had one advantage over the more normal lever types in that the lever was made so as not to impede the firer too much when he was in the prone position.

The first British breech loader resulted from a competition held at the instigation of the government to convert the large supply of muzzle loaders. The winner was an American, Jacob Snider, who, it is rumoured, had already had the system refused by the American government. The conversion consisted of fitting a side-hinged breech block to the cut off end of the barrel. The original lock-work was used. This, when combined with the Boxer cartridge, proved to be a very effective weapon. In 1871 it was decided to adopt a rifle that was not a conversion but of original design. The weapon chosen was the Martini-Henry firing the new .45 1871 cartridge. It combined the rifling that had been invented by Alexander Henry of Edin-

burgh, Scotland, in 1860 with the Martini lever action. It became one of the best single-shot actions and survives today as a target rifle, one of which is the BSA Martini International. Some single-shot pistols of the Free Pistol type also use a modified Martini action. The history of the Martini action itself, however, belongs to America.

Russia converted her muzzle loaders and produced what was, in effect, a poor copy of the Snider. The cast iron breech block was hinged on the left and seated into a bronze receiver-well. Lifting the block worked an extractor, unlike the Snider in which the firer had to pull the block to the rear to operate the extractor. Although this rifle was current from 1869, it is possible that the Russians were not altogether happy with it as they ordered 30,000 Berdan first model rifles from America in the same period.

The Berdan was developed by Colonel Hiram Berdan who was well known from having carried out work on the primer named after him. The

rifle was not nearly so successful. It had a forward hinged breech block which was simple enough, but the design was complicated by a relatively complex firing system, unlike the Springfield which used a simple exposed hammer.

The mid-1800s were a golden age for American designers who produced, directly or indirectly, many of the best actions. Christian Sharps began with a patent in 1848, the dropping block system with the block sliding in slots in the receiver walls. This basic idea was to be used in numerous applications. The early weapons used a paper cartridge and a percussion firing system, but in 1869 R. Lawrence developed a centrefire version. By 1881 the model 1878 was in full production. Production continued until 1881 but the basic type continued under other names such as Browning, Stevens etc.

Henry O. Peabody is probably one of the unluckiest designers of guns. His basic 1862 patent was the first to use the rear-hinged breech block mechanism. The actual weapon used the

Opposite: Early British breech-loaders. The first of the British breech-loaders was a conversion from the muzzle-loader. The Snider shown at the bottom used a new breech to which the old barrel was attached. For loading, the breech block was swung to the right.

Below: A Snider rifle manufactured by the London Arms Company in 1862. This is a carbine version and was not a conversion but produced from basic components.

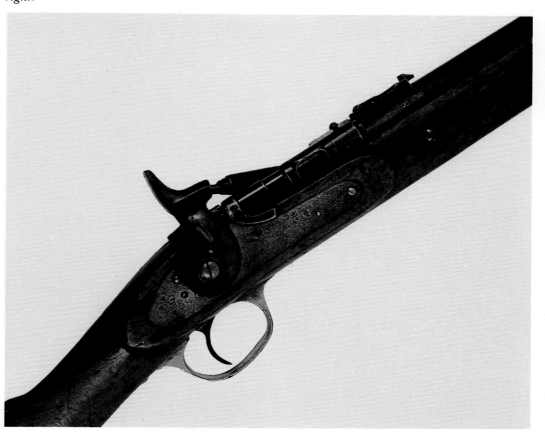

trigger guard as a lever to lower and raise the breech block. The rifle fired from an external hammer. The idea was tried as a military conversion of a muzzle loader but was not accepted. However, it was adopted in small quantities as a new weapon by a number of countries but never achieved any great success or fame for its inventor.

Along came the Swiss and Frederich von Martini, who redesigned the weapon using the basic hinged block. The hammer was dispensed with and the firing mechanism redesigned to take a striker inside the breech block. The first variant, the Peabody Martini, had used an external hammer but had made it self-cocking. With the adoption of the Martini-Henry by the British, Peabody's name was dropped. The action is now known exclusively as the Martini – an unfortunate result for Peabody, a brilliant inventor.

The Springfield 1873 was a conversion, designed by E. S. Allin, applied to the 1865 Springfield muzzle loader. The final version was not a conversion but a fully produced rifle and soon, because of its action type, it became known as the Trapdoor Springfield. The name came from the forward hinging breech block. Another well-used system was that of the Remington Rolling Block, first patented in 1863. The development period saw production of a modified type starting in 1867. The basic idea of the pivoted breech block being locked by the hammer as it fell forward was not only ingenious but also, like many good inventions, very simple. The action, despite some adverse reports, was very strong and saw use with powerful cartridges without problems. A number of armies adopted it in small quantities, the sportsmen in relatively large numbers and it eventually became a very popular rifle.

Bolt-action rifles

The adoption of the obviously better bolt action was delayed not so much because of unavailability or lack of designs but because of the soldier's old enemy, the politicians. Countries all had large stocks of single-shot rifles mostly in perfect working order. The politicians saw no reason to change, especially when the change would be a costly one.

Germany considered that the Dreyse needle gun did not require replacement as it had proved its worth. The Dreyse had indeed been successful and was able to fire a cartridge of sorts from a breech-loading bolt action. However, the gas action on the needle as it passed through the burning powder soon eroded it; and the sealing of the breech left much to be desired as the hot gases leaked profusely. This did not make the weapon popular with the firer.

The Dreyse was the start of development of the bolt action on rifles. In 1866, having seen the carnage of which the Dreyse was capable, the Swiss decided that they too must have a bolt action, and by 1867 the Vetterli was in prototype production. In Germany a degree of complacency had set in over the effectiveness of the Dreyse and because of this the Mauser family re-

Above: The French Model 1874 rifle, the Gras. This was the first French rifle to fire a metallic type of cartridge, the 11mm Gras. The rifle itself was in essence a conversion of the earlier Chassepot. The Gras was a single shot rifle and it was replaced by the much superior Lebel in 1886.

Right: The breech of the Gras, showing the manufacturer's name and the model type. This particular rifle was manufactured by Manufacture d'Armes de St Etienne, a firm that was founded in 1669.

ceived little response to their work so the first Mauser patents were taken out in the United States in 1868. The next year the Austrians flirted with the Fruwirth bolt-action rifle which had a tube magazine, but large stocks of Werndl single-shot rifles decided them against re-equipping. The Americans were very slow to accept, having had large stocks of a variety of weapons; they looked only briefly at the Hotchkiss in 1872 and at Lee's work in 1879. They were, in fact, the last of the major powers to adopt an effective bolt-action rifle, and they waited until 1892 to do so.

The French started development of the Gras in 1874 and modified it in a variety of models. In 1878 they adopted a repeating bolt-action, the Kropatschek. Russia adopted a Belgian-Russian combination in the Mosin Nagant, in 1883, and the British, admiring the work of Lee, adopted a variant in 1888. So by World War I the combatants were equipped with bolt-action repeaters, although some of the original single shots were still

around to be captured by the Germans many years later in World War II. The bolt action had come of age.

The years between the wars saw the sporting rifle take advantage of the bolt action's development, although the British double rifle was still considered by some to be the Rolls-Royce of game guns. The Mannlicher-Schoenauer and the Mauser in particular formed the basis of many sporting rifles, and top gunsmiths from all countries used basic actions on which to build.

The Americans, having failed to a certain extent with bolt action rifles, adopted the Garand automatic rifle in 1936. This weapon saw a great deal of service and without doubt, aided by the Russian adoption of a similar rifle in 1936 and 1938, drove the Germans into a frenzy of development. Yet World War II was fought by and large with the bolt-action rifle. Britain, for instance, did not abandon her No. 4 rifle until she adopted the FN in 1951. All military forces considered the bolt action to be at least as good as

any other type, and in many cases better, as a sniper weapon. The inherent accuracy of the good bolt action has led to its retention as the prime weapon of specialist marksmen.

Needless to say the sportsman did not adopt the self-loader with quite the same eagerness as his military colleague had done, but persisted with the bolt action not only of the old types but with many new developments. Typical of the latter was the work carried out in the Wetherby range of turn bolt weapons. Target ranges have yet to see in international competition anything other than the bolt action. Both the small-bore rifle and its full-bore cousin retain the designs of Lee and Mauser. Yet the self-loader itself is capable of great accuracy.

Development of the Lee type rear-locking rifles starts with a Scottish watchmaker to whom a son was born in 1831. Five years later the son, James, moved with his parents to Canada. He later went to America and started on his gunmaking career.

Lee came up the hard way with

A cased 10-bore centrefire rifle manufactured for the Wazir of Hyderabad by Holland and Holland. This under-lever opening double rifle was made in the best tradition of early rifles and even retains external hammers. The hunter of big game would feel safe with this weapon at his shoulder.

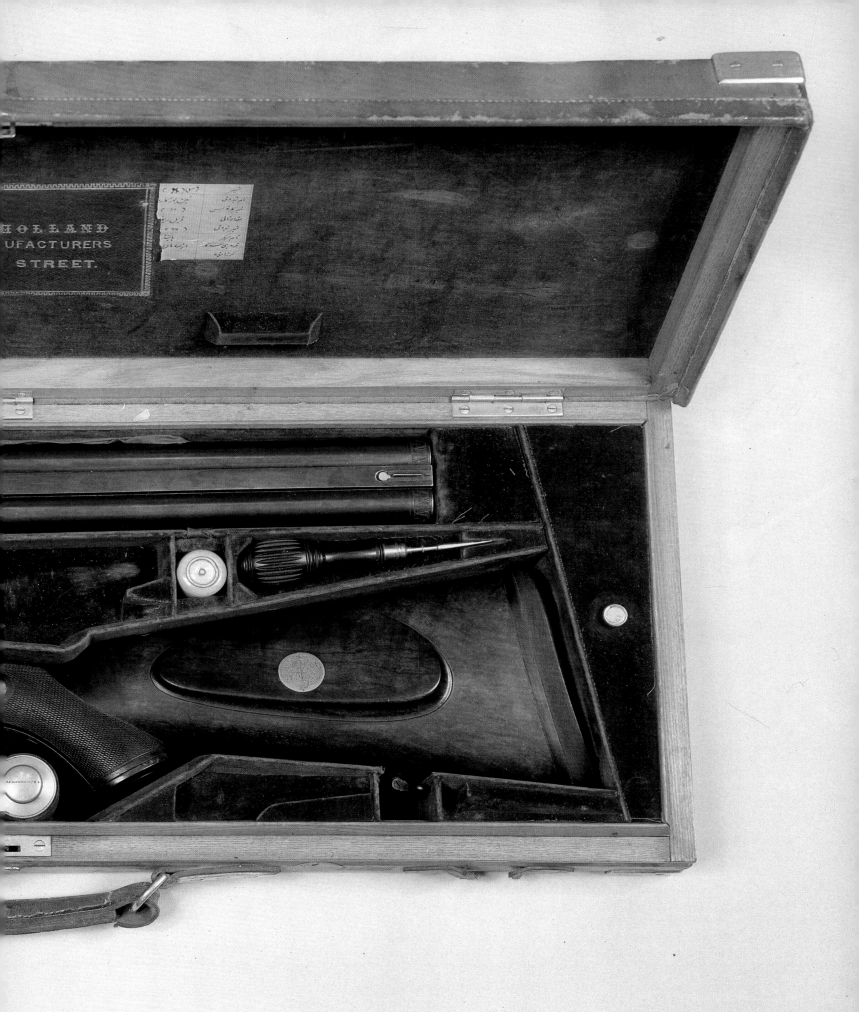

breech-loading conversions and lever-action rifles, some of which had been considered by both the American and the British governments. Work with Remington led to his patenting the Lee bolt-action rifle in 1874 which had the Lee patented box magazine. This rifle was produced for sporting use and for the American navy as the Model 1879. No sale of any great magnitude followed, however, and it was not until the 1887 trials held by the British government that the Lee became prominent. The Lee rifle was adjudged the best rifle in the trial and, combined with a Metford barrel, the British army accepted it as the Lee-Metford Magazine Rifle Mark I.

The first Lee-Enfield grew out of the troubles experienced with the Metford rifling and the subsequent adoption of the Enfield type in 1895. A large number of marques of the weapon were manufactured throughout its life but the major ones were the Short Magazine Lee-Enfield in 1900, known as the SMLE, and the No. 4 Lee-Enfield. The No. 4 resulted from development during the years between the two world wars and served the British army through World War II and for many years after. The Lee-Enfield action has shown superb accuracy in target events and it has also been used as a sporting rifle with some success. The action has proved sufficiently strong to enable it to be converted from the original .303 to the 7.62mm NATO round with complete success as both the sniper version and the numerous target versions have proved.

The Mauser brothers' first rifles were all modifications of the Dreyse and were single shot. The M71 was followed by its modification, the M71/84. This, although it had only the single locking lug, did cock on opening and in its later version had a tube magazine. The adoption in 1889 by Belgium of a clip-loading version followed the production of the first patented dual-locking lug variant of 1887. The Belgian version started the great FN factory on its way and their connection with the Mauser action was to continue. The introduction of the Infanteriegewehr M98 in 1898 was the start of the modern Mauser and its shortened version the KAR.98. This version was to see Germany through

two world wars and also equipped Belgium, Czechoslovakia, Yugoslavia, Spain and more than 20 countries.

For sporting use the Mauser has been valued as a game rifle and it is at present manufactured, with little change, by a number of factories under their own brand names. The action has achieved a reputation for strength and reliability second to none and will still be in production for a long time to come.

Some maintain that the straight-pull bolt system has never enjoyed the popularity that it deserved. Certainly the Swiss rifles manufactured with this bolt system are extremely accurate and the action of the bolt superbly smooth and very fast. The Austrians also adopted a straight-pull weapon, this time designed by Ritter von Mannlicher, who contributed to the design of the Mauser bolt-action rifles, especially in their magazines.

The Swiss rifle was the joint design of Colonel Rubin and Colonel Schmidt. The former carried out the cartridge development and the latter, after extensive study of existing models, designed the rifle. The Schmidt-Rubin rifles all worked on the same principle: the rearward pull on the bolt rotated either a sleeve in the first two designs or a bolt in the body itself in the last version, so that the bolt lugs were rotated out of engagement. The forward motion picked up a cartridge from a box magazine and then rotated the bolt lug back into engagement. The rifle used different positions for the bolt lugs. In the first model they were at the rear of the receiver, in the second at the front of the receiver and in the last they locked into the barrel extension. These changes were carried out to provide extra strength as the cartridge was modified to a higher pressure. There were no sporting derivatives produced but the rifle is still used as a sniper and on many target ranges, mainly in Switzerland.

The combination of the genius of Mannlicher and the production and development facilities of Steyr in Austria, produced some of the best rifles and development work to be carried out at the end of the 19th century. The Mannlicher designs began with the turn bolt but, as early as 1884, the first of his straight-pull types appeared. By 1886 the Austrian

government had adopted the modified rifle which was not only straight-pull but used a hinged block that was cammed up and down to lock the bolt into the receiver. This design survived with modification until 1890 when the action reverted to a rotating-lug type although retaining the straight-pull feature. The final 1895 Austrian service rifle used the same bolt with its rotating head carrying the lock lugs.

During this period Mannlicher had worked on turn-bolt designs and in 1888 had combined the revolving magazine with his turn-bolt action to make the first Mannlicher-Schoenauer rifle which was to become so well known. In the sporting field the straight-pull bolt disappeared but the turn-bolt work of Mannlicher lives on, still produced by Steyr.

In France the development of the bolt-action rifle started with a very close relative of the Chassepot; some were even conversions. This rifle relied on the bolt handle locking into a recess in the receiver as its only form of locking and was known as the 1866 Gras. In 1878 Alfred Kropatschek modified the rifle further by adding a tube magazine and its attendant feed mechanism. By 1886 the original design was not sufficiently strong to take a new cartridge which had been developed by Colonel Nicolas Lebel. The design was modified to include dual-locking lugs at the bolt head and was named the M.93 Lebel. By 1890 the outdated tube magazine was changed to a box type.

Different types of bolt-action rifles.
Top: The Gewehr 98. This rifle uses the front-locking lug system allied to a turn bolt. The theoretical advantage of front locking is that the stress path on firing is over a short distance and there is less chance of distorted action.
Centre: The straight-pull bolt type has had fewer adherents than others in the military and sporting worlds. Switzerland has produced this type in quantity and used it frequently. The Schmidt-Rubin rifles have been developed from the 1889 type illustrated here.
Bottom: The Lee type of bolt action as manufactured at the British Government factory at Enfield uses the rear-locking turn-bolt. The theoretical disadvantages of the longer stress path have not detracted from the reputation of the Number 4 rifle, illustrated here. This rifle and its derivatives in the target and sniping fields have shown excellent accuracy.

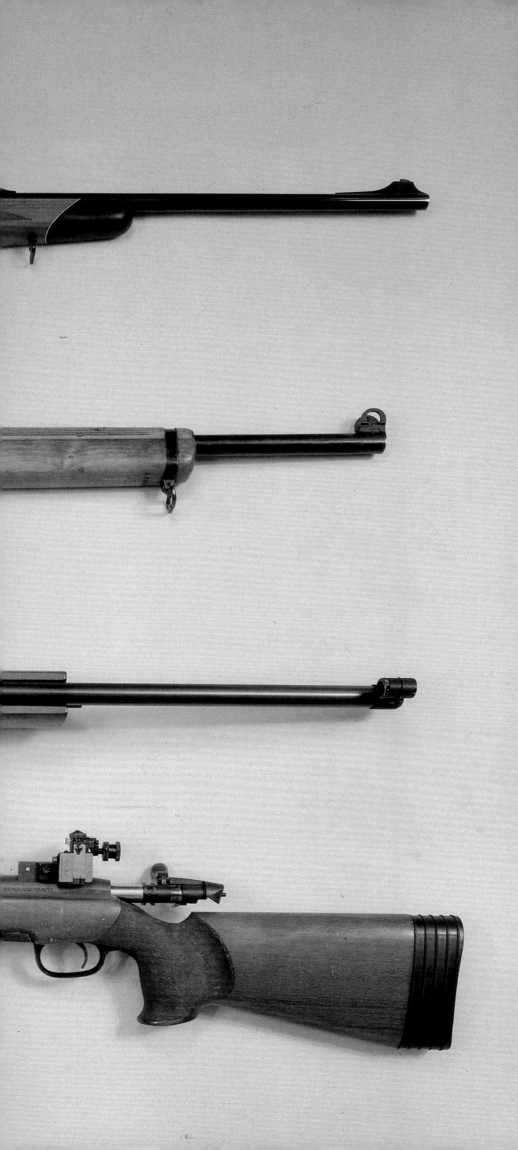

It was not until 1936 that a modern bolt action was adopted in the shape of the MAS M.1936. This was a turn-bolt type with the locking lugs well to the rear of the bolt locking into the receiver bridge. Other than a larger than normal bolt diameter, the design has little to commend it and was not copied nor developed in any way. No sporting derivatives of these rifles were made in any quantities, if at all.

As early as 1883 Russia decided that a modern bolt-action repeater was necessary. Two designers worked on the rifle, one a Belgian, Emile Nagant, and a Russian, Sergei Mosin. The rifle they developed was of the front-locking type. As the Russians could not produce the weapon in the quantity required it was manufactured in Switzerland, Austria and America. Russian forces served in two world wars with the Model 1891 and its progressive modification, the Model M1944. Communist troops in the Korean War were equipped with this rifle. The action has little advantage over others and little or no sporting use is made of it.

Many countries used the Mauser unmodified but some, such as Japan with Type 38 Arisaka, Italy with M.91 and the United States with the M1903, modified the action to suit their particular needs. The strength of the Japanese weapons is often viewed with great suspicion but types 38 and 99 were among the strongest actions ever manufactured when production standards were at their highest. Greece was among other countries that also adopted a modified Mannlicher-Schoenauer design. America adopted the Krag-Jorgensen, which was also used by the Danes and Norwegians during World War II. Not bad for a weapon which entered service as early as 1899. The action featured a single lug bolt locking at the front and an unusual magazine that was non-

A selection of sporting rifles, from top to bottom. A Colt–Sauer sporting rifle. The Number 8 is, in effect, a converted Number 4, and was adopted by the British army. The Walther V.I.T. is a specialist .22LR target rifle. A Steyr 'full bore' target rifle.

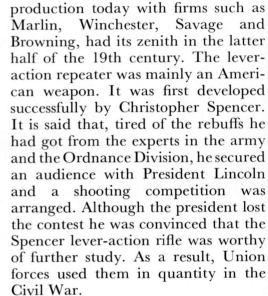

Although the bolt action has largely been superseded in the military field it still remains a favourite for the hunter. This scoped Holland and Holland rifle is an example of the best available. Note the foresight protection and the raised leaf type back sight. This Mauser action was made in 1908 by DWM of Germany.

detachable and was loaded from the right side of the receiver. This action with its single lug achieved a great reputation for smoothness and many were rebarrelled for other calibres and used as sporting rifles in the United States.

With the general adoption of the self-loading rifle the bolt action has been relegated to the target range and the game field. Many of the rifles, such as those made by Parker Hale, BSA,

Winchester and Sako to name but a few, are modifications of the basic Mauser dual lug forward locking system. Some such as the Wetherby, with its multiple-locking lug arranged in rows, and the Sauer, with its cammed locking lugs, are of modern design even if they owe a debt to early work. It will be hard for anyone to produce a totally new version of the bolt-action rifle but the popularity of the type with the target and sporting shot will probably encourage people to try.

Lever-action rifles

The lever-action rifle, although still in production today with firms such as Marlin, Winchester, Savage and Browning, had its zenith in the latter half of the 19th century. The lever-action repeater was mainly an American weapon. It was first developed successfully by Christopher Spencer. It is said that, tired of the rebuffs he had got from the experts in the army and the Ordnance Division, he secured an audience with President Lincoln and a shooting competition was arranged. Although the president lost the contest he was convinced that the Spencer lever-action rifle was worthy of further study. As a result, Union forces used them in quantity in the Civil War.

The Spencer had the magazine tube contained in the butt; the lever action acted only on the breech as the hammer had to be operated each time by hand. The next development had an action that cocked the hammer as well as operating the locking system. This was the Henry, patented in 1860. Although it was a more advanced rifle than the Spencer, it never got the orders it deserved. The magazine was a tube type fitted under the barrel.

Left: The Charter Arms AR7 (Armalite AR7). This interesting rifle was originally developed as a survival gun for the US Air Force. The basis is a self-loading .22LR rifle with the barrel attached by a screwed collar. The butt, which is also the container for the complete gun, is screwed on to the action. Two types of telescopic sight are shown. On the left is the Sight Unit Infantry Trilux (SUIT), used by British forces. The Pecar sight (right) is for sporting use. Opposite: The Leasley rook rifle. It was a type developed to fire several low-powered centrefire cartridges. It is in essence the same as the single-barrelled shotgun. The type is confined almost exclusively to Britain.

The first Winchester was a very minor modification and started the long chain of Winchester lever-action rifles. Although the lever action never became a military weapon to any great extent, it was effective nonetheless. A major development in the Winchester line was the use of a box magazine in the Browning-designed 1895. The early American settlers, cowboys and soldiers used the lever action Winchester whenever they could. Although of short range it was ideal for carrying all day and fighting off attacks of Indians, or for a shot for the pot at camp time.

One other lever action of note was the Savage 1899 which used a strong steel breech block moving in the steel wall of the receiver. The Savage also used the Steyr type rotating magazine. The action was extremely strong and capable of being used with any normal rifle cartridges.

The lever action was often used by the individual, for his own defence and for the hunting of game. Today the lever action manufactured by Marlin, Savage and Winchester is used purely for sport and is available in a number of calibres from the lowly .22 long rifle to the .308 Winchester. The up-to-date Winchester design uses a rack and pinion type lever and a rotating bolt head to modernize the action.

The pump or trombone action, or, to give it its correct title, the slide action has been generally relegated to the .22 LR cartridge although such manufacturers as Savage and Remington have manufactured centrefire cartridges of high-power types. The history of the type dates from as early as 1866 when W. Krutzsch patented a pump-action rifle in England. A Frenchman followed in 1880 with the Margot and, very quickly, the American arm manufacturers followed. From 1855 Colt and Winchester developed rifles and shotguns on the principle. One of the most famous was the Model 1890 Winchester .22 LR that became a firm favourite with shooting galleries. The type has been almost totally made for sporting use but a shotgun, the Winchester Trench gun, was used in World War I.

The various manual types of operation for rifles may have been overwhelmed by the self-loader but in some fields, notably target shooting and sporting, they remain supreme. There are those who look forward to the demise of the bolt action or any other manual action, but they will clearly have to wait a long time.

Famous Guns of the World

When a list of weapons that have ever been produced or developed is surveyed, the famous names such as Luger and Mauser Broomhandle are easy to pick out, but many more names both sporting and military are often almost unknown. As so often happens some weapons have names that have evolved from their true designation to a more popular term. Such is the case with the MP38 and MP40, which are commonly (if incorrectly) known as Schmeissers.

Some weapons are included not because they achieved large production and became household names but rather the opposite. The Dardick and the Gyrojet, for example, are noteworthy for attempts to change the basic concept of gun design. Failures or not, they deserve their place simply because of their difference and the job they attempted to do.

Every collector or student of weapons has his favourite and it is hoped that these find inclusion here. But of course what is 'famous' to one person may not be to another. Yet all the pistols, rifles and machine guns included in this chapter deserve such a designation.

AK47

The Soviet Union was the only country to appreciate the German research into the intermediate cartridge and act upon that information. The result was the development of the AK47 and the 7.62mm × 39mm cartridge that became almost universal throughout Communist countries and the guerilla organizations supported by them.

. The designer of the AK47, Kalashnikov, undoubtedly had access to the German MP44 and captured German personnel, yet the design of this rifle, with its simple long stroke piston and rotating bolt, displayed many original features. It was officially adopted by the Russian army in 1951 and soon proved to be an exceptional design. The use of a relatively heavy rifle, 9½lb (4.3kg), and the intermediate cartridge made it pleasant to fire both single shot and in bursts.

The replacement for the AK47, the AKM, employs the same basic design but simplifies it for mass production by using pressed components. The Israeli Galil is a modified version of the AK, firing the .233in cartridge.

Opposite: Although there have been a number of successful lever action rifles, the Winchester is probably the best known. This rifle has the lever in the down position which opens the breech, ejects the fired case and cocks the hammer.
Below: The Soviet AKM rifle is a direct development of the AK47 (shown here) which fires the 7.62 × 39mm round either single shot or automatically. The bayonet has become a multipurpose instrument, and serves as fighting knife and wire cutter.

Above: The Albini-Braendlin was a muzzle-loading weapon converted to breech loading by the addition of a forward-hinging breech block. It was a combined Italian-English conversion that was widely used in Europe.

Albini-Braendlin

This design, adopted by Italy, Belgium and Bavaria in the 19th century, was the work of Augusto Albini, an admiral in the Italian navy. The design was finalized in 1865 and manufacture was carried out by an English company, the Braendlin Armoury Company of Birmingham.

This rifle resulted from the requirement to convert large quantities of muzzle loaders. As with the Snider the rifle was produced in its entirety as a breech loader. The Albini-Braendlin was tested as a rival to the Snider but rejected.

The basic mechanism was a hinged breech block that pivoted at the front of the breech. This was operated by a handle on the right of the block and when the block was in the closed position the external hammer struck a firing pin that fired the .60 rimfire cartridge.

Arisaka

The series of bolt action rifles that were used in large number by the Japanese services from the turn of the 20th century onward through World War II were designed or developed from designs of Colonel Nariake Arisaka, superintendent of the Tokyo arsenal. His first design, the Type 30, came out in 1897 and had a calibre of 6.5mm.

The most common type, the 38 or M1905, was basically of the Mauser type having a dual front-locking bolt and a magazine similar to the Mauser. (Type 38 refers to the 38th year of the reign of Emperor Meiji.) The Type 99, brought out at the beginning of World War II, was similar to the 38 but was chambered for the 7.7mm cartridge. Contrary to popular opinion, the Arisaka action is a strong one when the manufacturing standard is reasonable.

Armalite AR15 (M16) and Sterling AR18

The rifle that has currently outsold any of its direct competitors in the military market is the Colt-manufactured Armalite-designed M16 rifle. Armalite were fortunate in securing the

services of one of the great designers of modern times, Eugene Stoner. One of the first of a series of designs which he worked on was the Armalite AR10 which was chambered for the 7.62mm NATO round. Because of the change in emphasis in calibre this weapon was not a success, although a small quantity were manufactured by NWM in Europe. The AR10 did, however, serve as the basis for the AR15.

Another important development was that of the M193, 5.56mm cartridge from the .222 sporting round. The new round used a longer case and a bullet developed by the Sierra Bullet company. The commercial designation is the .223 Remington. With this cartridge a number of AR10-type rifles scaled down were submitted for trial with the army. The results were very encouraging and the gun was favoured for adoption instead of the M14. The finalized weapon was ordered by both the army and the air force in 1961. The demand became so great that Colt was licensed to produce them then, at a later date, General Motors and Harrington and Richardson also contributed.

The action of the M16 uses a bolt carrier into which the gas from the barrel take-off is fed via a stainless steel tube. This direct-gas action system has disadvantages in that gas fouling can build up in the action, but development of both the gun and the propellant have largely cured this and users of the M16 and its variants report reliability.

At the beginning of 1960 it was decided to design a 7.62mm rifle, the AR16, which would not compete with those already on the market. The rifle was specifically designed to be manufactured with the minimum of sophisticated tooling and materials. Stoner was again one of the prime contributors. The swing away from the 7.62mm led to the project being switched to a 5.56mm version. The AR18 was the result and although Stoner had left the company by then the weapon was very similar to the AR16. After a number of attempts to manufacture and market the AR18 the licence was granted to the

well-known firm of Sterling in Britain. Sterling carried out extensive development work and at present have a full order book from all over the world. A number of developments such as a bullpup version and a light machine gun version have also been projected.

The AR18 uses a similar rotating bolt action to the M16 but instead of the gas action being direct it is operated via a conventional gas system.

Auto-Mag

The sole object of this huge pistol was to give the most powerful ballistics in a handgun that had ever been available. Even the Mars was eventually outmatched.

The basis for the concept was a cut down .308 Winchester rifle case using a 240 grain bullet and achieving a velocity of 1650fps. A further development was to neck the case down to accept a .357in bullet, and thus give the .357 Auto-Mag. The pistol was designed by Max Gera and used recoil operation to rotate the bolt. It went into production in 1970. The rarity of the pistol at one time prompted prices considerably in excess of the retail value. Although of very fine construction the pistol often gave trouble if not carefully tuned. For those requiring a powerful hand-cannon it cannot be surpassed. Once fired it is never forgotten.

Beretta Model 1934

Experts may argue about the effectiveness of the small-calibre pistol yet many European governments equipped soldiers, sailors and airmen with this type of weapon. The 1934 Beretta equipped the Italian forces from 1934 until the early 1950s, for example. The calibre .380 acp or 9mm short can hardly be placed in the magnum field, yet the pistol in a modified form is still in production today and is still in use with police forces.

The 1934 was the result of continual development of a range of pistols by Beretta which started with the Model 1915. Its direct pre-

decessor, the Model 1931, was made exclusively for the Regia Marina. The most readily recognized feature of the Beretta type is the exposed portion of the barrel between the slide nose and the breech.

The 1934 is a simple blowback pistol with an exposed hammer. It was also produced in .32 acp as the Model 1935. These pistols have markings that indicate their users: RE, Regia Esercito (army); PS, Publica Sicurezza (police); AM, Aeronautica Militare (air force); RA, Regia Aeronautica (air force); and RM, Regia Marina (navy). Modern production of the 1934 was carried out under the name Cougar and the replacements for the older range, the Model 70 series, still show the characteristic open barrel construction.

Below: The Auto-Mag is the most powerful pistol in the world. It is chambered for two special cartridges, the .44 Auto-Mag and the .357 Auto-Mag. Only a small number have been manufactured. Bottom: The Beretta Model 1934 was the standard service pistol for the Italian forces. A simple but reliable blowback design it is still the basis for some Beretta production.

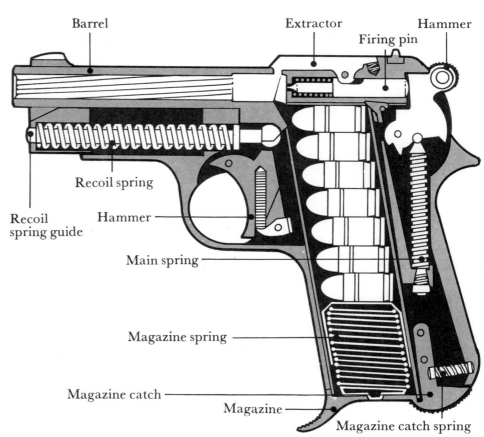

Barrel   Extractor   Hammer

Firing pin

Recoil spring

Recoil spring guide   Hammer

Main spring

Magazine spring

Magazine catch

Magazine

Magazine catch spring

Beretta M38A and M38/42 and M12 Submachine Guns

Starting with the Villar Perosa-inspired submachine guns, the firm of Beretta became the major designer and producer of this type of weapon for the Italian forces.

The Model 38A was a development of the M1935 which in turn had been based on components of the Villar Perosa. The designer, Marengoni, developed the M38A into a very successful gun that was produced from 1938 until 1950. Early production was completely machined and thus expensive; later weapons were modified to use stampings. Another development by Marengoni was designated the M38/42 and was similar externally to the M38A but was extensively redesigned to simplify construction. After modification by Salsa, this gun continued in production until the 1970s as the Model 5. An odd feature of these designs was the double trigger that used one for single shot firing and one for automatic.

After much research it was decided that the traditional Beretta designs with their characteristic wooden stocks and relatively expensive construction must be superseded. After a number of development models the Model 12 was finally put into production in 1959. The M12, which is still current, is constructed of steel pressings riveted and welded together. Easily recognized features are the built-in fore grip and a grip safety on the pistol grip. A single trigger with a selector button is used and the stock folds to the right of the gun.

Bergman Bayard Model 1908 (Model 1910)

This pistol was adopted by the Danish army in 1911 and named the Model 1910. Other countries such as Greece and Spain also used the Bergman Bayard.

The Bergman 1903 was manufactured in Germany at the Bergman plant but Model 1908 (Danish 1910) was manufactured by Anciens Stablissements Pieper at Herstal, Belgium. In 1922 the government arsenal manufactured a modified pistol, the M1910/21 and at the same time the Belgian production was updated to the same specification.

The pistol was recoil operated having a particularly heavy and strong construction. The cartridge fired was the 9mm Bergman Bayard or 9mm Largo. The only drawback was the somewhat clumsy external shape.

Berthier Rifle (Model 1892)

The Berthier rifle used the same bolt type as the M86 but employed the Mannlicher-type magazine. This magazine, initially of three rounds, used the clip as an integral part. In the M1916 the five-round clip was substituted. The most important change was when the Mannlicher-

type magazine was replaced by a Mauser type in 1934 to handle the new 7.5mm cartridge.

Besa

The Besa was adopted by the British army as a tank gun and became unique in that it used a non-standard round of ammunition, the 7.92mm Mauser. As with the Bren LMG the Besa was a Czech design and was known in its native country as the Zb53.

The Zb53 was a gas-operated gun with a recoiling barrel. The gun fired as the barrel was on its way forward. The additional energy required to turn the barrel round made the recoil particularly light. The system has been employed by the Americans who are applying it to the development of artillery pieces under the title of 'soft recoil'.

Initial guns had dual rates of fire from 450–800rpm but this was deleted by BSA who carried out some redesign before producing the weapon. The fire rate was fixed at 800rpm and then later slowed to 500rpm. The gun had originally been a ground gun and was used as such by the Czechs and the Germans in World War II. As such it was considered for British service but the calibre was inappropriate and time for redevelopment was lacking. The Besa achieved an enviable reputation for reliability and accuracy and served with British tanks until superseded by the Browning.

A derivation of the basic gun was the Zb60, essentially an enlarged version chambered for a 15mm round. This heavy machine gun was produced only in small quantities for armoured cars. It was known as the 15mm Besa.

Borchardt C.93

The Borchardt has been seen by many as simply a forerunner of the Luger but of little value in its

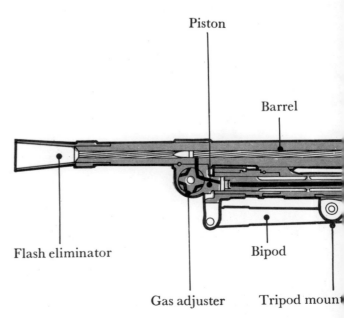

Piston

Barrel

Flash eliminator

Gas adjuster

Bipod

Tripod mount

time as a commercial pistol. The facts, however, show that it was designed in the early 1890s and appeared as a production pistol in 1894. It was a true production weapon with more than 3,000 manufactured. This was a figure unrivalled at that point in the 19th century.

The basic design of the toggle lock was derived from that of Maxim but worked upwards instead of down. The box magazine owed much to the American James Lee, but the combination of all the necessary attributes for a successful automatic pistol was Borchardt's work.

The first pistols were manufactured by Ludwig Loewe at their Berlin factory but after only a few weapons had been made, work was transferred to Deutsche Waffen und Munitionsfabriken (DWM). Production stopped in 1899 when the development of the Luger was well under way.

The Borchardt C.93 is an ungainly weapon with a near vertical butt and a pronounced overhang at the rear. It was frequently offered with a shoulder stock that was clamped to the back. It proved to be reliable and accurate but the overall length of nearly 14in (355mm) and its weight of 46oz (1,304g) prevented it from being a total success.

Boys Antitank Rifle

World War I had ended with the tank beginning to show its possibilities and development of the first antitank weapons. The Mauser 13mm antitank rifle was developed from the standard infantry Mauser and proved effective against the thin armour then used. The interwar years saw the Germans develop the tank and the British develop no antitank weapon. When in 1934 thought was given to the matter the rifle that was developed had a performance not much better than the Mauser. The handbook for the Boys recommended firing at the joint between the turret and the body. Easier said than done, and hardly likely to give confidence to the firer.

The basis for the design that was developed under the direction of Captain Boys was a bolt-action rifle firing a .50in bullet from a large-capacity belted case. This bullet attained a velocity of 3250fps and could at best penetrate 1.3in (35mm) of plate. The recoil was fearsome and a number of efforts were made to try and make the gun more practical for firing. The butt was heavily padded, the barrel recoiled in a cradle and a massive muzzle brake was fitted. The result was never popular as it was often ineffective as well as unpleasant to use. Adoption of a cored bullet (tungsten, following the Polish antitank rifle) did little to improve performance and in 1943 the weapon was withdrawn from service.

Bren Gun

The successor to the Lewis Gun was to come from the favourable report of a military attache who had seen the Zb26 in Czechoslovakia. The only problem that presented itself, after many tests against various other types, was that it was in 7.92mm calibre which was a rimless round rather than the British .303 rimmed. The Czech designers Holek and Marek redesigned the Zb26 to fire the British round which could in retrospect be considered a mistake but because of the stocks of .303 the British could not afford to change calibre. The new weapon was called the ZGB.

With great difficulty, because of the change from metric to Imperial measurements, the Royal Small Arms Factory at Enfield tooled up and by the end of December 1936 the first gun had been produced.

The Bren was, and still is, a firm favourite

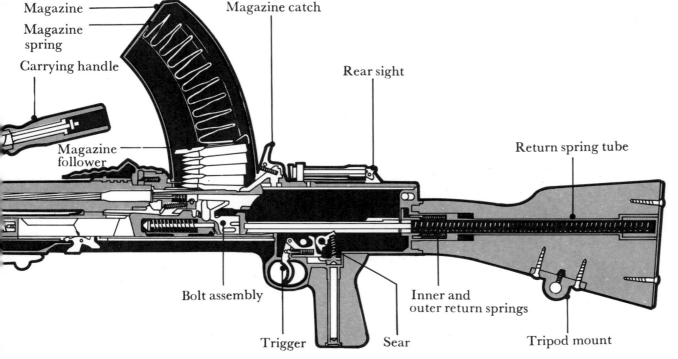

Magazine — Magazine catch
Magazine spring
Carrying handle
Rear sight
Magazine follower
Return spring tube
Bolt assembly
Inner and outer return springs
Trigger
Sear
Tripod mount

Left: The Bren gun is probably the best light machine gun ever produced. It combines Czech design with British manufacture. Still in service and converted from its wartime .303in calibre to 7.62mm NATO, the Bren remains a popular weapon.

Right: The Browning Automatic Rifle or BAR. Almost too late for World War I it has seen service in both the United States and other countries over many years. FN have also produced it in modified form.

with a reliable gas action and top feed magazine. The interchangeable barrel provided the capability for sustained fire. Renamed the L4 and rechambered for 7.62mm NATO, the Bren is still in service.

Browning Automatic Rifle (BAR)

The BAR was designed for use in World War I and survived in service with the American army in Korea. The concept was that of a magazine-fed, gas-operated, self-loading rifle. The overall weight of later versions, 19½lb (8.8kg), made the BAR more of a light machine gun. The BAR was designed by John Browning in conjunction with Colt and Winchester. Later the FN factory carried out a redesign programme and incorporated an interchangeable barrel.

Browning .30 (Model 1919) and .50 (M2) Machine Guns

John Browning's first machine gun, the Model 1895, while relatively successful had the disadvantage that the link mechanism protruded from the bottom during firing, thus earning for the weapon the name Potato Digger. Browning's next guns were, if not perfect, then good enough to see service with the United States, Britain and many other nations. The firm of FN have announced that the .50 is to go back into production.

The Browning machine guns were recoil operated using the recoil of the barrel to unlock the breech and eject the empty round. The recoil spring returned the mechanism forward, chambering a fresh round from a canvas belt. Both the .30 and .50 were air-cooled and used relatively heavy barrels and gave a reasonable rate of fire.

The .50 was an enlarged version of the .30 using a newly developed cartridge. The Ameri-

Left: The M2 Carbine is a selective fire version of the famous M1 Carbine. Although the cartridge is of doubtful effectiveness the carbine proved very popular and a number of companies still make versions of it.

can forces at the end of World War I wanted a heavy machine gun that would have good penetration. Successive developments using the French 11mm round and various home developments were unsuccessful. Luckily, captured German antitank rifle ammunition was tried and found to have the desired characteristics. Some development was done and the .50 Browning cartridge was born. It is a most successful cartridge/gun combination.

The Brownings served not only as vehicle and ground guns but also were adopted as tank and aircraft weapons. Both are still in use in front-line service in many forces, including those of Britain and the United States.

Browning Model 1935 Hi Power
John Browning was not an inventor who sat back with satisfaction on the completion of a project. The Colt Model 1911 had proved a success but his fertile brain decided that it could be improved upon and so, in collaboration with Fabrique National in Belgium, he embarked on what he felt would be its successor. The patent for the Browning Hi Power was granted in February 1927, two months after Browning's death the previous December. Browning had decided that the link system of the Colt was not ideal and so he replaced it with a cam system. The separate barrel bushing was replaced with a fixed one and the use of a double column magazine allowed a larger cartridge capacity. He used a complex lever system in the trigger and added a magazine safety. These complications of the original design may be considered a decided disadvantage. The original prototypes were striker fired but this was soon dropped in favour of the more normal hammer.

The final pistol was introduced in 1935 by FN and has remained in production ever since.

The John Inglis company of Toronto made the pistol for the Chinese and the British in World War II. The Browning, adopted by the British army, has remained in service as it has indeed with other armed forces.

The pistol is accurate for one designed as a service side arm and with any reasonable ammunition it is extremely reliable. The Canadian army tested it: they took two pistols, stripped them, put them in a bucket of sand and then reassembled them. The pistols fired without a hitch.

Carbine .30 M1 and M2
The M1 Carbine, not to be confused with the M1 Garand, was developed to provide an all purpose weapon to replace the pistol, submachine gun and in some cases the rifle. This aim was impossible to achieve, but the resultant weapon has been in production, with gaps, since 1940.

The original development was on the cartridge which was developed by Winchester. In effect the .30 carbine cartridge is an enlarged .32acp round using a heavier bullet and a longer case with a bigger powder capacity.

The carbine itself was also a Winchester development but had to win a 'shoot off' with other designs. Using the gas system developed by 'Carbine' Williams, Winchester developed a prototype in 14 days and a final development weapon in 34 days – a truly remarkable achievement that enabled the final trial in September 1941 to show its outstanding superiority.

The M1 Carbine is under 36in (914mm) long and weighs under 5½lb (2.4kg). A number of different versions were developed including one with a folding stock and another, the M2, with selective fire capability. The M1 saw much use in Vietnam.

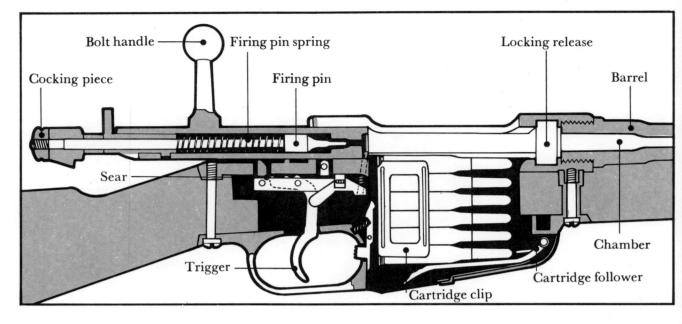

Bolt handle — Firing pin spring

Cocking piece   Firing pin   Locking release   Barrel

Sear

Trigger

Cartridge clip   Cartridge follower   Chamber

Right: The Carcano rifle was the standard Italian service issue. It is a combination of Mauser-type action and Mannlicher magazine. It went into production with the Model 1891 (illustrated) and ceased with the Model 1941.

Below: When the muzzle loader became outdated a flood of inventors designed breech-loading conversions. The same can be said of the bolt-action when the self-loading rifle came into use. The Charlton, shown here, was the only conversion to be even remotely successful.

Carcano Rifles

This group of rifles, developed at the Turin arsenal, spanned the period from before the turn of the century through two world wars.

The Carcano, which is a Mauser-type action, is often called the Mannlicher Carcano because of its magazine type. The first Model of 1891 was chambered for the 6.5mm cartridge. The following models, 1891/24, M1938 and M1941 all follow the basic design and differ only in furniture and barrel lengths. The Model 38 was designed specifically for a new cartridge, the 7.35mm. The outbreak of war, however, resulted in many M38s being made in 6.5mm.

CETME Assault Rifle (M58)

The Spanish CETME rifle programme, an off-shoot of German World War II development, was to spawn the H & K range of weapons which have been sold and manufactured under licence in many countries world-wide.

The German StG 45M was taken as the model and the Cetro dos Estudios Technicos de Materiales Especiales, with the help of an ex-Mauser Werke employee, Volgrimmler, modified the controlled roller lock system into a delayed blowback type. Cartridge development was also intense and an unusual bullet with a very long spire point was initially used. This was replaced by a cartridge identical to the 7.62mm NATO except that it had a lower propellant charge. A modification to the rifle will allow the use of the standard round.

Charlton Machine Gun

At the start of World War II most rifles in use were of the bolt-action type and numerous attempts were made to convert the stocks to self loaders. Only one of the conversions actually saw any real production, and this was the Charlton.

The basic conversion was simple enough. The bolt action was retained but operated by a cam attached to a gas system. The return movement of the bolt was controlled by a recoil spring. The magazine feed was similar to the standard weapon although some guns were manufactured to use the Bren gun magazine with its larger capacity. The conversion added a gas port to the barrel and then the gas piston and cylinder system. A bipod was added and in some cases a muzzle brake.

The Charlton was designed by the Charlton Automatic Arms Company in New Zealand but the company had insufficient production capacity to produce the gun so manufacture was carried out by the Electrolux company of Australia. Production ran to only some 500 units before more important work intervened. This small number nevertheless earns the Charlton its significance as the most successful conversion from bolt action to self loader.

Chauchat M1915

The Chauchat has received the dubious distinction of being voted the worst machine gun of World War I and is probably the worst ever taken into service. Rudolf Frommer, the designer, had incorporated a long recoil system operating a rotating bolt in a .32acp pocket pistol, and he designed the Chauchat on a similar principle.

The quality of materials and the manufacturing shortcuts employed added to the basic design deficiencies. The use of the 8mm Lebel round led to a magazine that was semicircular in shape and bottom-mounted. The Americans, desperate for machine guns, purchased the Chauchat first in 8mm Lebel then converted to 30-06.

Colt Single Action Army

If gunmen such as Hickok, Masterson, Billy the Kid and the Earp brothers were alive today they would all be glad to see that their favourite pistol was still available. Although it was withdrawn for a short period, public demand caused the reintroduction of the Single Action Army.

The demand for more and more powerful cartridges meant that the open frame of the early Colts, while sufficiently strong for the original types, proved too weak for these new developments. The introduction of the solid frame in 1873 made the single-action revolver possible.

Early production stopped in 1840 and did not resume until 1856 so the pistols may be considered in two groups. The first production pistols have two distinct models: the first has a rounded top to the top strap and the second a flat top. The early weapon is the standard frame and the later one is known as the flat top. The flat top, developed in 1888, was largely a target version with a sight set into the top strap. The name of the famous target range at Bisley was incorporated in the title of the target version.

In its basic form the pistol was adopted by the United States government which accepted 37,000 units. There were many variations of barrel lengths, from 3in (76mm) to the famous Buntline of 12–16in (304–405mm). Calibres also varied and more than 30 different ones were used on the Single Action Army.

The call for the reintroduction of the pistol was strongly reinforced by the fact that copies of the original had started to appear. Colt decided to re-enter the market and this proved a success. The pistol was announced as a New Frontier Model, which had a similar frame to the flat top. It was available in modern pistol calibres (centrefire). Ruger produced an extremely successful single action .22 and Colt retaliated with the Frontier Scout. This too was a success. Whatever the personal preference, for single or double action, no one can deny the appeal of what some consider to be the real revolver, the single action – and this means the Colt Army.

Colt .45 Automatic

The American GI has been able to rely on the Colt .45 since World War I. The continuous service that this pistol has seen since then, and the fact that there are no plans to supersede it, make this weapon unique.

The early Browning designs carried out for Colt were relatively successful but were of .38 calibre, but the army preferred a larger

Above: The Chauchat earned itself a reputation as the worst machine gun ever produced. Despite this, many saw service in World War I.

121

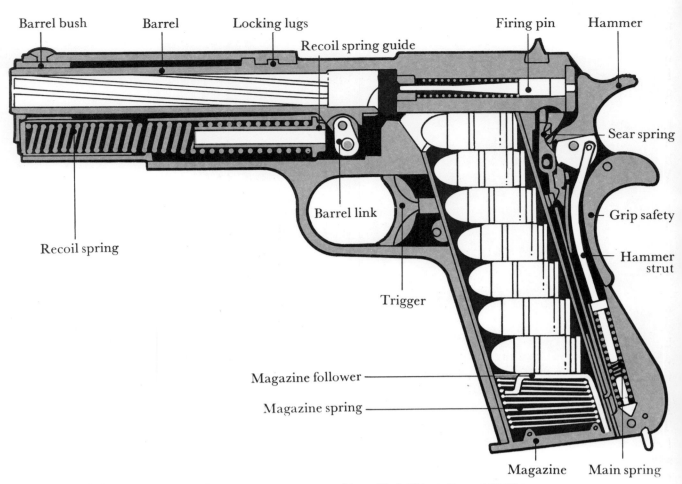

Right: When J. M. Browning designed the Colt 1911 he could hardly have envisaged its success. It still serves the US Army nearly 70 years later.

Barrel bush — Barrel — Locking lugs — Recoil spring guide — Firing pin — Hammer — Sear spring — Grip safety — Hammer strut — Barrel link — Trigger — Recoil spring — Magazine follower — Magazine spring — Magazine — Main spring

calibre and Winchester and the government set about developing a new round. Colt had Browning modify his model of 1902 with its twin-link recoil system to handle the new cartridges. One of the main weaknesses of the early design was that the cross-pin which allowed the weapon to be stripped for cleaning was the only thing that held the slide on. The twin-link system was complicated.

Browning carried out a large number of experiments using different features such as a concealed hammer, no grip safety, and various forms of manual safety before the army accepted the final design, the Colt Model 1911. The 1911 had a single-link recoil system, a grip safety, a manual safety and a spur hammer. A major change was the adoption of the 1911A1, which featured a modified safety grip; hammer and trigger were used.

The model 1911A1 continued in production throughout the war and reached a total production during that time of over 2½ million. Production was carried out by Colt, Remington Rand, Union Switch and Signal, Remington, Ithaca and Singer.

One minor disadvantage of the barrel bushing has always been the variable amount of free play and the effect this has on accuracy. The Colt Mk5 Series 70 has modified this with the use of a barrel bush with fingers that hold the barrel tight at lock-up. Other versions of the basic gun are the National Match Target version, the Ace .22 LR conversion and innumerable copies.

Dardick Pistol and Rifle

When a truly innovative piece of design appears on the market it is often not given the support it would appear to justify. This can be said of the 'tround' concept used by the ill-fated Dardick system.

The basis of all Dardick work was the belief that a triangle provided a better shape for the cartridge case. This was based on the open chamber concept where the cartridge was supported by the cylinder in a revolver type mechanism only on the two inner faces, leaving the main body of the gun to support the outer, third side. The advantage was that the cylinder could be fed by a conventional type of magazine and the ejection of the empty round was easy. This revolving cylinder gave the round its characteristic shape with the sides of the triangle being made to conform to the cylinder's outside diameter. An added advantage was that the rounds fitted together in the magazine much better than the conventional type.

The Dardick Model 1100 went onto the market in 1954. This pistol not only had an unconventional method of operation, but also an outward appearance that was quite unattractive. A carbine version could utilize the tround to fire any round smaller than the basic calibre of .357 by using a different barrel and the tround as an effective adapter to hold the cartridge. This feature was much discussed as a military advantage for the pistol could fire any calibre captured from the enemy by using a new barrel and a handful of trounds. But the public did not find the concept of any value and military interest was not followed up. The Dardick concern went into liquidation and the guns became collectors' pieces.

De Lisle Carbine

The De Lisle carbine has long been superseded by the L34 Sterling Patchett, but during World War II it served with distinction.

It was designed at the Royal Small Arms Factory and featured a modified SMLE action. The basis of the true silent weapon is the use of a bullet that is either subsonic (the De Lisle) or is reduced to this velocity by gas bleeding (the Sterling Patchett). The De Lisle used the Colt .45acp cartridge with a complex baffle system which made the shot inaudible within a few yards. The SMLE action had a .45in calibre barrel fitted and the bolt shortened. A magazine was fitted and the silencer was integral. Both fixed and folding stocks were utilized.

Erma MP38/40

The range of Erma-developed submachine guns has often been credited to Schmeisser and the soldiers' name for the German submachine guns of World War II was invariably 'Schmeisser'. The first designs from the Erma factory were the Heinrich Vollmer and the EMP, both introducing the telescoping mains spring guide and cover.

The German government felt the need for a light weapon to equip armoured vehicle crews and paratroops so asked Erma to produce a suitable weapon. It was lucky that Berthold Geipel, the founder, had continued with the development of the basic Vollmer designs as he was very quickly able to provide what was to become the new standard in submachine gun design, the MP38. This was not in itself a massive production success for it was not simple to manufacture. It did, however, have an easily folded stock manufactured from metal, a telescoping spring guide and used plastic and metal pressings.

An interim variant was produced which was a modified MP38 and had the unofficial designation of MP38/40. The MP40 was the final version and while the basic weapon had not been changed in concept the design was specifically orientated to wartime production. The major components were stamped from low-carbon steel and welded together. The foregrip was moulded from a phenolic resin which not only was light and strong but provided a better grip in adverse weather conditions.

In an attempt to provide more fire power than the 32-round magazine normally fitted, a side-by-side sliding arrangement was fitted with the designation MP40/2. This used two standard

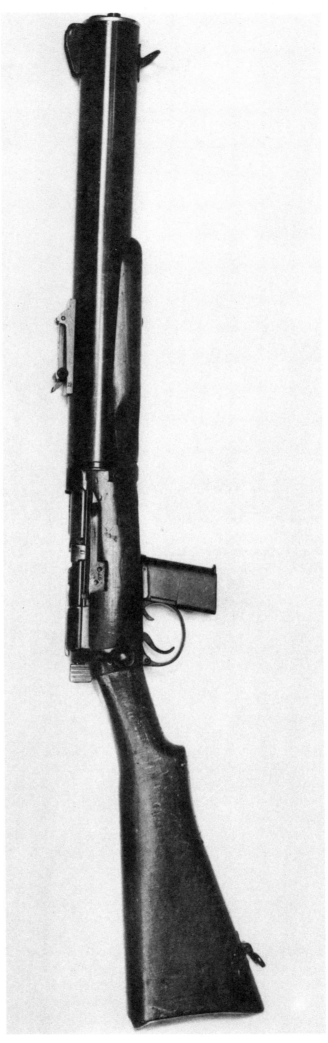

Left: The De Lisle Carbine was a simple solution to the problem of providing a silent gun. A standard bolt action rifle was converted to .45acp and fitted with an efficient silencer.

magazines and allowed the empty to be slid out of the battery and the full one in. The Americans tested the MP40 and found it very reliable and accurate, and it was greatly respected by other Allied troops in the field.

Experimental Model 2 (EM2)

When World War II drew to a close Britain remained the only major power without a self-loading rifle in service. The design project that was set up to rectify this was composed of four teams. EM1 and EM2 reached hardware stage while EM3 and EM4 were only drawing-board exercises.

The weapon finally chosen was the EM2, which was a gas-operated rifle with a two-projecting-lug bolt. To obtain the required barrel length with compact overall dimensions it was decided to employ the then radical bull-pup layout. An optical sight was fitted in the carrying handle. The cartridge that was developed was of the short case type using a 7mm bullet called popularly the .280/30. (The .30 referred to the case base being the same as the 30-06.) The official designation was 7mm Mk1Z and it was adopted in 1950. In April 1951 the government adopted the rifle, calling it the No. 9, but later on the decision was reversed and the FN rifle adopted instead.

FAMAS and MASAR (Le Fusil Automatique MAS)

In 1967 the French General Staff decided that the army should have a new group of infantry light weapons. The initial choice that had to be made was ammunition and after extensive tests it was decided in 1970 that the 5.56mm M193 Armalite round would be suitable. In 1971 MAS was given a development contract for a rifle to meet the General Staff's requirements firing the 5.56mm round.

The rifle developed was a bullpup in configuration giving the required barrel length with the compact overall package demanded. The operation is delayed blowback but unlike a number of other rifles and machine guns it uses a lever rather than rollers. The fire mechanism is designed to offer the option of not only single and automatic fire but also of a three-round burst. Grenades can also be launched from the standard weapon.

This rifle is now equipping certain French army units as well as a limited number of police. It means that the French are the first in Europe to adopt a small calibre rifle and cartridge as standard.

FG42

The FG42, which was manufactured by Krieghoff for the German paratroops during World War II, marked a worthwhile advance in weapon design. The concept replaced the rifle and light machine gun with a single weapon. The initial weapon developed was of high grade materials and had a metal butt. The action was gas, using a long stroke piston and a two-lug rotating bolt. The weapon was designed by L. Stange.

The later version which went into production had a simplified construction using wood for

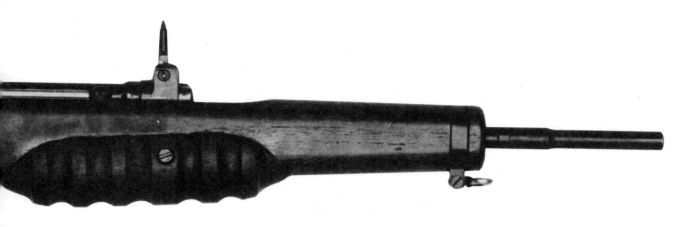

the butt. The use of the full power 7.92mm cartridge with a short barrel led to a violent muzzle flash and considerable recoil. The complex muzzle break-cum-flash hider helped but the gun was still unstable when fired in long bursts. The rather feeble bipod contributed to this. The trigger mechanism allowed open bolt on auto, closed bolt on single shot. All in all, although only 5,000 were produced, the FG42 was a clever design.

FN FAL and L1A1 SLR

The basic design work for the FAL and SLR was carried out in pre-war Belgium, during the war in Britain and after the war back in Belgium. The design team at FN, headed by M. Saive, slipped out of Belgium ahead of the German forces.

The initial work led to a rifle, the SAFN or Model 49, that was very much in the Tokarev mould. It was gas operated with a tipping bolt firing a full power rifle round such as the 7.92mm Mauser. The weapon was sold in large numbers in countries such as Egypt and equipped Belgian soldiers in Korea. It was at one time considered for service with the British army but the EM2 project intervened.

The FN company developed the M49 and during the late 1940s and early 1950s the first FAL-type rifle appeared. This was again basically designed with a full power cartridge in mind although the .280in was used on prototype weapons in competition with the EM2.

When the EM2 proved unsuccessful in 7.62mm NATO the British took 1,000 of the developed FN FAL rifles for trial. Although it was accepted by some countries the British decided on a number of modifications and the resulting weapon was designated the L1A1 rifle and manufactured at Enfield and BSA.

Galil

The Galil is very similar to the AK47 in many respects. After the Six-Day War the Israelis decided to adopt the 5.56mm cartridge and tested a number of rifles including those from many major companies. The result of the test was that a design from Yaacov Lior and Israel Galili was judged the best. The rifle represents the best points of the AK amalgamated with those lessons that can only be learned from the hard experience of war. Galil has been entered for the NATO trials by the Dutch firm of NWM.

Gaulois Pistol

This odd pistol achieved a degree of popularity around 1900 as a personal defence weapon. It was manufactured by Manufacture Francaise d'Armes et Cycles de St Etienne in relatively large quantities.

While the 8mm cartridge was of doubtful effect it is probable that at the distance envisaged by its users the Gaulois would at least distract a would-be rapist or assailant. The pistol was a mechanical repeater using the squeeze action of the hand to operate it, thus giving it the nickname Palm Squeezer. The firing cycle was as follows. The pistol was gripped in the hand with the chamber empty. The inward motion chambered a round from the magazine

Right: The Gaulois mechanical repeating pistol was designed to provide the lady or gentleman with pocketable protection.

and then fired it. As the grip was released the gun opened under the force of a spring and the empty case was ejected. The removable magazine had space for five cartridges. Today the weapon is much sought-after by collectors.

Gras Rifle (Model 1874)
The French Model 1874 rifle was a single-shot bolt-action weapon firing an 11mm cartridge. Designed by Basile Gras it was based on the Chassepot but converted to fire the metallic cartridge. A number of different versions were produced varying little except in furniture and barrel length. A major development was the 1878 Kropatschek rifle that employed the Gras breech allied to a butt-held tubular magazine. This was used by the French navy.

Gyrojet
The rocket-firing Gyrojet achieved no success, militarily or commercially, although its de-

velopers had high hopes. R. Mainhardt and A. Bexiehl formed the company of MBA Associates in California to develop promising ideas that came available and they took an interest in the design of small arms. Not wanting to use conventional cartridges and weapons, they decided to use rockets. The idea was not new, but the technical problems had until then limited actual production of weapons.

The rocket consisted of a steel body with a variety of shaped heads. The body was filled with propellant and a centrally mounted primer was situated in the rear cover. The cover had angled vents for the rocket gas so that the projectile would spin and thus stabilize. Apart from the basic problem of accuracy, the rocket had two inherent problems. It started very slowly and muzzle velocity was therefore low, which made the energy lower at point blank range than further away. Moreover, the light steel case or projectile lost velocity very quickly after burn out.

The pistol itself was little more than a smoothbored launching tube with a pistol grip. The firing was novel in that the hammer did not deliver its blow to the primer but struck the front of the projectile and drove it back against the fixed firing pin. The rocket's forward motion recocked the hammer. The calibre was 13mm. Although the pistol achieved production in the 1960s it was short-lived.

Hotchkiss Model 1914
The name of the Model 1914 was all that Benjamin Hotchkiss contributed to the gun. The design was based on an Austrian Captain Odkojek's patents which were purchased by the

Right: The Gyrojet was the only rocket-firing pistol to achieve production but was nevertheless a commercial failure. The inaccuracy of the weapon coupled with its expense were major contributing factors.

Left: The Ingram M10 submachine gun has attracted a great deal of publicity largely because of its bulbous screw-on silencer. Although it is not totally effective the silencer and the compact dimensions of the gun has ensured sales to specialist users.

Hotchkiss company. By the late 1890s the design had been perfected and in 1904 the Japanese used it successfully in their war with Russia.

The French, finding the German Maxim disastrously defective, needed an effective machine gun and were soon equipping with them. The gun proved so successful that the American and British troops also used them in World War I.

The first model operated with a gas system that utilized a long stroke piston and a lug lock. The later M1914 used a rotating 'nut' or collar lock operated by a similar gas system. The feed system is similar to the Breda, but the tray is articulated every three rounds. To assist with the air cooling a distinctive five 'dough nuts' were fitted round the breech end of the barrel. The Hotchkiss saw service in World War II.

Ingram Model 10 and 11

The Ingram Models 10 and 11 have achieved a certain notoriety for they have been used with their silencers as both clandestine and terrorist weapons. They are good examples of modern production techniques and function well.

Gordon Ingram, the designer, gained practical knowledge of weapons in World War II. His basic philosophy of weapon design was that, apart from efficiency, it must be possible to manufacture them as simply as possible out of basic materials. After the war the market for a new submachine gun was limited. It was not until the formation of Police Ordnance Company in 1949 that he had any success. The Model 6 was sold in small quantities in the United States and Peru, with his help, established a production line.

Ingram left the company in 1952 to work in Thailand where it was decided to produce his Model 8 submachine gun. He joined Sionics Inc. in 1969 as a designer. The management of that firm were keen to produce weapons and decided to form a separate company. Thus Military Armament Corporation came into being in 1970 and the Model 10 and 11 Ingrams appeared.

These weapons were constructed of simple box section steel pressings. The tooling was simple and the machine requirement such as would be available almost anywhere. They were made in three calibres, 45 acp, 9mm P and .380 acp; the models were basically identical other than in calibre. Many of the weapons were fitted with silencers. Production stopped in 1973 and the firm closed, although the weapon was put back into production by a new company in 1976–7 and is still on sale.

Kimball .30 Pistol

The designer of the Kimball, John Kimball, started his work on the premise that as the American army already had in use the .30 M1 Carbine and its pistol-type ammunition they would be better to drop the .45acp Colt and have but the one round for both weapons. The idea of a common cartridge throughout the army has always been attractive as an idea but most designers have settled for the rifle and machine gun to have the one round and for the pistol and submachine gun to have another. The rifle may well be amalgamated with the submachine gun, as the full-sized cartridge of the small-bore type can be fired from a small weapon. But no designer tries to fire the rifle cartridge from a pistol even when the cartridge is as low powered as the M1 Carbine type.

The weapon was not a success and in tests carried out with a revolver chambered for the M1 round most firers were so dismayed by the heavy recoil, loud noise and flash that they ended up firing with eyes shut.

The Kimball was designed as a delayed blowback pistol. It used two methods to delay the opening of the breech. Firstly the barrel and slide recoiled together for a time and when the breech block was free to open itself the round was delayed in the chamber by grooves machined round the chamber into which the case was designed to extrude and thus slow the opening. This feature depended on a very hard case material and its effect was erratic. The final

127

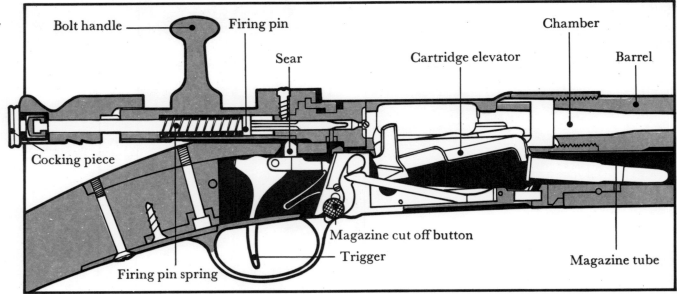

Right: Although the main claim to fame for the Lebel is the fact that its cartridge was the first to use smokeless powder and a small, 8mm, bore, it did serve France from 1886 through to World War II. The tubular magazine, similar to the Winchester's, is noteworthy.

Bolt handle — Firing pin

Sear

Chamber

Cartridge elevator

Barrel

Cocking piece

Firing pin spring

Magazine cut off button

Trigger

Magazine tube

downfall of the pistol was hastened after the lack of interest shown by the army. The frame had a habit of fracturing and letting the breech block come free – not something that guarantees happy customers.

Kolibri

The Kolibri is undoubtedly the smallest automatic pistol and also the least effective. This weapon and its two different cartridges were marketed by a Herr Grabner around 1914. The actual designer is unknown and the weapon, a simple blowback, has little to recommend it in design. The two calibres were 2.7mm and 3mm. Taking a standard .22 bullet they generated a power of about one-fiftieth of the energy. The magazine of the Kolibri contained five of these miniscule bullets which were of the centrefire type.

Lahti L35

Apart from the fact that it is one of the most robust and reliable pistols ever manufactured, the Lahti is unique in that it uses an accelerator to speed the bolt on its way rearward rather than relying on the momentum. The pistol was produced in its native Finland and also in Sweden.

The designer, Aimo Lahti, worked for the state-owned Valtion weapon factory. This design was begun in 1929 and after acceptance, with modifications, production started in 1935. The Finnish army adopted it as the L35. Production was interrupted by the war but resumed again until 1950. A small batch of hybrid Swedish/Finnish pistols was manufactured in the late 1950s.

In Sweden the Lahti was built under licence mainly by Husqvarna Vapenfabrik. This product lasted from 1942 until 1946 and resulted in more Swedish pistols being produced than the original Finnish design. The Swedish designation was M40.

The outward appearance of the pistol gives it some resemblance to the Luger, but the mechanism is totally different. The Lahti has a massive rectangular bolt sliding inside a square section receiver; its recoil action uses a vertically sliding locking piece and an accelerator. The massive size and comfortable shooting position make it a pleasant gun to use.

Lebel Rifle (Model 1886)

To the French Lebel rifle must go the credit of being the first small bore, 8mm, rifle using a cartridge with a smokeless propellant. Lieutenant Colonel Nicolas Lebel was not the designer but he was a member of the French commission which decided the configuration of the new weapon. The rifle had a similar bolt action to the Gras and used a tubular magazine, as had the Kropatschek. The magazine was under the barrel as opposed to in the butt. A modified version with a strengthened action called the 86/93 was still being used in World War II.

Lee-Enfield

The first Lee-Enfield entered service in 1902 replacing the Lee-Metford. The Enfield rifling that replaced that of Metford led to the Lee-Enfield Mk I. The Mk I was somewhat overlong and after use in the South African War the rifle was shortened by 5in (127mm) and appropriately renamed the Short Magazine Lee-Enfield or SMLE.

Various marks followed, including conversions from the original Lee-Metford. The SMLE saw Britain through World War I and the final Mk VI became, under new nomenclature, the No. 4 rifle which was used by British troops in World War II and until the adoption of the FN self-loader. The No. 4 had the wood fore-end stop before the end of the barrel, unlike its predecessors.

One development that did not see adoption was that of the Pattern 13 rifle, which was a Mauser-type firing a new 7mm bullet. Although World War I prevented its adoption, it was manufactured in the United States both for Britain, as the Pattern 1914 (.303), and for America as the Model 1917 (30-06).

Liberator Pistol

One million of these peculiar devices were manufactured for the American government by Guide Lamp Corporation in 1942. The basic idea was that there were in occupied territory numerous guerillas who would be glad of any weapon, and that vital strategic materials and manpower were not available to produce a conventional type.

The pistol was based on the crudest of metal stampings and used a smooth piece of tube for the barrel. The breech mechanism was held in place by the firing pin which was attached to a cast hammer/striker. There was no ejector or extractor and so a piece of wood came with the cased set. The box contained cartoon type instructions and spare ammunition. If fired at very close range they would be just as effective as any proper pistol.

Luger (Pistole Parabellum Modell 08)

Few if any weapons have elicited as much enthusiasm and devotion as the Luger. As a weapon of war it had some drawbacks yet over 3 million were produced and most saw service at some time or another. It was replaced by the P38 mainly because it was expensive in time and machinery to produce under wartime conditions.

The development of the Luger from the Borchardt has never been proved to have been the work of any one person but evidence points to the fact that George Luger, when asked to produce a more acceptable pistol, did so, with or without the cooperation of Borchardt. The Borchardt Luger of 1898 contained the major modifications that were to make the Luger a success. The development of the 7.65mm Luger cartridge is also attributed to Luger as the longer Borchardt round would have posed problems when the recoil spring was placed in the rear of the grip. Switzerland adopted the Luger in May 1900 and accepted some 5,000 from DWM, thus becoming the first nation to adopt an automatic pistol as their standard side arm. The later Swiss pistols were locally produced.

Resistance to the small calibre 7.65mm round led Luger to develop the 9mm successor. This round was to achieve what even the Luger did not – it became almost the universal cartridge for submachine guns and, in many cases, pistols. Many variations of the Luger were developed, such as the Artillery version with its 8in (203mm) long barrel and its shoulder stock. This version was also fitted at times with the Trommelmagazin 08 or Snail drum 32-round drum magazine. The various 'look alike' copies of the Luger and the demand for pistols in the collectors' market led the postwar Mauser Jagdwaffen factory to resume production of a slightly modified Luger in 1971.

M1935 and M1950 Pistols

These pistols are manufactured on the Browning-Petter system. The original 7.65mm cartridge was ineffective but the M1950 uses the 9mm Parabellum.

The M1935 dispenses with the conventional locking grooves in the barrel top and slide (used on the 1935A). The locking is achieved by the barrel locking surface mating with the slide in the ejection point opening. The 1935 models were manufactured in quantity by MAC, MAS, MAT and SACM. The Model 1950 is an amalgamation of the Browning Hi Power and the Colt .45 along with the slide mounted safety of the M1935. The adoption of the 9mm Parabellum cartridge has made the French automatic pistol a weapon worthy of more serious consideration.

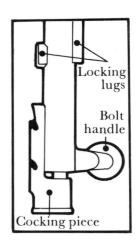

Locking lugs

Bolt handle

Cocking piece

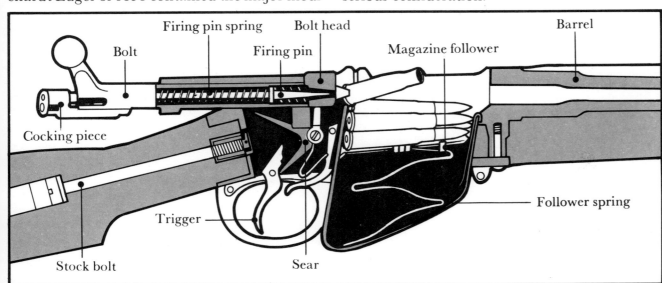

Firing pin spring — Bolt head — Barrel

Bolt — Firing pin — Magazine follower

Cocking piece

Trigger

Stock bolt — Sear

Follower spring

Left: The SMLE or Short Magazine Lee-Enfield and its successor, the Number 4, served the British army in both world wars. The use of a near locking system for its bolt action may have theoretical disadvantages but this has never detracted from the rifle's accuracy and reliable performance. The near locking lugs are shown above.

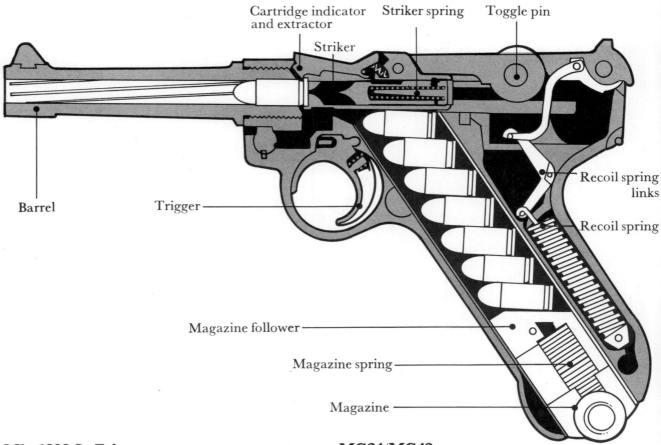

Right: The Luger has achieved a reputation enjoyed by few weapons. The Mauser factory is once more manufacturing Lugers for sale although the pistol no longer serves any army as a front-line weapon.

Cartridge indicator and extractor

Striker spring

Toggle pin

Striker

Recoil spring links

Recoil spring

Barrel

Trigger

Magazine follower

Magazine spring

Magazine

Mle 1892 St Etienne

The adoption of the 8mm calibre revolver for their service issue by the French in 1889 led to an initial order of 50,000. The first revolver in the development was a scaled down Chamelot-Delvigne Mle85 and only 1,000 or so were produced. This was a double action revolver with a loading gate for a non-swing-out cylinder and a pivoted ejector rod housed integrally with the cylinder pivot.

The inspector general of the arsenal carried out a redesign of the Mle 87 and by the autumn of 1892 the new revolver was in production. The new weapon was a swing-out cylinder double-action revolver with the ejection rod mounted through the cylinder pivot to give simultaneous ejection as with the Colt and S&W. The old loading gate on the right side of the frame was made to operate the cylinder catch, a neat piece of improvization. The cylinder swung out to the right rather than to the left. In this respect it differed from its rivals.

The frame design was also unusual in that the side plate, normally attached to the frame with screws, was hinged at the front so that the whole of the left side of the pistol could be opened up. This made maintenance of the weapon extremely convenient.

The actual numbers of the Mle92 produced is not known but 340,00 has been estimated. The revolver was to serve the French until it was replaced in 1935 by an automatic. The mechanical design of the Mle92 was good but the cartridge was ineffective. But it undoubtedly served its purpose well.

MG34/MG42

To Germany must go the credit for the first General Purpose Machine Gun (GPMG). The idea of the GPMG is that it can replace both the light and the heavy machine guns, being portable yet also capable of sustained fire. The MG34 was a recoil-operated gun that had a rotating bolt head with interrupted thread locking. The normal method of feed was with metal nondisintegrating belts of 50 rounds. With the adoption of a special top cover the gun could fire the Double Drum magazine and in this specification was often used as an antiaircraft gun. The main drawback was the fine tolerances to which the MG34 was manufactured, which resulted in occasional problems with dirt ingestion jamming the action. Nevertheless the MG34 was the standard tank gun and remained in army service until the end of World War II. Since then the MG34 has equipped many countries, including Israel.

The successor to the MG34, the MG42, was and probably still is the most successful GPMG ever built. Designed for easy manufacture with metal pressings and featuring a recoil-operated roller-locked breech, it proved its worth on all fronts in World War II. The belt feed system has been copied by most of the successful machine guns since, such as the M60, FN MAG and SIG. The belt feed combined with the simple and effective barrel change earned the weapon much respect and many countries after World War II took captured weapons into service.

The German army uses it at present as the

MG3 or MG42/59. The Italians have also produced it under licence. Both of these weapons have been converted from the original 7.92mm calibre to the NATO 7.62mm. The Germans have entered the gun for the NATO trials for the 1980s – not bad for a 35-year-old design.

MP44 Maschinenpistole 44, Sturmgewehr

The MP44 is one of that elite group of inventions that start a trend that is eventually followed world-wide. The Germans had decided before the outbreak of World War II that the intermediate cartridge with an attendant weapon was worthy of development. Initial work concentrated on the cartridge but by 1940–1 the basic 7.92mm short or Kurz cartridge design was finalized and development then began on the rifle to fire it.

Two designs emerged, one from the Walther company and one from Haenel. Both were put into limited production but neither was successful. Using the experience gained from these, Schmeisser modified the Haenel version into the MP43. The rifle was soon being produced as fast as the Germans could manage under war conditions. It was gas operated and featured extensive use of metal pressings, many of which were produced at sub-contract plants. The designation was changed twice, the first time to MP44 then allegedly at Hitler's insistence as a battle honour to Sturmgewehr.

Even today the MP44 looks a modern weapon and it is surprising that it has taken so long for countries other than the Soviet Union to adopt the concept.

Above: The MG34 was manufactured to high standards but because of over-close tolerances it was susceptible to jamming through dirt ingestion. Below: The Sturmgewehr or MP44 was the world's first true assault rifle. It was manufactured from steel pressings, used an intermediate powered round, the 7.92mm × 33mm, and had selective fire.

Madsen 1902

The Madsen has been described as the machine gun that should not work. The fact that it has been used by countless forces at one time or another with never failing efficiency speaks for itself.

It was named after the Danish minister of war and developed by the forerunner of the Dansk Industrie Syndikat, DRRS. The basic action of the Madsen is that of the Martini with the block movement extended to an above the breech position, and controlled by a stud running in a camway on the left of the gun body. The action is actuated by recoil and the feed is by box magazine mounted on the top. The Germans also produced a belt feed version.

Martini-Henry

The Snider rifle that equipped the British army was the result of a competition to utilize the old muzzle-loading rifles with a breech-loading conversion. In 1866 a committee was set up by the War Office to decide on a replacement. The result was the Martini-Henry rifle.

The American Peabody lever action was the basis for Friedrich Martini's patent of 1868. The Martini action used an integral firing pin with no hammer rather than the external hammer of the Peabody. The action was a dropping block operated by the lever which was also the trigger guard. For the barrel the Henry seven groove type was used. The bore was .45in. This single-shot breech-loader saw good service with the British forces until it was superseded by the Lee-Metford in 1891.

MAS38 and MAT49

The French were very late to start making sub-machine guns and did not start production of modern weapons with a good cartridge until after World War II. The MAS 38 had one major disadvantage that could not be overcome; this was the cartridge. It was 7.65mm long and a development of the American Pedersen cartridge for the Pedersen device. Although accurate, the low power made it of doubtful use as a combat cartridge.

The gun itself, although of simple blowback design, had a number of interesting features. The main design work had been carried out on the MAS35, which was developed in prototype form only. The magazine well-cover was spring-loaded to cover the opening when there was no magazine in place. The cocking handle was non-reciprocating and actuated a breech dust cover. The safety must rank as one of the most unusual ever, for the trigger was pushed forward to actuate it.

Production started in 1939 and the French army still had the MAS38 as their main sub-machine gun in Indo China decades later.

After 1945 it was decided that the next sub-machine gun should drop the 7.65mm cartridge and use the almost universal 9mm P. It was also decided that two manufacturers should produce competitive designs; these were MAC at Chatellerault and MAS at St Etienne. The MAC did not result in any volume production but a number of the later MAC48s were used by the army.

MAT also involved themselves in a development programme and an early type was the C4 which used the delayed blowback system popular with French weapon designers. Unlike competitive designs that use rollers to operate a two-piece bolt, the French use a lever. Their GPMG and the present service rifle, the FA MAS, both use the system.

The MAT1949, which is the present sub-machine gun of the French, once again has certain features not altogether normal. The calibre is the standard 9mm P but the magazine for the ammunition is pivoted so that when in the firing position it acts as a foregrip and when folded forward is compact and safe. The ejection post has a spring-loaded cover and there is a grip safety. The weapon fires only on fully automatic.

Mauser 1896

Today the weapon designer looks towards mass production with the minimum of production problems. The C.96 has all that today's designer would despise. It is a pistol that is machined from solid steel and dispenses with pins and screw. It is held together with neat interlocking parts and integral pivots. It could never be a mass-produced weapon in the true sense.

When Paul Mauser sold his business interest he concentrated on weapon design. Under his control in the Mauser design office was Fidel Federle and his brothers. Mauser worked with them during the period 1893–4. The patents for the pistol were taken out in Mauser's name in 1896 and covered the basic design that was to remain throughout the production life of the pistol.

The prototype was chambered for the Borchardt pistol cartridge and because of the low power of this round had only one lock lug on the bolt. The Mauser cartridge was dimensionally identical but used a considerably heavier charge and so with its development, a second lug was added. The frame of the pistol changed three times during production; the firing pin twice; the extractor twice; the trigger twice; the safety three times and the hammer three times. The changes were of minor importance.

The pistol was produced in two other calibres, the powerful 9mm Mauser export and the 9mm Parabellum. The latter was not only produced as standard but also as a conversion so that the standard cartridge could be used. Another deri-

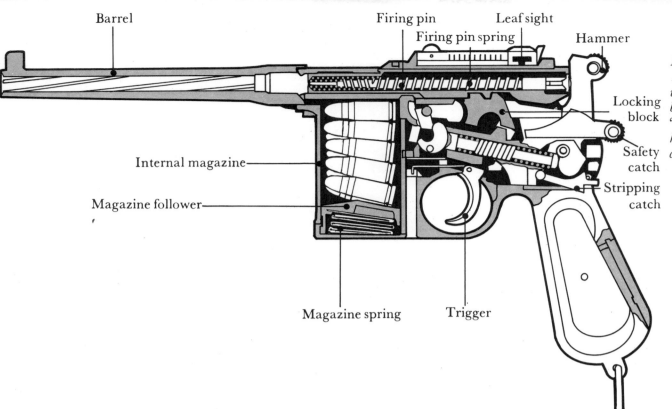

Left: The Mauser 1896, because of its unusual shape, has been given the name 'Broomhandle'. It has had a distinguished career.

vation was the Schnellfeuer or fully automatic version. This, while being of little practical use, saw service in World War II.

The Mauser was never a military success and was not adopted by any country in large quantities, but many were sold commercially.

Mauser Rifles M71, M71/84, M89, M98

The taking out of the patent for their first bolt action rifle in the United States brought the attention of the German government to the Mauser brothers. The result was a design that would become a classic and be copied by almost every arms making concern at one time or another. It still forms the basis for many sporting rifles.

The first Mauser developed for the German army was the Infanteriegewehr M71, a single shot bolt action. This was modified to a magazine loader by adopting the tube magazine that was so successful on the American rifles. This model was the M71/84. Although it had been in pro-

duction since 1880 it was not adopted until 1884 by the German army.

The most important development was not initially used by the Germans but by the Belgians. The Belgian M1889 was the first of the Mausers to introduce the one-piece bolt, locking with its two lugs at the bolt head. The magazine was an integral box-type loaded with a stripper clip. The other advance was the use of a small-calibre cartridge loaded with smokeless powder.

The final major development was the German M1898 which used the cock-on opening bolt system for the first time. It used the German 7.92mm cartridge and although a number of variants were produced such as the carbine K98k the basis remained the same.

The Mauser served the German and other armies through war after war and is even now still turning up wherever there is fighting. In the sporting field and on the target ranges, the Mauser action is still prominent.

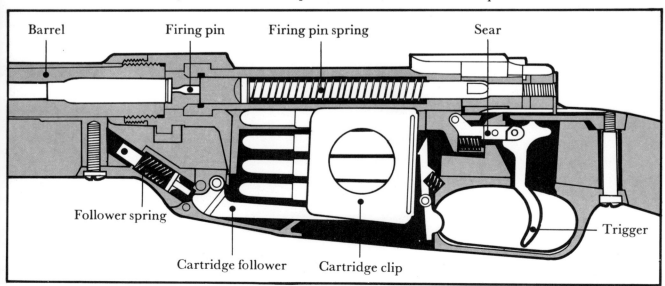

Left: Early Mausers such as the 1884 used a tube magazine. Another variant, the 1888 (illustrated) used the Mannlicher clip type. This is loaded and remains in the action until expelled through the bottom of the gun on the last shot.

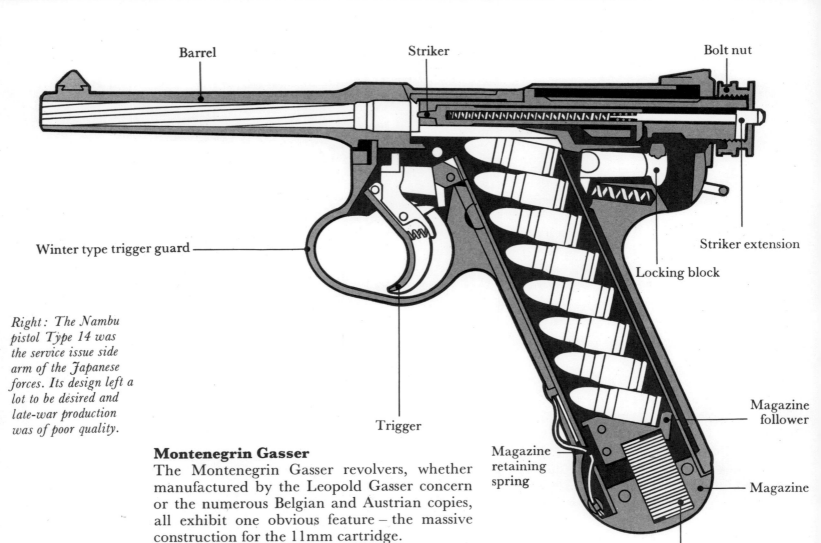

Barrel   Striker   Bolt nut

Winter type trigger guard

Striker extension

Locking block

Right: The Nambu pistol Type 14 was the service issue side arm of the Japanese forces. Its design left a lot to be desired and late-war production was of poor quality.

Trigger

Magazine follower

Magazine retaining spring

Magazine

Magazine spring

Montenegrin Gasser

The Montenegrin Gasser revolvers, whether manufactured by the Leopold Gasser concern or the numerous Belgian and Austrian copies, all exhibit one obvious feature – the massive construction for the 11mm cartridge.

The original M1870 Gasser used the 11mm Montenegrin cartridge and was of the hinged-frame, automatic ejection type. It was of cast iron but in 1874 a new model of steel construction was introduced. The locking system for the frame was accomplished by crosspins operated by levers at both sides of the standing breech. Numerous variations of the basic revolver were made, some double-action, some single and some with the most ornate engraving and precious metal inlays.

Nambu Automatic Pistols

The first pistol design by Colonel Kijiro Nambu, the Model 1904, introduced the standard Japanese automatic pistol cartridge, the 8mm Nambu. This was a very underpowered round which, considering some examples of the Nambu range, was just as well. The Model 1904 was recoiled-operated and featured a grip safety on the front of the grip. The pistol is often found with a slot for a shoulder stock but the stock itself is rare. A miniature version chambered for a 7mm cartridge was also manufactured and is normally known as the 'Baby Nambu'.

The Type 14 adopted by the army in 1925 was a modification of the 1904 deleting the grip safety and substituting a magazine type. A later variant which had a larger trigger guard to facilitate its use with gloves was fitted with an external spring to help hold the magazine in

place – testimony to the frequently very poor standard of manufacture. The final pistol of the prewar era was the Type 94 which began production in 1934. A recoil-operated pistol firing the 8mm round, it can only be described as one of the worst ever produced.

Owen

The inability of either Britain or America to supply a submachine gun in any real quantity made the Australian army look to a locally developed weapon. Prototypes of the Owen were not available from Evelyn Owen until the end of 1940 and the patents were not taken out until the next year. The gun was adopted for the Australian army in November 1941 and the production order was given to Lysaght in New South Wales. Production continued until 1944 by which time 45,000 of the various types had been produced. A number were refurbished with small modifications in 1952.

The most interesting feature of the Owen is that, unlike most submachine guns which have the magazine either side or bottom mounted, its magazine was on top. The theory was that this placement was more convenient in jungle conditions and when firing prone, without the need to hold the gun high because of a bottom mounted magazine. The top-mounted magazine is obtrusive, however.

Soldiers were unanimous in reporting the Owen reliable under arduous jungle conditions. The weapon was well built but heavier than its rivals. The double grip with the foregrip attached to the barrel and the top mounted magazine will always distinguish the Owen.

P38 (Pistole 38)

In their search for a replacement for the Luger the Germans were shown a number of pistols, none of which proved totally successful. The Walther prototype, produced in 1935, led to the AP or Armée-Pistole being patented in 1936. The AP was an enclosed hammer pistol and this was one of the features objected to by the army. The next pistol offered was the HP which had the same locking system as the AP but featured a cleaned up frame and slide and the required external hammer. This was submitted in mid-1938. The design was accepted and after trials production was authorized. The final production pistol, named the Pistole 38, featured small changes in the firing pin and extractor but was essentially the same as the HP.

Left: The Owen is a submachine gun that is easily recognized because the magazine is placed on the top. It was a strong and reliable weapon.

Right: The Russian army used more submachine guns than any other force in World War II. This was to offset the loss of weapons and production facilities. The PPSh41 has a drum magazine containing 71 rounds.

Delivery started almost immediately production got underway in 1939. Demand grew and Walther was unable to supply the needs of the army on its own. So Mauser and Spreewerk became manufacturers as well as a number of other firms who made components.

Although production of the P38 stopped at the end of World War II it was resumed in 1957 for the Bundeswehr by Walther. The postwar version is almost identical but features an alloy frame. German forces are once more issued with the pistol as are the police. It is also on commercial sale – a fine tribute to Walther design.

PPD34, PPD40, PPSh41, PPS43 Submachine Guns

More than any other country during World War II, the Soviet Union adopted the submachine gun or Pistolet Pulyema (machine pistol). The main reason was the ease of manufacture which was necessary because of the lack of materials and production facilities.

The first submachine gun adopted in quantity was the PPD34 (Pistolet Pulemet Degtyarev). This weapon, designed in 1934 by Degtyarev, was based closely on the German MP28:11; as a result it was a relatively expensive weapon to manufacture. The major difference from the German gun was the adoption of a 25-round drum magazine. This original magazine had a weak mounting and this was modified on the PPD40. The magazine capacity was increased to 71 rounds.

The PPSh41, designed by Shpagin, also used the 71-round magazine, but although of similar outward appearance it was very different. The expensive construction of the PPD40 was replaced by a riveted and welded set of steel pressings.

The final wartime development, in fact the last Russian submachine gun development, was a design by Sudarev, the PPS43. The design was undertaken during the siege of Leningrad and as a result the weapon reflected the constraints of the time. The complete weapon was constructed from steel stampings welded and riveted together. Unlike its predecessors the stock was an all steel folding type, and the magazine, because of the unavailability of the drum, was a 35-round box type. A modified version was developed by Sudarev.

In Russian service the submachine gun had a short but eventful career before it was superseded by the AK47 rifle.

Pedersen Device

The Pedersen device was manufactured because it seemed a good idea at the time. During World War I, American soldiers were equipped with the Springfield bolt action rifle. The use by the Germans of early submachine guns led to a

Above: The RPK light machine gun shares the major components of another Russian weapon, the AK47 rifle.

demand for a rapid fire weapon.

The result was the top secret 'Automatic pistol calibre .30, Model 1918'. This was not a pistol but a device that fitted into the Springfield rifle instead of the bolt. The device was fitted with a 40-round magazine firing an elongated .32 acp cartridge. An ejector opening was cut in the receiver of the Springfield to line up with that on the device.

Some 65,000 were manufactured. It was thought that infantrymen could fit the device in 15 seconds but in the heat of battle and the mud of the trenches it would have proved impossible. The device was scrapped after the war.

Radom VIS-35

The Radom is often dismissed as yet another Browning copy. While this is true of the locking system, which is that of the Browning Hi Power, the pistol has modifications that take it out of the ordinary.

Two Polish arms designers, Wilnewczyc and Skrzypinski, at the request of the Polish government submitted a design that was, after a competitive trial, adopted in 1935. The pistol went into production at the Fabryka Broni Radomu factory in Radom in 1936 and was known as the VIS-35.

It had no safety catch and relied on firstly the grip safety and secondly the unusual feature of being able to drop the hammer by means of a lever on the slide. The depressed lever moved the firing pin forward and the hammer then hit the frame. A loaded round could be kept in the chamber. The recoil spring was mounted on a guide rod unlike the Colt design.

Production continued during the German occupation as the P35(p) and was only ended by the Russian advance in 1944. German production was of poor quality compared with the original and parts such as the hammer dropping lever and the stripping catch were deleted to ease production. Components were also manufactured at other factories. This pistol was a derivation that deserved a better fate for it was never put back into production.

RPD (Ruchnoi Pulemet Degtyarev) and RPK (Ruchnoi Pulemet Kalashnikova)

The use by the Soviet Union of the intermediate 7.62mm × 39mm round for both the rifle and the light machine gun has made their logistical problems much simpler and has led to a most efficient weapon construction. As a result of the present NATO trials it is probable that Western nations will adopt the same solution.

The RPD, which is no longer in front line service with Russia, was designed by Degtyarev and used the same gas system and hinged lugs of his earlier designs. The weapon is belt fed from 50-round non-disintegrating metal link belts. These are often carried in a drum attached to the gun. The gun has gone through a series of modifications during its life, to make the belt feed more positive and to ease vibration experienced when firing (a buffer was fitted). Although the barrel is fixed, there is little overheating problem if the fire rate is reasonable. It is a relatively heavy ($15\frac{1}{2}$lb or 7kg) weapon.

The RPD has been replaced by the RPK which is a modified AK47 rifle. The majority of the major components are interchangeable.

Schmidt-Rubin

Switzerland is one country which has remained faithful to the straight pull type of rifle. The Schmidt-Rubin is still in service although front line troops now use self-loading weapons.

Colonel Rudolf Schmidt designed the basic action in 1883 and it entered service as the M1889. Three basic developments took place to parallel the cartridge development carried out by Colonel Rubin. The original rifle had the locking lugs at the rear of the receiver, leaving a very long bolt length ahead of them. The M1911 which was chambered for the standard 7.5mm M11 cartridge had the lugs moved to the forward part of the receiver bridge. Although this was an improvement it was not until the M1931 that the locking lugs on the bolt head were introduced. The Schmidt-Rubin rifle is superbly manufactured and the action very fast and smooth.

Schwarzlose Machine Gun

This machine gun was invented by Andreas Wilhelm Schwarzlose, a German from Charlottenberg, just after the turn of the century. A delayed blowback weapon using both mechanical disadvantage and a heavy recoil spring, the Schwarzlose was the first, and for many years the only, delayed blowback machine gun. Early models, because they were blowback weapons with powerful cartridges, had to have an oil pump to lubricate each cartridge as it was

chambered. The last model, the M1912, saw service in both world wars. It had a large flash hider on the muzzle.

Schwarzlose Standardt

The Schwarzlose, designed in the last years of the 19th century, was one of the pistols that, given the right circumstances, could have achieved success. It was a pleasant pistol to handle.

Andreas Schwarzlose's development work on pistols began in the early 1890s. The first design deemed suitable was one patented in 1897 and put into production the following year. The locking system used is one that is popular on modern rifles, the multi-lug turning bolt. In the case of the Schwarzlose it had four lugs and was actuated by the recoil energy as the barrel and bolt moved to the rear from a short distance. The cartridge was the 7.63mm Mauser. The pistol achieved a small sale but soon disappeared from the market. The Schwarzlose company was closed at the end of World War I and with it died any real chance of further development.

The other pistol of note to be produced was also of unusual design in that it worked on the blowforward principle – the barrel moved forward to actuate the cycle. This pistol, the Model 1908, also achieved some sales and was even exported to the United States. Schwarzlose was perhaps most successful with his machine gun, which was used by the Austro-Hungarian army.

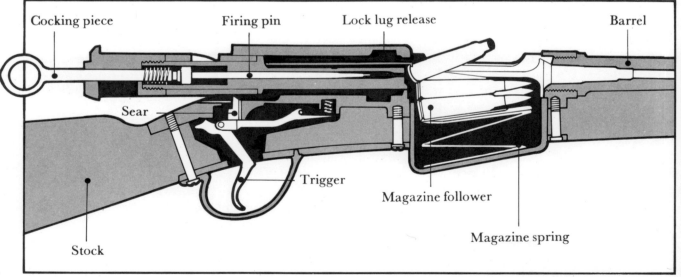

Right: The Schmidt-Rubin straight-pull bolt-action rifle is the only one of its type to be adopted for long term service as a military weapon. The reciprocal movement of the bolt handle (shown separately) is converted to rotational movement by a camway.

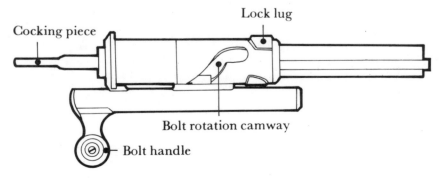

Sten Gun

The Sten may have been the most unloved weapon ever developed, but it certainly filled a need. Britain was struggling for her very existence and required something reliable, quickly.

The British army prior to World War II had been reluctant to acquire what they considered to be a gangster's weapon, but reluctantly accepted what was available at the beginning of the war. The navy, however, adopted the Lanchester which was a German copy of the MP28 and the army followed suit. A decision was made that a simplified weapon should be developed and the result was that in a hut at Enfield the Sten was developed.

Designers Shepherd and Terpin patented the weapon on 17 April 1941 and by September of that year they had a Mk I and a Mk II on trial. Production started in late August 1941 at the BSA factory at Tyseley. Over 100,000 were made of the Mk I and its modification, the Mk I* (a star was used by the British to denote a modification not sufficiently extensive to warrant the adoption of a new mark number).

Efforts to produce the weapon more cheaply led to continued development. The Mark II became the basic weapon and production exceeded 2 million units. The government asked a toy manufacturer to produce the Mark III and Lines Brothers modified the design to make it almost totally a stamped and welded weapon. This was the cheapest of the Sten guns and was produced in Canada at the Long Branch arsenal. Small firms could make the required stamping and assembly was simple so that the Sten was ideal for wartime manufacture. It was, however, not the safest of weapons and suffered intermittently with feed problems caused by poor magazines. The postwar variant remained in service until it was replaced by the Sterling in 1953.

Sterling L2A3

Designed at the Sterling Armament Company by George Patchett during the latter part of World War II, the Sterling has been supplied all over the world and produced under licence in some countries.

The L2A1 version was adopted in 1953 as standard for the British forces after a long trial. The weapon worked on the blowback system with advanced primer ignition. The functioning in adverse weather conditions has been one of the major strong points of the Sterling. This has been aided by the use of spiral grooves cut on the bolt. The magazine is side mounted on the left of the gun and a simple but very ridged folding stock is fitted.

The L34 silenced version uses a drilled barrel to allow the escape of propellant gas, making the 9mm Parabellum into a subsonic round. The large silencer that is integral with the main body of the gun ensures that the Sterling Patchett is the most efficient silent gun manufactured.

Above: The Schwarzlose Standardt pistol was designed in 1897 and went into small-scale production.

139

Steyr M12

This pistol was the standard side arm of the Austro-Hungarian forces in World War I. The Germans rebarrelled a number and used them in World War II. Both the cartridge, the 9mm Steyr, and the pistol could and-should have enjoyed even more popularity but the awkward clip loading was not popular.

The recoil operation used a rotating barrel and produced a very strong pistol. The magazine was integral with the butt and the pistol was loaded in the manner of the Mauser with a clip. An interesting addition to the system was a button that, when depressed with the slide back, allowed the cartridges to spring out and empty the pistol. The 9mm Steyr is one of the most powerful pistol cartridges. The pointed bullet and large powder charge give very deep penetration. The Germans rechambered the gun for 9mm Parabellum.

Right: The Steyr M12 would, had it not been for its clip loading, achieved greater success than it in fact enjoyed. Its strong locking system and powerful cartridge are noteworthy features of the design.

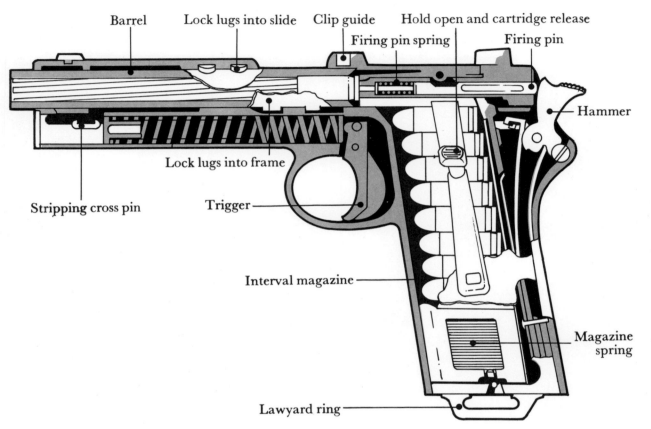

Barrel — Lock lugs into slide — Clip guide — Hold open and cartridge release — Firing pin spring — Firing pin — Hammer — Lock lugs into frame — Stripping cross pin — Trigger — Interval magazine — Magazine spring — Lawyard ring

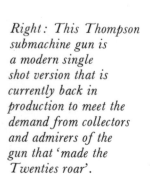

Right: This Thompson submachine gun is a modern single shot version that is currently back in production to meet the demand from collectors and admirers of the gun that 'made the Twenties roar'.

Thompson Submachine Gun

The Thompson may have brought fame to the name of General J. T. Thompson but it certainly did not bring him a fortune. The 'Tommy-gun' made its name in the United States in the Roaring Twenties, in the battles between the Bootleggers and the Revenue men. Until the outbreak of World War I the numbers produced were small.

Auto Ordnance was formed in 1916 but it was not until 1919 that a definitive model was produced. The shape of the weapon would remain easily recognizable throughout production. The early weapons had the Blish lock. This was an H-shaped piece that simply provided a doubtful form of hesitation. It was deleted in later models.

Colt production of the Model 1921 amounted to some 15,000 but these, because of slow sales, lasted Auto Ordnance nearly 20 years. The famous Cutts compensator designed by Colonel Richard Cutts was introduced in 1926. The advent of World War II changed everything. The British asked for any available weapons and the Thompson was supplied. The bulky drum magazine beloved of the gangster was dropped and soon even the combined efforts of Auto Ordnance and Savage were insufficient. The design was simplified first in the Model M1 and then in the M1A1, which saw the deletion of the Blish lock. Over 500,000 of these types were produced and so the gun at last achieved true mass production. Today the Numrich Arms Company,

which purchased the Thompson in 1951, have put the weapon back on the open market with a number of versions designed to appeal to the collector and enthusiast.

Tokarev Model 1930

At first sight the Tokarev would seem to be one more copy of the Browning type of locked-breech pistol typified by the Colt 1911. This is true as far as the basic operation of the pistol is concerned but the Russian service pistol had important features.

Fedor Tokarev based the weapon on the swinging link locking of the Colt with the locking lugs machined on the top of the barrel. This was modified in 1933 with grooves turned round the barrel's circumference. This model is sometimes given a separate designation. The cleaning and maintenance of the hammer and sear group has always been a problem in the solid-bodied pistol and assembly very much a workshop job. The Tokarev has incorporated into its design a removable group which is of great help if cleaning or maintenance is to be carried out. The Tokarev has its feed lips machined into the body so that no damage can occur.

The cartridge chosen for the pistol was the 7.62mm Tokarev which was a copy of the 7.63mm Mauser. It uses a higher propellant charge than its predecessors and firing is often accompanied by flame from the muzzle.

All in all, regardless of the somewhat rough and utilitarian exterior, such as the pivot pin

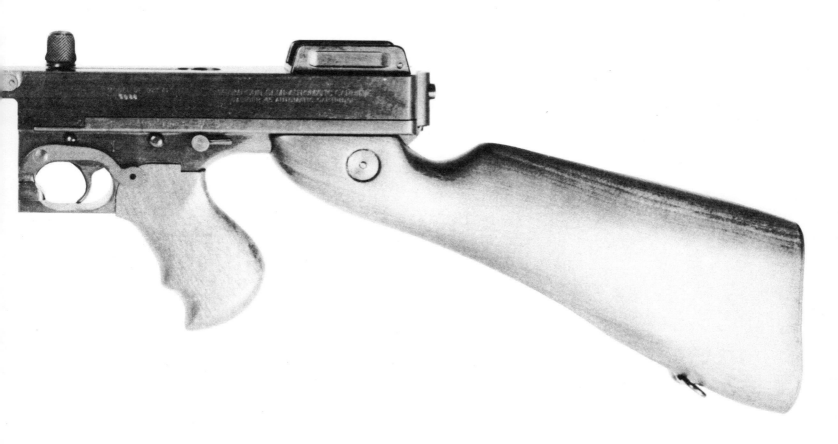

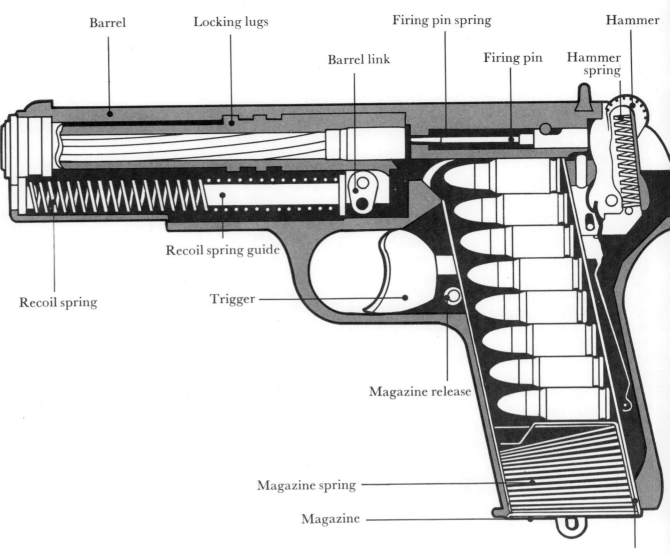

Right: The Russian Tokarev Model 1930 shows the strong influence of J. M. Browning's work. The adoption of a removable sear group and machined-in feed lips are original features that improve the design.

Barrel   Locking lugs   Firing pin spring   Hammer

Barrel link   Firing pin   Hammer spring

Recoil spring guide

Recoil spring

Trigger

Magazine release

Magazine spring

Magazine

Magazine follower

Below: The Uzi is a weapon born of need and developed in battle. It is a submachine gun that is reliable, robust and easy to use. It has been produced in its native Israel and also in Belgium by FN.

being held in by a spring clip, the weapon is reliable and has been produced not only by the Russians in large numbers, but also by many of her allies in one form or another.

Uzi Submachine Gun

The Uzi was designed as part of the Israeli programme to make the country less dependent on the supply of weapons from outside sources.

The designer, Major Uzielgal, finished his work in 1950 and the Uzi was soon in full-scale production. The weapon is constructed from relatively heavy steel stampings and incorpor-

ates a telescoping bolt. The use of the pistol grip as the magazine well has the advantage that in the dark 'hand finds hand'. The initial wooden stock has been replaced by a metal folding one. The Uzi has been a very successful submachine gun, having been produced not only in its native country, but also by FN in Belgium. The rather heavy construction has proved an asset and it is extremely reliable. Many countries have adopted it, if not for the armies at least for special units or police use.

Vickers Machine Gun

The Vickers medium machine gun is a most efficient weapon that gives accurate and sustained fire. The design was a modified Maxim that Vickers developed during and after their production of the Maxim. The toggle was inverted so that it broke upwards unlike its predecessor. The general construction was changed to use the advances in metallurgy. The work was carried out during 1911–12.

The water cooling, along with the ability to change the barrel every 10,000 rounds when it wore out, led to its unrivalled fire power. Many regretted its passing after its use in two world wars and countless smaller conflicts.

Villar Perosa

The Villar Perosa is often said to be the first sub-machine gun to be designed and put into service, but it was not designed for that purpose or used as such. The weapon did, however, have the basic characteristics of the modern submachine gun in that it was compact, capable of automatic fire and fired a pistol-type cartridge.

It has been known under a number of names depending upon who is given the most importance, the manufacturers, Officine di Villar Perosa; the designer, Revelli; the other manufacturer, Fiat; or the Italian military who named it the Model 1915. The common name is after the original manufacturer and is often shortened to VP. It was also produced for the Italian government by General Electric in Canada.

The weapon consisted of two parallel actions mounted side-by-side and feeding from two magazines mounted in the top. The action was a delayed blowback using a cam track that caused the bolt to rotate 45 degrees as it reciprocated. The combination of a heavy recoil spring and a light breech block led to a very high rate of fire. Each barrel fired in the region of 1,200–1,500 rounds per minute. The noise was considerable as the two barrels emptied their magazines in about one second.

The firm of Beretta were given the job of making the VP into a more practical weapon

and their designer, Marengoni, developed a single-barrelled version with the stock that the VP lacked. It was adopted by the Italian army and thus became one of the earliest, if not the earliest, submachine gun in general issue. The weapon was known by the name Beretta Model 1918. After World War I the stocks of VP guns were returned to Beretta who used many of the components to produce the Model 1918.

Walther PP and PPK

The PP and PPK share with the P38 the honour of being the most successful products of the Walther factory. Production of the PP and PPK under licence in France after 1945 helped provide funds for the rebuilding of the Walther empire when they themselves were forbidden to produce pistols.

The Model 8 Walther pistol produced in 1920 was of the ineffectual 1.25 acp calibre, but because it was one of the few pistols in production in Germany at that time it was used extensively by the police. More importantly it paved the way in design for the PP. The Walther PP or Polizei Pistole, introduced in 1929, had advanced design. Although of conventional blowback construction it featured a double action trigger and indicator pin to show that the weapon was loaded. The streamlined compact shape was an immediate success and has remained so.

Left: The Villar Perosa is often called the precursor of the submachine gun. It certainly had many of the necessary attributes but the application was not altogether appropriate, resulting, for example, in a machine gun type bipod.

143

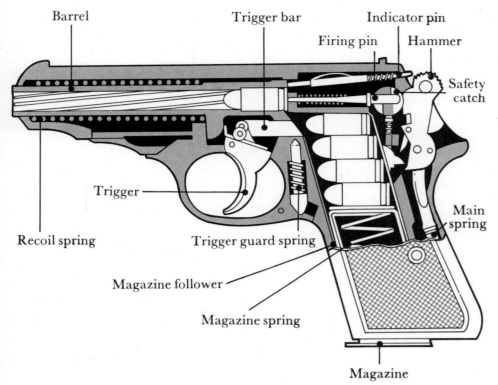

Barrel   Trigger bar   Indicator pin

Firing pin   Hammer

Safety catch

Recoil spring

Trigger

Trigger guard spring

Main spring

Magazine follower

Magazine spring

Magazine

Winchester Lever Action Models 66, 73, 86, 94

The Winchester lever action rifles along with the Colt revolvers have entered history. Films are made, books written and hunters and sportsmen still tell their tales of the impossible shots that they made, all with a Winchester. The forerunner was the Henry rifle. B. Tyler Henry was an employee of Oliver Winchester at the New Haven Arms Company that preceded the Winchester Repeating Arms Company. He designed what was to be the standard weapon with the tube magazine and a lever action for reloading. Although the name had changed, the 1866 Winchester was very much a Henry, but the modifications made enabled it to be fired at a rate of 30 rounds a minute. A cast brass frame was used on the majority.

The Winchester that established the fortune and the reputation of the company securely was the Model 1873. The 73 was a centrefire that used the 44-40 cartridge, as did the Colt Single Action Army of the same year. These weapons provided both sides of the law with their weapons up to the turn of the century. The company hit upon an advertising ploy that would bring one model of the 73 more fame than any other. Selected guns with selected barrel and match triggers as well as a special finish were sold as 'One of One Thousand' Winchesters.

The successor to the 73 was the 1876 which was followed by the first of the John Browning-designed lever actions in 1886. This was the first lever action made by Winchester that could accept a high-power cartridge and as with most of the Browning designs was immensely successful. Total production was in the region of 160,000. The Browning-designed 1894 was to be the pick of an already good series. The factory proudly called it the best lever action and the production run of more than 80 years and 3 million guns is impressive testimony indeed.

Above: The PPK is a small blowback pistol well suited to police use.

Below: A typical Winchester rifle showing the underlever action and tube magazine so characteristic of Winchester. Lever action rifles are still produced by Winchester.

The PPK or Polizei Pistole Kriminal, announced in 1931, was in effect a smaller brother to the PP. The mechanism was similar and it was available in the same calibres as the PP, .32 acp, .22 LR and occasionally in .25 acp. Production during World War II of both weapons shows the effect of poor materials and slipshod finish.

After 1945 the French firm of Manhurin built the pistols under licence from Walther before Walther themselves were able to resume production. Other countries such as Turkey have built copies. An interesting derivation of the pistols used parts of both models to try to circumvent the American import restrictions on pistols. A PP frame was used with a PPK slide. The final accolade to come for the Walther PPK was its adoption by no less a character than James Bond.

Opposite: Walther OSP/GSP. Above the complete weapon are alternative barrels, and below are alternative trigger mechanisms and magazines. This enables the weapon to fire three different calibres.

Automatic & Semi-Automatic Weapons

The desire to fire faster and to be able to have more ammunition in the gun soon led to the adoption of the self-loading weapon with a self-contained magazine, or in the case of the machine gun the belt feed. Even in the sporting field a large market was waiting to be tapped. John Browning stated that he only worked on military weapons so that he could work on sporting ones without being constantly harassed by the army.

The actual development of the self-loading weapon spans a relatively short space of time. The first ones were designed just prior to the turn of the 20th century and the majority of the present designs were available in one form or another by the 1930s.

The self-loading pistol has been known by various names. The correct one is simply the self-loading pistol, but the most commonly used is 'automatic pistol'. This is technically incorrect as an automatic would fire all rounds in the magazine at one pull of the trigger. Some authorities have tried to show the difference by using the term 'pistol' for the self-loader as opposed to the revolver. This is wrong by dictionary definition if by nothing else. Throughout this chapter the term 'automatic' will be used to designate the self-loading pistol.

The first attempts to produce automatic pistols were prefaced by a short lived and remarkably useless development, the mechanically self-loaded pistol which relied on the firer to operate the mechanism rather in the manner of the lever action rifle. This was a retrograde step from the double action revolver, but pistols were made in prototype or even limited produc-

tion by Schulhof, Reiger and Mauser.

Although the principle of recoil operation had been postulated long before, it was not until the 1890s that the first pistols appeared. The Schonberger was developed in Austria by Laumann in 1892. This used a system that has been tried intermittently ever since with varying degrees of success. The primer setback system used the primer in the cartridge to operate the mechanism. In a normal weapon the designer spent time and money trying to ensure that the primer stayed in the cartridge but in this system the primer is encouraged to move rearward in the case. This movement actuates the mechanism. But to be fully effective and reliable special ammunition is necessary, although it can operate with standard types. The primer moves a block and allows the mechanism to operate by the residual gas pressure. The pistol also featured metallic cartridge clip loading.

Four years later in 1896 Andrea Schwarzlose, after working on a number of designs, developed a short recoil-operated rotating bolt pistol. The short recoil system works by using the energy of the recoil of the weapon to operate the breech-locking mechanism. In the short recoil system the breech remains locked for only a short time before the breech block recoils to the rear. In a long recoil system which is rarely used, the breech remains locked for most or all of the recoil movement. The cartridge used in the Schwarzlose was dimensionally identical to the one that Mauser and Borchardt were using, but similar in power to the Borchardt rather than the more powerful Mauser derivative.

Left: An early self-loading was the Mexican-designed Mondragon. Produced in Switzerland by SIG this rifle was gas operated. The large and unwieldy drum magazine would have been a disadvantage. Although there was a production run the weapon was little used and surviving examples are rare. This particular example is in the Royal Small Arms factory collection, Enfield.

Opposite: The Luger 'artillery model' or 8in barrelled version. This pistol is complete with holster, which contains in the top a stripping tool and at the side a cleaning rod. The pistol is fitted with a detachable shoulder-stock that can be buckled to the holster. The standard magazine has been removed and the 32-round 'snail drum' fitted. Although it unbalances the pistol the magazine boosts the firepower of the weapon.

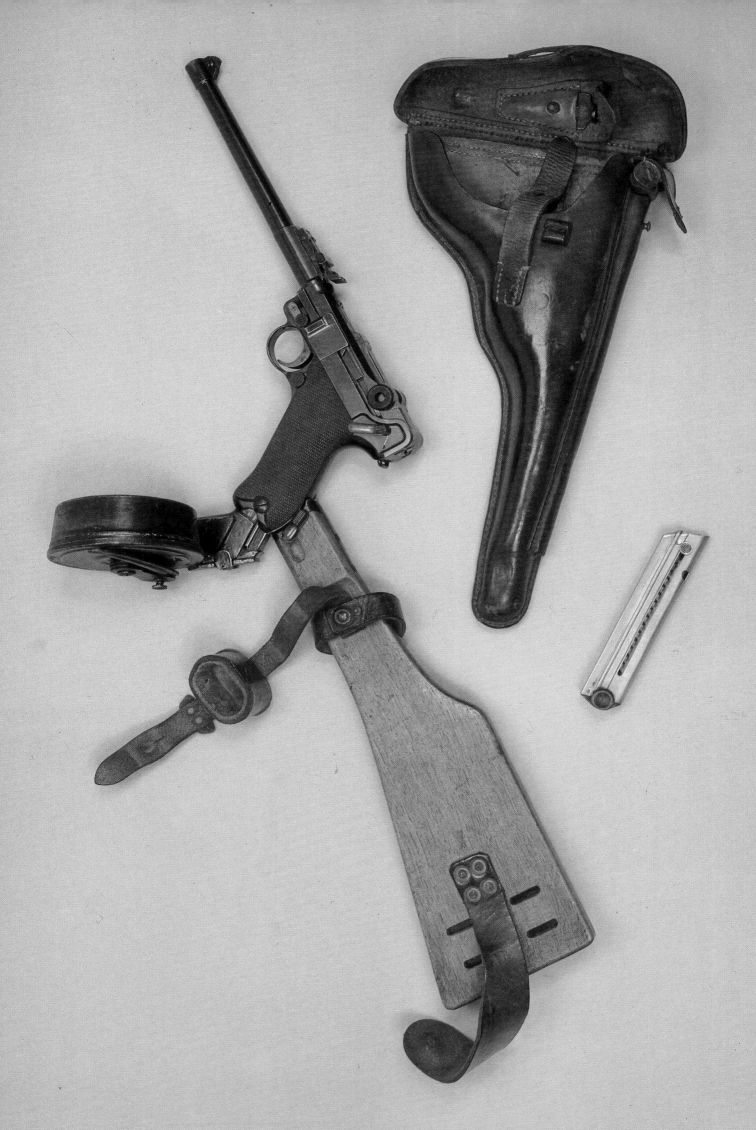

Top: Mauser C96 Broomhandle pistol. The C96 was a Mauser design that was to be used in one version or another through several wars. This was the pistol chosen by Sir Winston Churchill to replace his sword in the Boer War. The C96 was often supplied with the holster of hollowed-out wood and which could be attached to the butt of the pistol to make a short-range carbine. Length: 312mm; barrel length: 139mm; weight: 1.25kg; magazine: clip-loaded internal 10-round.

Left: The Lahti, although basically a Finnish design, was also manufactured by Husqvarna in Sweden. It was produced specifically for the army and some 84,000 were made.

The Borchardt pistol. This weapon is best known as the forerunner of the Luger and it was designed by Hugo Borchardt. This particularly fine example is shown (right) cased, with its full range of accessories. The pistol was designed to be used with its shoulder stock as a carbine as well. Ungainly and ill balanced, the Borchardt was produced in small numbers and was sold on the open market. The accessories in the case include the shoulder stock and holster and two spare magazines. The item that resembles a wooden magazine is in fact a cleaning device that allows the breech to be kept open. The other small wooden block is a check piece that attaches to the stock. The Borchardt was issued chambered for a pistol and also a submachine gun cartridge, which was to have the longer life. Length: 279mm; barrel length: 165mm; weight: 1.16kg; magazine capacity: 8 rounds; calibre: 7.63 Borchardt.

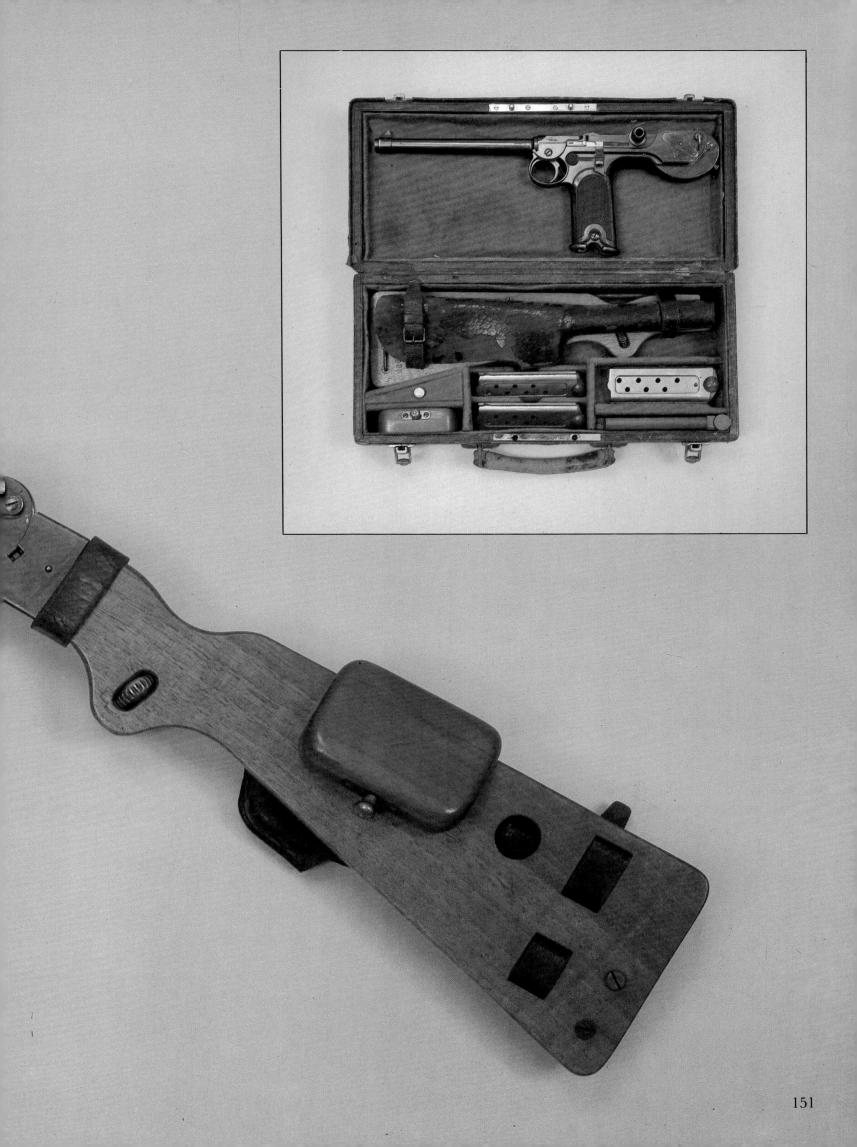

The forerunner of the Luger was the Borchardt which was developed by Hugo Borchardt in 1894. The C.93 was a toggle-operated pistol which used a 7.63mm cartridge. It was the first pistol to achieve a reasonable commercial sale although it did not achieve military success. The Luger was part of a continuous development programme carried out by Luger on the Borchardt pistol. The Swiss adopted the developed model as the Model 1900 and thus became the first country to adopt an automatic pistol for its forces. This also made the Luger the first military automatic to be adopted.

The Mauser C.96 was to see use in two world wars but because of the lack of official military adoption in any numbers it was predominantly a commercial success. The Mauser was made to the highest manufacturing standards and was very expensive. Its shape was almost clumsy and its clip loading was less than satisfactory.

Two designers whose work led to quantity production were Theodore Bergman, who worked on a number of pistols between 1893 and 1897, and Mannlicher, who worked at the Steyr company at the turn of the century. An interesting Mannlicher was the Model 1894 which used a system of operation that is rare. In the blow-forward system the barrel is blown forward off the cartridge by the gas pressure and the fresh cartridge collected by the chamber as the barrel returns under spring pressure. The blowback system, which is the universal system for low-powered pocket and target pistols, works in the opposite way in that the barrel is stationary and the breech block recoils under the pressure of gas. There is therefore no locking of the breech in either system and the gas pressure must drop to a safe level in the time that the inertia of the system and the return spring pressure can keep the breech block closed. In fact the breech block starts to move very quickly and this, together with the weight of the breech block and/or recoil spring, normally limits the system to low-powered rounds of the .32 acp and .380 acp type. The Mannlicher Model 1901 was adopted by the Argentinian army and was used by officers on a personal basis in Europe.

Bergman managed to persuade the Spanish, Danish and Greek armies to use his Model 1910 but, unable to produce it himself, he arranged for production to be carried out by Pieper who used their trade mark, Bayard, and so the pistol became the Bergman-Bayard. Another commercial pistol designed by Bergman was the Simplex. It was produced in a number of different calibres. The Bergman cartridges and also, for that matter, the pistols to fire them ranged from 5mm to 11mm. Only those mentioned above were produced in any quantity but it was nevertheless a major achievement.

Many pistols have not been particularly pleasant to fire, but few achieved the distinction of having this officially reported. One pistol which did have this doubtful honour was the British designed and manufactured Mars. The designer, Gabbett-Fairfax, seemed to

Above: The cheapest and probably crudest pistol ever officially manufactured is the Liberator. This assembly of steel pressing fired the standard .45acp round as a single shot. Opposite: Left side, from top. The Beretta model 1934, which became the standard service side arm of the Italian forces fired a cartridge of calibre .380acp. The Russian service pistol of World War II and the postwar years was a modified Browning design by Tokarev. The calibre was 7.63 Tokarev. A rare Webley automatic chambered for the 9mm Browning long cartridge. This model was supplied to the South African police under contract. The blowback pistol has an unusual slide release, a button on top of the slide. Right side, from top. The Steyr military pistol served the Austrian forces well and was used in small quantity by the Germans. It is clip loaded with an internal magazine. The 8mm Nambu automatic was the service pistol of Japanese forces in World War II. Webley .32acp pistols equip many units of the British police.

want to produce a pistol more powerful than any other. This he achieved but only with massive size and complexity so that nobody wanted to use it. The pistol worked on the long-recoil principle and was chambered to fire a number of specially developed cartridges. Attempts to manufacture and sell it were a disaster. The only good to come out of the whole scheme was the fact that Webley, having been involved on a contract basis to work on the project, decided that they could produce a practical pistol.

The Webley automatic pistols ranged from the blowback .25, .32 and 9mm Browning to the massive locked breech .455 which was adopted as standard by the British navy. The .32 model achieved success as a police pistol and was still in use until after World War II. This use by the British of an automatic was to be their last until recent times, as the revolver became the standard until adoption of the Browning Hi Power.

Advances by Browning
It was an American, John Browning, who brought about the greatest change in the pistol and made it the standard weapon in many armies and on the target range. Browning's first pistol, the Model 1900, was of the simple blowback type and was produced by the Belgian firm of FN. This was a massive success, as were its successors, but a more important advance was in the field of the short recoil locked breech type of pistol. The locked breech recoil operated pistol used the recoil energy to move the slide or bolt back a short distance during which time the breech was locked. After a short movement the locking system was operated and the slide or bolt continued rearward on its own. The time taken allowed the high pressure in the gun to drop to a safe level.

Development of the Browning system, the most popular ever to have been designed, was undertaken by Colt. The first models, the Colt 1900 and 1902, were chambered for the .38 Colt cartridge which was a lower-powered version of what was to become the .38 acp. The pistol operated by having twin links which pulled the barrel downwards as the slide recoiled. The slide and the barrels had interlocking lugs that locked them together when the barrel was in the uppermost position. The design was carried forward into the Model 1905 which was in .45 calibre. This model, while enjoying some measure of commercial sale and an army test, did not become a success. The twin links were dropped and a single link at the breech end substituted, and the Model 1911 was born. This design was to become the standard operation not only for Colt but also for innumerable developments and copies. The cartridge became the famous Colt .45 acp.

The Colt/Browning copies or developments include those produced by Star and Llama in Spain (the Star became standard army issue), the Radom in Poland, the Tokarev in Russia (the use of a separate hammer group that can be removed for cleaning was noteworthy) and the Ballester Molina in Argentina.

The last of Browning's line of pistols did not go into production until after his death. This was the Hi Power. It discarded the link altogether and substituted a cam that worked to pull the barrel down and push it up. A derivation of this, the Petters patents, are used by the French in the M1935 and the Swiss SIG in their service pistol where the cam is a slot in the barrel lug through which a cam pin fits. The SIG is considered the best service pistol in the world by many, but it is also the most expensive.

In Germany the Luger had been used as standard with its toggle-operated recoil action. This was replaced by the simpler and more reliable Walther P.38. This pistol, still in service today, uses a recoil-operated falling locking piece, cammed in and out of engagement with the receiver by the breech block, and has a feature that was a first in a military pistol – the double-action trigger. The advantage of the double-action trigger in an automatic pistol is debatable but it has become something of a 'desirable' feature today.

Other than the simple blowback, of the various types of pistol to be developed by different countries the Aus-

Browning-designed pistols. Top left: The Browning .25acp 'Baby' manufactured by FN. Top right: The Browning Hi-Power by FN. Bottom left: The Colt .45acp model 1911. Bottom right: The Colt .32 'pocket automatic' manufactured by Colt and FN.

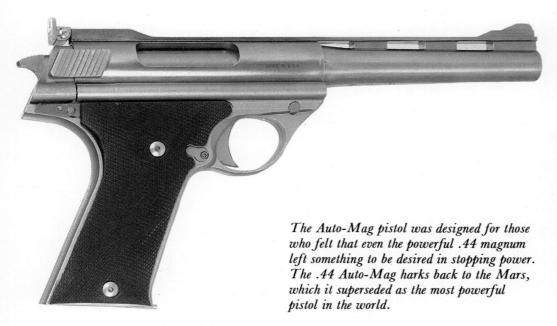

The Auto-Mag pistol was designed for those who felt that even the powerful .44 magnum left something to be desired in stopping power. The .44 Auto-Mag harks back to the Mars, which it superseded as the most powerful pistol in the world.

trian Steyr is by far the best. This pistol is short recoil operated but uses a turning barrel with the locking lugs on it. The Model 1912 would probably have been a greater success if it had not been chambered for an odd cartridge, the 9mm Steyr, and clip loaded. A derivative of the system is used today by the French firm of MAB. The American Savage uses this type of system but as the rotation is only 5 degrees the effect is of a simple blowback, German research work having shown that the breech opened as quickly if not more so than a simple blowback. The Steyr is a most pleasant pistol to shoot but was driven off the market after its use as a service pistol by the Austrian army.

The Italian Glisenti has a form of locked breech but the construction of the weapon necessitated the use of a low powered version of the 9mm Parabellum. The Japanese Nambu was similar and suffered from a low powered cartridge and often very poor manufacture. One military pistol, the Hungarian Frommer, chambered for the .32 acp round, must go down as the most complex small pistol of all time in that it uses a breech system suitable for high power ammunition. The pistol works on the long recoil system with a rotating bolt. The designer must have had other things on his mind when he put pencil to paper.

The Browning system is used in both military and sporting fields as much today as it has ever been. The H&K pistol has broken ground with the use of the roller locking system applied normally to its rifle and machine guns. This system was also used by the Hungarians. The pocket pistols still use the basic blowback system as do the many .22 LR target pistols. Construction of the pistol has changed little but the use of steel pressings is on the increase as are investment castings.

Submachine guns

The submachine gun has, in present times, had its identity somewhat blurred by the appearance of rifles of comparable size and weight. The original concept was a light, compact weapon, capable of automatic fire and using a pistol-type cartridge. The weapon often given credit for being the first submachine gun is the Villar Perosa Model 1915. This was a double-barrelled weapon, recoil operated, firing the 9mm Parabellum round. The fact that it had two of everything, including triggers, disqualifies it from being considered a true submachine gun.

Nearer the true concept were the various attempts to fit shoulder stocks and oversized magazines to pistols such as the Luger and the Mauser 1898. The Germans persevered with this project and the first true and, most important, practical submachine gun was born, the Schmeisser-designed Machinen Pistole 18. The MP18 was the first weapon to have all the basic ingredients of a submachine gun: it was compact, used blowback operation and had simple construction. The Germans, however, tended to overlook the tactical advantages of this type of weapon and formed squads that carried spare ammunition in hand carts – hardly the thing for rapid or clandestine operations. Nevertheless the fact remains that the weapon was in service in quantity by the end of World War I.

An interesting divergence from the submachine gun, but still an attempt to fulfil the basic functions, was the American Pedersen device. This was an insert device that fitted into the breech of the Springfield 1903 rifle after the removal of the bolt. It was in effect a small blowback pistol that fired a pistol-type cartridge through first its own barrel then the barrel of the rifle. It was fed from a 40-round magazine and could be inserted in a very short time. The device was dropped because it was felt that the soldier could, in the heat of battle, lose either part of the device or the original bolt of the rifle. It never saw active service and was put aside after World War I.

The other major powers took little heed of the submachine gun apart from banning the Germans from using it again. In fact, Britain stated in government reports that 'it is a gangster's weapon and not suitable for

Opposite: A Heckler and Koch MP5 submachine gun. This 9mm weapon developed from the CETME-inspired G3 rifle. This compact submachine gun has achieved large sales although, unlike most of its competitors, it fires from a closed bolt position.

soldier's use'. This attitude was probably fostered by the development of the Thompson submachine gun in the United States. Although the Thompson was a heavy weapon it was a practical submachine gun firing the .45 acp round. The American forces took small quantities and it was not until World War II that large quantities were ordered. The relative complexity of the Thompson gave way to the simplicity of the 'Grease Gun' which served the army through that war and subsequent conflicts.

The Russians, with the rest of the world, were slow to adopt the weapon but having made the decision, they manufactured upwards of 7 million submachine guns in a relatively short period. From a start in 1926 the Russians produced a series of classic submachine guns all of which were simple and easy to construct. A typical feature was the use of a rifle barrel cut in half to produce two barrels. The cartridge harked back to the Borchardt/Mauser type but was a most powerful derivative of the 7.63mm. The other point which the Russians understood only too well was that, with production facilities damaged or destroyed and the need to arm soldiers particularly for house-to-house fighting, the submachine gun was ideal. The PPD, PPSh41 and the PPS42/43 served throughout World War II and were only abandoned for general issue when the self-loading rifle became available in quantity.

Germany started to develop the submachine gun to replace the solid MP18 type before 1935, the major firm being Erma. It must be noted that Schmeisser did not develop the MP38/MP40 range as has often been stated. In fact a law suit was taken out against him for patent infringements on the basic designs of Vollmer and Erma. The MP38 was a truly modern weapon constructed from steel pressings and had a folding stock. Although other types of submachine gun were available, many soldiers of all nationalities preferred to appropriate the MP38 or its successor, the MP40, for their own use. Although long since out of production and issue, these weapons still crop up from time to time in small wars.

The Italians were quick to see the

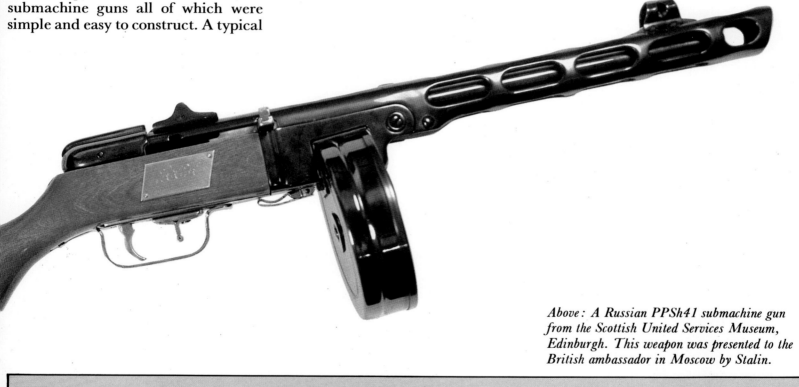

Above: A Russian PPSh41 submachine gun from the Scottish United Services Museum, Edinburgh. This weapon was presented to the British ambassador in Moscow by Stalin.

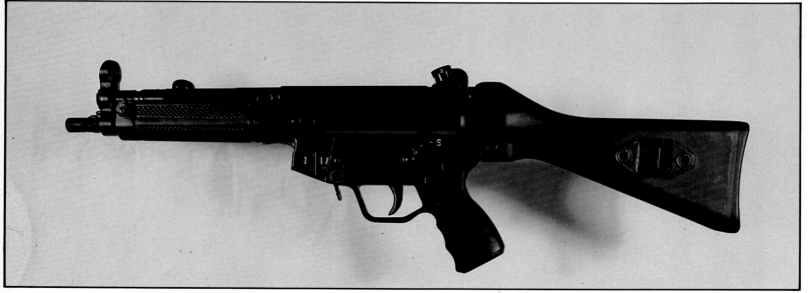

Opposite: The MP40 submachine gun (top) and the Thompson submachine gun (bottom). The Maschinenpistole 40 was developed from the earlier MP38 and featured a number of improvements to ease production. Often known erroneously as the Schmeisser, the MP40 was designed by Erma. Machined parts were kept to a minimum and wherever possible lower grades of steel were used. The folding stock is one of the more effective employed, and the weapon was often preferred to the issue Sten gun and its equivalents. The MP40 can be considered not only a forerunner of the modern submachine gun but also a very effective one. Length: 832mm (extended), 629mm (retracted); barrel length: 248mm; weight: 3.97kg; magazine capacity: 32-round detachable; cartridge: 9mm Parabellum.
The Thompson submachine gun had a long and chequered history. If war had not occurred in 1939 it would probably have been produced only in small quantities. The early guns used the Blish lock that was, in theory at least, a form of delayed blowback. To simplify production it was dispensed with and large numbers of wartime guns functioned with a simple bolt. The drum magazine gave way to the box type. The Thompson is on sale now as a single-shot weapon. Length: 857mm; barrel length: 266mm; weight: 4.9kg; magazine capacity: 20 or 30 round detachable box, and 50 or 100 round detachable drums; cartridge: .45acp.

Opposite: The MP18/1 submachine gun (top) and the PPS43 submachine gun (bottom). The MP18/1 was designed by Hugo Schmeisser in 1916 and was the first to see service in any volume. Although heavily built it was reliable after deletion of the 'snail drum' magazine. Many early weapons of this type are very similar and it was not until the MP38 that the basic design changed. Length: 812mm; barrel length: 196mm; weight: 4.26kg; magazine capacity: 32-round drum or 20 and 32 round detachable box.
The PPS43 appeared about the time of the siege of Leningrad but remained in service with the Russian army for several years after World War II. The basis of this gun is an assembly of crude pressings and stampings that produce an effective and easily manufactured submachine gun. Length: 820mm; barrel length: 272mm; weight: 3.39kg; magazine capacity: 35-round detachable; cartridge: 7.62mm Tokarev.

possibilities and had Beretta modify the Villar Perosa into the Model 1918, which used many components of the Villar Perosa. Italy continues to use the Beretta submachine gun to this day. One oddity of their weapons is that they still have a fixed wooden stock reminiscent of the original MP18.

Britain entered the field very late and decided on a derivative of the Schmeisser MP28:11 called after the developer, George Lanchester. Lanchester worked for the Sterling Armament Company and although they did not design the successor to the Lanchester, they were to be the designers and large-scale producers of the present issue weapon, the Sterling. The government factory at Enfield developed what was to become the Sten gun. Sten is an acronym formed from the names of the two people concerned with its development, Shepherd and Turpin, plus Enfield. It was the ultimate in simplicity and could be produced on sub-contract by any engineering works or even small workshops. Certainly it had its disadvantages, the most important being that it was far from totally safe – it had a nasty habit of firing if dropped, a problem often found in a weapon that fires from the open bolt position.

Open bolt refers to when the bolt is held back in the open position when it is ready to fire; the trigger action lets the bolt slide forward and chamber a round on the way. The weapon then fires as the bolt meets the breech face. (The advantage for a rapid fire gun is that the chamber is empty until the point of firing and thus can cool.) Another disadvantage of open bolt firing is the jar of the large mass of the bolt moving forward on firing. While this is relatively unimportant on a machine gun, where there is weight to damp it, it can be disconcerting on the lighter submachine gun.

Every nation and many guerilla groups have designed and manufactured submachine guns, but interest in the weapon has waned since the introduction of the short small-calibre assault rifle. Two postwar designs of note are the Ingram and the Uzi. The Ingram is a simple steel-pressed gun, notably compact and offered in a number of calibres. It has been used as a police weapon as well as a military one and is often fitted with a silencer.

The Uzi was designed in Israel and is manufactured both there and by FN in Belgium. The design is reliable and relatively easy to manufacture and has been battle proved by its country of origin. It can be seen in use worldwide by military and police units.

Self-loading rifles

The history of the self-loading rifle is somewhat complicated, as is also that of the bolt action. It developed not because the military wanted it, but because the sportsman was much more interested. So both rifle and shotguns were adopted in large quantities, especially in the United States.

The basic principles of the self-loading rifle had been dealt with earlier but it was left to a band of inventors in the late 19th and early 20th centuries to carry out the practical work. Hiram Maxim was one of them, and in the period 1881–3 he worked on an existing design, the lever-action Winchester, to provide what was the first practical rifle. It was recoil operated and used a butt plate connected to the lever action. The recoil of the weapon against the butt plate which rested on the firer's shoulder pushed it in and this worked the lever; a powerful return spring then pushed the plate and the lever back to the original position. This received no interest in America although a number of Winchesters were converted in Europe. Maxim diverted his energies to machine guns and took out his recoil operated patent in 1884. He returned to the rifle with a gas-operated model.

There are two gas-operation types; one uses the short stroke piston operation and one the long stroke piston action. They can be described simply. The short stroke piston is not directly connected to the action and delivers a short stroke or blow to the action then returns to its rest position leaving the action to cycle. The long stroke piston is attached to the action and delivers its impulse and then continues with the action for the full cycle. The short stroke piston is lighter although it requires more components.

A designer whose contributions to the design of weapons, and to self-loading rifles in particular, have often been underestimated, is Ferdinand Mannlicher. Between 1885 and the early 1900s he not only worked on a

Below: The FG42. This was designed as a weapon to fire the full power 7.92mm Mauser cartridge either as an automatic rifle or as a light machine gun. It was intended for equipping parachute troops, and the weapon was developed outside the normal army channels by the Luftwaffe. Two types were manufactured, with the early metal butt, as in the photo, and a later and cheaper type with a wooden butt. It was an effective weapon but unstable when fired off its weak bipod in an automatic mode. Length: 940mm; barrel length: 508mm; weight: 4.53kg; magazine capacity: 20 rounds detachable; cartridge: 7.92 Mauser.

Opposite page, bottom: The Gatling gun marked probably the high point in the development of the hand-cranked machine gun. This 10-barrelled version with its large capacity magazine is fitted to a relatively complex mount. It is part of the famous collection at the Royal Small Arms factory at Enfield, England.

Above left: Sterling L34A1 (Sterling Patchett Mk 5). The Sterling Patchett is an example of a very silent weapon. The complex silencing system requires a barrel drilled to lower the velocity of the round to less than the speed of sound, and a baffle system breaks up the gas column and disperses it quietly. This weapon has exceptional accuracy and it can put a bullet within a 190mm square at 90 metres. Length: 856mm (extended), 644mm (retracted); barrel length: 198mm; weight: 3.54kg; magazine capacity: 34-round detachable; cartridge: 9mm Parabellum.

Left: The MP44 (Sturmgewehr). The MP44 and its predecessors, the MP43 and MP43/1, demonstrate the concept of the assault rifle and, considering the development that was carried out during World War II by the Germans, it can be rated an exceptional achievement. The basis for the rifle was the adoption of a special cartridge of reduced power compared to the standard 7.92mm Mauser. This cartridge, the 7.92mm pistole patronen 43, enabled the rifle to be reduced in size and to fire bursts with ease. This weapon used steel pressings extensively. Today the weapons being designed for the 1980s reflect the Sturmgewehr concept. Length: 940mm; barrel length: 418mm; weight: 5.12kg; magazine capacity: 30-round detachable; cartridge: 7.92mm pistole patronen 43.

recoil-operated rifle but also on a delayed blowback. The delayed blowback works in the same basic way as the simple blowback but to make possible the use of a higher-powered cartridge a delay in the opening of the breech is used. A final design used a gas operation and was similar in operation to the much later Garand. It was unfortunate that little encouragement was forthcoming to develop the undoubted potential of his designs into practical production rifles.

Mauser also entered the field but achieved little of the success that his bolt action rifles had attained. Initially he used the long recoil system which had the disadvantage of the large recoiling mass. This system has met with no success in small arms, although weapons of the type have been produced in quantity.

Another system that has been tried from time to time with little success is the muzzle trap system. The gases are trapped at the muzzle and, via a cone, work the action. Browning carried out a simple experiment to prove the theory. He placed a block of wood with a hole big enough for the bullet to pass through at the muzzle of the gun and then fired it. The block was blown across the room by the gas even though the bullet had passed through the hole. The system has practical disadvantages and has had no real success although Mauser manufactured a rifle, the G41(M), to that same design during World War II.

Designs such as the Griffith and Woodgate rifle of 1894 were produced in Britain. The Italians developed the Cei-Rigotti at the turn of the century. This was a very advanced rifle as it featured a piston-operated gas system and a front-locking rotating bolt. At

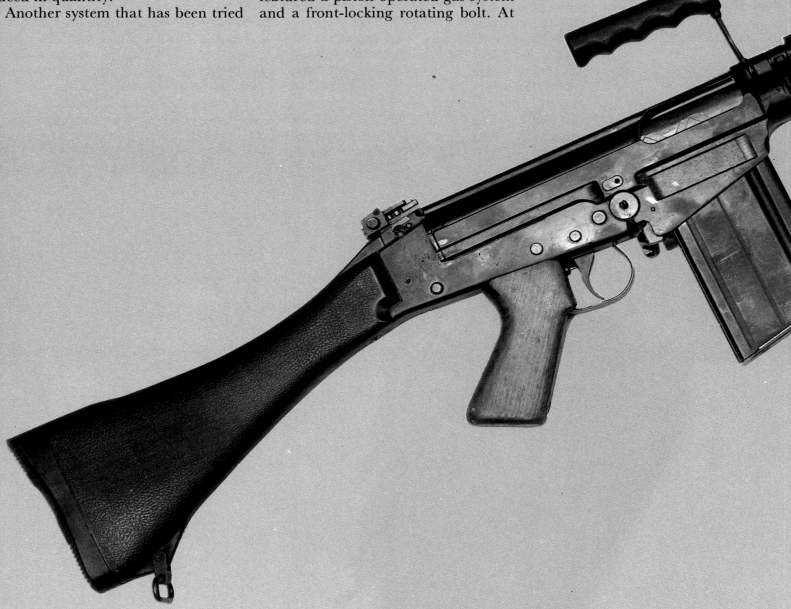

St Etienne in France a number of interesting designs were put on the drawing board and one model even went into production and appeared in World War I in small quantities. On the sporting side the Winchester blowback-operated 1903 model chambered for the .22 LR started a long line of similar weapons manufactured by innumerable concerns.

World War I could have seen, at least on a limited scale, a self-loading rifle in use. But there was little official enthusiasm. The interwar years saw much development carried out, but stockpiles of bolt action rifles stopped governments from adopting anything else. An exception was in America where the Garand was adopted after competitive trials with other types. A prewar development which saw service in World War II was the Johnson rifle, the only recoil-operated self-loading rifle to be adopted and used in any quantity. The Garand had one undesirable feature. It was cliploaded through the top with a clip that remained in the action until empty, when it was expelled. Apart from the problem of loading single rounds to 'top-up' the weapon this Mannlicher system gave rise to the occurrence, possibly exaggerated, in the Korean

War of the Communist soldier listening intently to the GI firing and upon hearing the 'ping' of the clip being expelled and hitting the ground he would rush him, for he knew that the gun was empty.

When World War II ended the vast majority of weapons in use were bolt action and although for a time most countries remained committed to the type the basic groundwork for much of the present day weapons had been done.

The Germans in World War I toyed with the Swiss-manufactured, Mexican-designed Mondragon and the Mauser aircraft self-loading carbine Model 15. But they did little between the wars and in 1939 had no self-loading rifles. This was not only because of the pressure of work on machine guns, tanks and the like, but also because of the belief that, as in 1914–18, the machine gun would be a powerful influence. When the effectiveness of the American Garand and the Russian Tokarev 1938 and 1940 models was felt, work began with a rush.

The first German designs were not successful. Instead of looking closely at the Tokarev and Garand they started almost where they had left off, with muzzle trap designs. The M41(M)

Mauser variant and the M41(W) Walther variant had different locking systems. The Walther locking system used a bolt with two lugs cammed out into the receiver by one of the two pieces of the bolt. The result of experiments combined a gas piston assembly with this locking system and was named the G43 or K43. This rifle proved relatively effective even when the standard of production dropped drastically during the closing months of the war.

The development which was to have most impact was the assault rifle concept. The first necessity was the adoption of a less-than-full-power cartridge, the 7.92mm Kurz. A design competition produced two winners, and the MKb42(W) Walther and MKb42(H) Haenel went into production. These were both fairly compact selective-fire rifles, the first of this type. The development weapon, the StG44, a re-work of the Haenel rifle by Schmeisser, was very close to the ultimate for a type.

Many attempts have been made to develop an ultra cheap rifle. The prototype was a gas delayed blowback design known as the Volkssturm Gewehr 1-5. This used the low-powered round, and postwar tests have shown

that it works relatively reliably and would have been the cheapest weapon to produce under wartime conditions.

The final German development which was to have a profound effect on postwar design was the Mauser StG45 (M). It used a system of rollers in the bolt that engaged with recesses in the weapon body. This was developed after the war into a delayed blowback system that has been adopted in the H&K rifle, CETME rifle and SIG rifles as well as machine gun derivatives.

Russia learned from German developments and acted on them. She started with the Fedorov Automat M1916, and continued with the Simonov 1931 and the Tokarev 1932, 1938 and 1940. Then, having been impressed with the German assault rifle and cartridge concept, she adopted it as the basis for postwar rifles and developed the 7.62mm × 39mm cartridge and the SKS rifle. The SKS was superseded by what was to become one of the world's most used rifles, the AK47. This not only became the Russian standard rifle but also that of most of the Communist world, being manufactured by many countries either in standard form or with minor modifications. The Chinese adopted it and use it as their current service issue. The Russians have since re-equipped with a simpler version, the AKM.

Military self-loading rifles. From top to bottom: Vickers Pedersen rifle; Garand rifle M1; M1 Carbine; Sterling-Armalite AR18 rifle. Pedersen's rifle worked on a brilliantly conceived delayed blowback action using a complex toggle link. The calibre was .276in and it was a superb cartridge and but for political and economic reasons could have become the American standard. The Garand rifle M1 was the first self-loading rifle to be adopted as standard by any country when, in 1922, the US Army re-equipped. In a modified form it is the standard Italian rifle, the BM59.
The M1 Carbine, although firing a cartridge of doubtful military efficiency, was very popular because of its light weight and low recoil.
The Sterling-Armalite AR18 rifle, manufactured under licence by Sterling, is a successor to the AR15. The action differs from that of the AR15 as it has a piston type of gas system rather than direct gas. This particular example is fitted with a Snider scope.

167

In the West, the idea of the assault rifle and reduced-power cartridge received little encouragement and the Americans developed a modernized version of the Garand with an interchangeable magazine named the M14 which fired the 7.62mm NATO cartridge that was a full power round. Britain decided to follow the assault rifle route after the war and developed a 7mm cartridge known as the 280/30 which was allied to a 'bull pup' rifle. (The term 'bull pup' denotes a weapon that has no butt or stock and thus has the pistol grip forward of the magazine.) This rifle was officially adopted by the British, but the Canadian and American governments persuaded them, in the interest of standardization, to adopt the 7.62 cartridge. This they did but then found that their EM2 rifle needed considerable alteration to take the cartridge and so the Belgian FN rifle was adopted instead.

In Italy the firm of Beretta, with commendable foresight, saw the num-

bers of surplus Garands on the market and, no doubt looking at the American experiments, used the basic weapon and modernized it with a change to the NATO cartridge and a detachable box magazine. The BM59 became their standard issue and was sold to several countries.

Under a reciprocal trade agreement the Germans took over the Spanish CETME rifle and produced the Heckler and Koch range of delayed-blowback weapons. This range included submachine guns, rifles and machine guns, all based via the CETME on the Mauser developments. The G3, as the rifle is known, has been manufactured not only in Germany but under licence in a number of countries and sold to others. Along with the Belgian FN it jointly provides the bulk of the 7.62mm NATO rifles.

Belgium has had, in the firm of FN, one of the foremost weapon developers and manufacturers in the world. When John Browning died the design department under the direction of Dieudonne

Saive continued to develop rifles and at the outbreak of World War II they were working on a design for a self-loading rifle using a gas-operated short-stroke piston and a tilting bolt that is cammed up and down to lock and unlock. The German invasion stopped the work but the team relocated and, under the direction of the British government, continued work in Britain. The resulting weapon was tested by Britain but rejected in favour of the EM2 design. Postwar it became standard equipment for the Belgian army as the M1949 or SAFN. Although not of very modern design, it led to the development of the FAL which was to be adopted by Britain and many other countries as a standard rifle.

In America the Garand and the M1 carbine were both successful weapons. The M1 carbine was developed by its designer, Williams, while he was in prison for shooting a government official. The term 'carbine' has been applied to various types of weapon but the original meaning was 'a shortened firearm for the use of the mounted soldier'. This led to the term being applied to a short version of the standard rifle and then by usage to any short rifle. In this day of short light weapons the term has less meaning.

As has been noted, the only country to apply the doctrine of the short/low powered cartridge after the German wartime example was Russia. Under the influence of America the West decided to retain the full-power cartridge and therefore, of necessity, the heavy and bulky rifle to go with it, al-

Above left: The Vickers submachine gun. This gun served British forces from 1912 until it was finally phased out in 1968. It could fire continuously for long periods with remarkable reliability. Length: 1155mm; barrel length: 723mm; weight: 18.1kg; belt fed from 250-round, non-disintegrating fabric belt; cartridge: 303in SAA (also in 30–06 and others).
Opposite: The Maschinengewehr 08 Maxim. The German army was the first to realize that the machine gun was a devastating weapon when correctly used on the battlefield, and the Maxim-designed MG08 possessed a deadly fire. This particular example is fitted (not correctly because of damage) to the schitten or sledge mount. Length: 1175mm; barrel length: 719mm; weight: 26.5kg; belt fed from 250-round non-disintegrating canvas belt.

though Britain's abortive .280/30 could have been a successful answer.

In America, Armalite employed a very talented designer, Eugene Stoner, who designed a number of rifles for them. They were at first in 7.62mm but after experiments with small-bore sporting cartridges, a .223in/5.56mm round was adopted for the AR15 rifle. The cartridge with its small bullet relied on the high velocity of 3,200 fps as opposed to the 7.62mm at 2,800 fps. The smaller cartridge enabled Stoner to design a very compact weapon of light weight, 5lb (2.2kg).

The rifle worked on a direct gas principle with a rotating bolt with multiple lugs. The direct gas system feeds the gas from the take off on the forward end of the barrel along a stainless steel tube back into the bolt itself to operate the action directly. This is contrary to the normal system of the piston or tappet being operated at the point of the gas take off and an operating rod in the short stroke type, or the piston itself in the long stroke type transferring the impulse into the bolt. The cartridge and the rifle were adopted by the US Air Force in small

quantities but the army, involved in jungle-type war, decided that it was ideal and adopted it as the M16. The main contractor was Colt and to date somewhere in the region of 5 million M16-type rifles have been produced by them or other licencees. Adoption of the M16 after a declared intent to adopt NATO standardization and pressurizing Britain to do likewise has been viewed by many as hardly cooperative.

The NATO countries and a number of other interested parties during the late 1970s have been testing new weapons and ammunition. The intention is to adopt at least common ammunition for the rifle and light support weapon or machine gun. The ideal of a common rifle seems unattainable as countries such as France (not in NATO, but involved) have already adopted 5.56mm ammunition and a 'bull pup' rifle, the FAMAS. The rifle of the future will be of small calibre, compact size and light weight. There is a very effective 4.85mm cartridge and attendant rifle of 'bull pup' design from Britain and a development rifle firing caseless ammunition

from H&K of Germany.

The most popular self-loading sporting rifle has been the .22 LR which has been produced by countless firms in many variations but exclusively of blowback design. Apart from the purely military designs and their commercial derivatives produced by such firms as Colt, H&K, SIG, Springfield Armory and Valmet, there are few designs for large-calibre cartridges as the hunter and target shot tend to prefer the bolt action. The rifles available are of American origin except for the Browning. Harrington & Richardson, Remington and Ruger all make hunting rifles of the self-loading type.

Development of the machine gun
Although the mechanically operated machine gun was a very effective weapon, the self-loading machine gun was not far behind. Hiram Maxim started work on other weapons before his machine gun, but working from London between 1883 and 1887 he not only invented the first practical recoil-operated machine gun but also manufactured it. The weapon used a toggle lock in the same manner as the Luger pistol and had a device for varying the rate of fire. Maxim also perfected a belt-feed which used a canvas belt with the bullets looped through it and fed automatically into the gun.

Vickers manufactured Maxim guns for trial but, although the gun proved itself in 'brush fire' wars, the British army did little to encourage it. The Germans, on the other hand, appreciated its true worth and adopted it in quantity. Appalling slaughter resulted in World War I as the Allies tried to inch forward under the crossfire of the Maxim. Ironically when the British did adopt a machine gun it was that manufactured by Vickers, which was in turn a development of the Maxim. This Vickers Medium Machine Gun was water cooled and stayed in service until the 1950s.

In America John Browning started machine gun development using the gas principle. In 1895 he demonstrated the weapon. Because an operating joint came below the gun as it was firing and could, if the gun was mounted too low, dig into the ground, this weapon became known as the Potato Digger. Successive Browning

developments resulted in air-cooled and water-cooled machine guns that are still in service and production today. The Browning machine gun was used not only as a ground gun but also in many aircraft. The Fifty Calibre, as the .50in version was called, is produced by FN.

Britain needed a light machine gun and during World War I an American, Colonel Isaac Lewis, offered his drum-fed gun to the firm of BSA. This soon became the standard light machine gun as well as being the first gun to be fired from an aircraft. The British used it as an aircraft gun and, during 1939–45, as a light antiaircraft gun. Between the wars the Brno Arms firm of ZB in Czechoslovakia, together with the British government factory at Enfield, developed a magazine-fed, gas-opera-ted, light machine gun with change-able barrels. It was named the Bren gun, an acronym of Brno and Enfield. Changeable barrels allowed the gun to be fired for long periods without the need for water cooling as in the Vickers. This made the gun truly portable. The Bren is still in service with the British army among others, although it has been converted from the original .303 calibre to 7.62 NATO.

Three countries that have produced machine guns with little real success are France, Japan and Italy. The French designed the Chauchat, a long-recoil weapon. Because of the odd shape of the extremely tapered Lebel cartridge the magazine under the gun into which this had to be fed was there-fore very curved. A grave error of judgement or possibly sheer despera-tion led the Americans to use a number of these 'Shosho' machine guns. The present French machine gun, the ATT Mle52, is a delayed-blowback gun using a similar two-piece bolt to the H&K/SIG/CETME, but instead of a roller it uses a lever to activate the components.

Japan managed to produce a num-ber of badly manufactured and appal-lingly designed guns that are now museum pieces. The Italians have contributed guns which were some-times reliable, such as the Breda Model 1937, but also some incredibly useless devices such as the clip feed that not only fired the cartridges as the clip moved through the weapon but re-

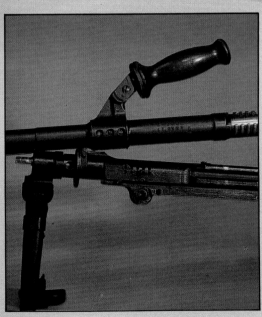

Above: The Bren light machine gun. The Bren gun Mk 1 was similar to the Zb26, from which it was developed. The Bren that was produced in a number of different Marks including a conversion from the original .303in to 7.62mm NATO is probably the best and most popular machine gun ever made.
Length: 1155mm; barrel length: 635mm; weight: 10.15kg; magazine capacity: 30-round detachable; cartridge: .303in (also 7.62mm NATO in 14 versions).
Left: The barrel of the Bren can be easily removed.

placed the empties so that the battle-field was nice and tidy! Today Italy uses the MG42/59.

One gun which must be mentioned is the Madsen, one of the most reliable and longest-lived weapons. The basic action is of the Martini single shot rifle but the breech block is controlled by a cam. The weapon is of the long-recoil type and is fed with the breech block down and ejected with it up. It was produced from 1903 until the 1950s and served with over 30 countries.

The Russians stayed with the Max-im, adopting it in the Imperial days of 1900 and keeping it through both world wars. They discarded it only after World War II. When they decided to develop they did so with their usual type of weapon, of poor external finish but reliable in service. As they possessed the short case rifle cartridge it gave this machine gun a tactical role that was not usual because of the full-powered cartridge employed by the rest of the world. Early postwar developments such as the DP, with its upside-down gas system (the gas piston was under the barrel) caused by

the fitting of a drum magazine, were dropped in favour of the RPD, a modi-fication of the DP. The RPD fires the short 7.62mm round from a belt carried in a drum under the gun. It uses a long-stroke piston with twin locking pieces that are cammed into a recess in the side of the gun body. Also used is a version of the AKM rifle, the RPK. The AK47 rifle was turned up-side down, and with an added belt feed was named as a light machine gun, the PKS.

The Germans decided that there was a case for a machine gun that could fire for reasonably long periods at a time but which would be of port-able weight. This ruled out water cooling and dictated interchangeable barrels and led to what is now called the General Purpose Machine Gun or GPMG. Cynics say that this gun can-not carry out either of its functions because it is too heavy for a light role and not heavy enough for sustained firing. This particular argument has been revived in the present NATO trials and different solutions have been put forward. The German solu-tion to the problem was to design

portable weapons with belt feeds which fired a full-power cartridge. The MG34 was recoil-operated and used a rotating bolt; it could also take a magazine. The final weapon, the MG42, was roller-locked, recoil-operated and featured a belt feed that was to be copied extensively. It was also manufactured from steel stampings wherever possible. The fire rate was very high, was not affected by the limitation of a belt feed, and reached 1,200 rpm. The gun was so successful that it was adopted by post-war German governments as the MG 42/59 or MG3.

An interesting wartime development was the FG42, a selective-fire magazine-fed weapon which was a little heavy for a rifle and was often used as a light machine gun by the paratroops to whom it was issued. One very desirable feature was that it fired accurately on single shot from a closed bolt and from an open bolt on auto-matic to promote cooling and prevent cook-off. An odd and debatable feature was its side-mounted magazine.

The bolt system similar to that of the Lewis is used by the current American machine gun, the M60. At present the Swiss use the very successful SIG with its roller-delayed blowback, the British and many others the Belgian FN MAG which is a development of the Browning, and other countries the H&K or Communist bloc guns. The future choice of the Western NATO countries and their allies will depend upon the results of the NATO trials. The British have entered a magazine-fed derivative of the 'bull pup' rifle, the Belgians a 5.56mm belt/magazine-fed Minimi and the Germans the MG3.

The self-loading weapon has become universal in the military world except where there is a need for a specialist weapon. The pistol and sub-machine gun, the rifle and, at the top end, the machine gun – all are of the self-loading type. In the sporting and target field the transfer has been far from total. The target pistol has, with the exception of the free pistol, evolved into a blowback-operated self-loader. The service pistol or practical pistol is dominated by self-loaders such as the Browning Hi Power and the Colt .45 acp. The target rifle remains bolt action or even single shot whether full bore or small bore. In sporting guns there has been little change apart from the .22 LR which has been developed as a self-loader in blowback form in every conceivable shape and size. The hunter with his full-calibre weapon still prefers the bolt action or, in the case of more dangerous game, the double rifle. In America the self-loader has made some progress owing to somewhat easier gun laws and it is also used for hunting. All in all the self-loader has changed the face of firearms design and development will continue to try to find an even better type.

The SIG AMT rifle. This rifle is a sporting derivative of the SIG 510 military series which, as the Sturmgewehr Model 57, equips the Swiss army. Chambered for the 7.62mm NATO round for commercial sale, this rifle is considered by many to be the best of its type in the world. Traditional SIG excellence is evident in the quality of production. The AMT has the grenade launcher and bayonet lug omitted and the trigger fires single shots only. An upper hand-guard is fitted but the military bipod is retained. This is one of the most pleasant rifles to fire and is superbly accurate, especially when fitted with the optional scope sight.

Shotguns

The precise British legal definition of a shotgun as a smooth bore weapon having a barrel length of at least 24in (609mm) is hardly correct, as the barrel length has no important bearing. Smooth bore is the most important attribute and the firing of shot as opposed to solid is the next. This is not to say that the firing of solid shot from a shotgun makes it any less of one except in the eyes of the law. Equally, the firing of a shot cartridge from a rifled weapon does not make it a shotgun.

In the early days almost any of the smooth bores, whether military or sporting, could and often did double as a shotgun. It was as easy to load them with shot as with a bullet because the bore sizes were reasonably large allowing a sufficient charge of shot to be loaded.

The shooting of game birds in the early days was very different from today. Wing shooting of any sort was virtually unknown. This is not surprising considering the slow 'lock time' or time taken for the weapon to fire from the pulling of the trigger. It is difficult enough to shoot a bird with today's consistent and fast cartridges and shotguns, let alone with a weapon that allowed a priming flash to frighten the prey before the main charge eventually went off. The shot itself was far from regular and the lack of any choke boring made the normal practice of stalking one's target and shooting it in the tree or on the ground without warning very difficult. Indeed many early drawings and paintings show a horse being used as a mobile 'blind' or cover. This was not, however, shooting for pleasure or sport, but very much 'for the pot'.

As the game of the land normally belonged to the king, it was natural that early gun laws were directed to ensure that no one shot for the pot without his consent. Henry VIII made it an offence to shoot without royal consent and thus limited game shooting to the very rich or to the poacher. By an Act in 1542 citizens and land-owners were allowed the privilege of shooting sitting birds. However, shooting was still mainly for food and the gentry did not get involved.

The flintlock shotgun in the early days was notable for one outstanding feature – the long barrel. The weapons often had an overall length of more than 60in (1,524mm). The reason for this was that the early powder was so slow-burning that a very long barrel was necessary to ensure that the powder was all burnt by the time the shot left the muzzle. Needless to say the loading, as with the military musket, was slow. The powder charge had first to be measured and then placed in the barrel. This was always a slightly worrying moment because, if a glowing remnant of the previous wad or powder granule was still lurking in the barrel, the new powder

Opposite: One of the rare Dickson round action over-and-under shotguns.

Below: In an attempt to make the flintlock an all-weather, go-anywhere gun a number of different systems were tried. This double-barrelled sporting gun has the locks concealed in boxes on the side of the gun.

Right: A double-barrelled percussion shotgun that was manufactured by Westley Richards about 1845. The barrels are of the Damascus type. Below: A four-barrelled sporting gun with separate flintlocks for each barrel. The owner must be patient to load this gun and also strong to mount it. Opposite: An advertisement from an old Sears catalogue.

charge would ignite giving, at the least, a very nasty fright. It was not unknown for the charge to ignite the powder flask and for this to blow up in the shooter's hand. The charge safely in the barrel, the overpowder wad was rammed down on top of it and then a measured quantity of shot poured down. The application of a thin overshot wad was followed by priming the pan with fine priming powder. The shotgun was now ready for use.

Nearly all of the early guns were single barrelled. Perhaps the weight and bulk of a double-barrelled gun, 60in (1,524mm) long, deterred even these intrepid hunters.

The earliest form of non-live bird shooting was Popinjay. This involved shooting at a model bird on the end of a pole. As sitting birds were the rule, this sufficed as practice. It was, however, not until the 18th century that shooting was established as a sport for enjoyment and not just 'killing to eat'. The hunting party, accompanied by servants burdened with shot flasks, powder flasks, wads and all the odds and ends that were so indispensable in those days, became a form of sport amongst the landed gentry.

Advent of the double barrel
Although the double-barrelled shotgun was being produced in Europe during the first half of the 18th century it did not become popular until the end of the 18th or beginning of the 19th century in Britain. The main reason for this was the more practical size made possible with the improvements in powder and design. The use of a regular and faster burning powder helped, as did the use of special breeches such as that designed by Henry Nock in 1787 which increased the breech pressure and helped the clean burning of the powder. This contributed to the shortening of the barrels to 34in (863mm) or even 30in (762mm). The flintlock double gun became a weapon of considerable technical merit with waterproof locks, well-made Damascus barrels, good woodwork and in many cases intricate and elaborate decoration.

The double barrel did bring with it one additional hazard to the sportsman. If, in the heat of the moment, with game flying all around, the weapon should misfire or the shooter forget that both barrels had not yet been discharged, it was all too easy to double charge one of them. The effect of this could cause a most unpleasant surprise, even total disintegration of the gun. It was recommended that a check be made to see if there was already a load in the barrel. Needless to say, as the action got hotter the shooter's ability to load regular amounts of shot and powder became less reliable and the results were,

to say the least, variable. Because of the problem of the corrosive effect of the powder and its ability to attract whatever moisture was in the air, it was recommended that the weapon be reloaded immediately on firing while the barrel was still hot. This was good advice – as long as it was remembered to look out for a piece of burning wad.

With the lack of choke-boring, numerous attempts were made to produce a tight shooting gun. One of the most successful types was the Eley shot basket. This was a wrapped wire basket with a shot inside, cushioned by powdered bone, and loaded after the powder. It needed no overpowder wad. It was relatively successful in holding the shot together over short distances and was continued even after the shotgun cartridge came into use as a unit.

The prime reason the Reverend James Forsyth invented the percussion system was so that he could have a weapon which had a fast enough lock time to make wing shooting a more practical proposition. The military application of the percussion system was delayed for some time, but after Forsyth's invention the gradual conversion to the percussion system began. Many fine flintlocks were modified as well as original weapons manufactured. By 1830 almost all guns manufactured were of the later type but as with any innovation some still demanded the tried if not altogether trusted flintlock.

The sport of shooting as opposed to live game shooting became popular and the shooting of live birds released from boxes was given formal rules. Although the clay pigeon has largely replaced the captive live bird, the latter is still shot today.

The early 19th century saw the development of the shotgun cartridge and with it the breech loader. Once again the sporting gun took the lead in the development of firearms. The breech

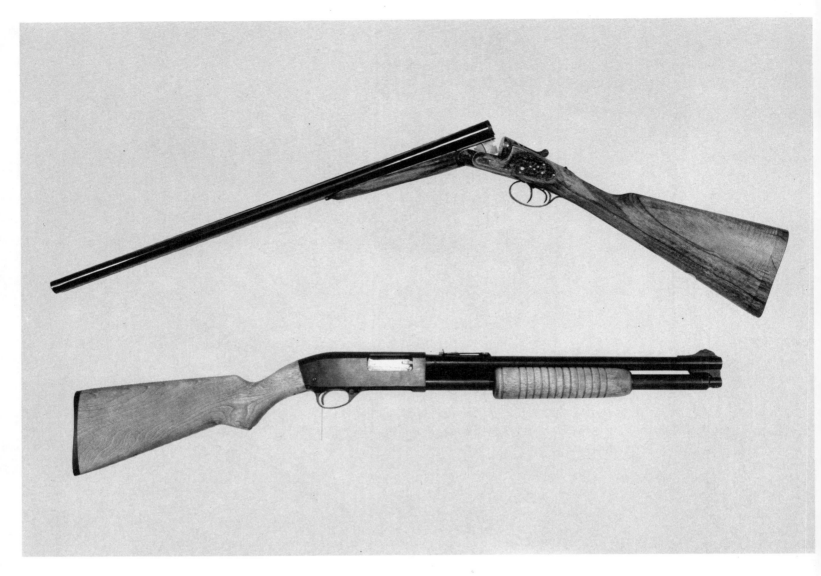

loader was viewed with suspicion and some
eminent authorities dismissed it as too heavy
and unreliable. Their reaction may have been
coloured by the fact that, as respected makers
of shotguns, they were not at that time making
this type.

By the mid-19th century the shooting of game
became a popular sport and started a chain of
attempts by record breakers who spent days
trying to amass the largest total of birds in a day's
shooting. The use of a matched pair of guns with
a loader standing behind to pass the loaded gun
and take the empty made the shooting of these
immense bags far removed from sport.

Just as the flintlock took time to die, so did the
hammer gun. Many breech-loading cartridge
guns were made with hammers and it was not
until the late 1880s that the hammerless gun
became the norm. At this time the old and much
respected Damascus barrels were being superseded by the stronger steel ones. The shots of the
day, however, still often demanded not only
hammer guns but steel barrels made to look as if
they were Damascus. The tradition of the top-
class shotgun had begun and still continues.
Customers are willing to pay many thousands
of pounds and wait two, three or even more
years for their shotgun.

Modern weapons

The design of the modern shotgun has become
standard. There are a number of specific types
manufactured externally to a pattern regardless
of their mechanical functioning. The barrel layout has three basic types with the addition of
the drilling. The single barrel is still much in
demand as the cheapest form of simple game
gun. It has in addition the wide range of automatic and pump action guns to its credit. Some
competition clay shooting is also carried out
with the single barrel.

The double barrel has two layouts. The traditional side-by-side is still looked on as the game
gun. The English double, or more properly,
pair of doubles, especially if by one of the better
known makers, commands the highest respect
and money. Actions such as the Scottish Dickson

round action are as good as, some would say better than, their English counterparts. The over and under, with the barrels mounted one on top of the other, has become a firm favourite on the clay pigeon range. While not considered by some as the ideal game gun it still can hold its own in the field.

The drilling is an odd combination of the shotgun and the rifle. It was, and still is, popular in Europe where the habit of shooting both birds and animals on a shoot was normal. There have been many different combinations. The two most common are two shotgun barrels mounted side by side with the rifle barrel underneath in the centre. The over and under, with the shotgun on top and the rifle underneath, is also used. The calibre of the rifle varies but many of the European high-power cartridges of the hunting type appear, as well as others less powerful, even the humble rimfire.

With the use of the cartridge breech loader one new problem arose and this was the removal of the case from the chamber. It led to the development of the extractor and the ejector. In the first development the cartridge case was merely raised from the chamber by an extractor and then removed manually. This system is still in use on the cheapest of guns. It was desirable that the case be automatically removed and so the ejector gun was born. The ejector threw the case clear of the gun. Needless to say the ejection of the live round from a double was not desir-able, so the selective ejector was developed. On a modern ejector gun, the empty case is flung clear and the live one merely raised so that it can be removed if desired. One of the first ejector guns was the Needham, patented in 1874. On the expiry of the patent many types were developed by top English gunsmiths and some are still in use today.

The placing of the hammer and sear mechanism in the shotgun gives rise to two descriptions. The Box lock has the entire mechanism contained within the main body of the gun. The Side lock has the lock located on plates fitted to either side of the weapon. The Box lock has often differed little from the Anson and Deeley patent of 1875. The abrupt line of the Box lock can be offensive to the eye compared to the flowing lines of the Side lock.

The fitting of the Side lock to the stock must be more accurate as the cutting away of the wood where the stock joins the action, if badly done, can weaken the joint. The attractive appearance of the Side lock has been combined with the Box lock on occasion by the use of a Box lock fitted with false side plates. The side plate has the advantage of giving an area for the master engraver to present his art.

The inside of the lock, while technically protected from the ravages of the weather by the close fit of the woodwork, is, in the top class of gun such as the Dickson, gold plated for added protection. Nothing must be left to chance. This

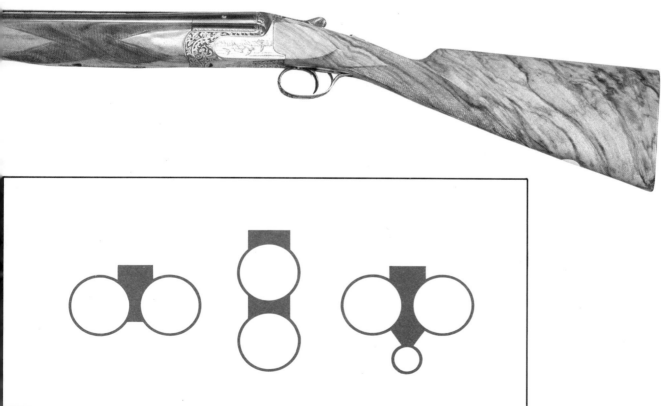

Above left: A Holland and Holland over-and-under shotgun.
Left: Shotgun barrel configurations.

*Right: The French
Darne shotgun is
unique in that it uses a
sliding breech block
operated by a lever on
the top. This particular
shotgun is highly
engraved and
beautifully stocked.*

is why the age of the top guns is to a large extent immaterial as they are built to outlast their owners.

Some sportsmen who shoot for game consider the use of a gun other than a side-by-side, far less the over and under, to be a breach of etiquette. Yet many people derive immense pleasure and great success from the use of the auto or pump action shotgun. We have to thank that genius John Browning for producing the automatic shotgun, a gun that not only set the standard for today, but is still in production in one guise or another. Pump action shotguns, in which the firer must move a grip under the barrel back to eject and forward to chamber a round, provide a cheap and reliable multi-shot weapon.

The bore of a shotgun is not, as in the rifle, measured by a dimension but by a gauge. This is derived from the old method of measuring the barrel by the use of lead balls. The theory was for a ball to be cast which exactly fitted the barrel then it was weighed. The number of such balls that would make up 1 lb weight (0.45kg) was calculated and this number recorded as the gauge of the weapon. Thus a 12-gauge bore shotgun has a bore in which 12 balls from it would make 1 lb. Today the bore of the 10, 12, 16 and 20 have reasonably precise dimensions although they do vary slightly from make to make.

The standard dimension of the 12 gauge is .775in (19.68mm). The exception that occurs is the 410 that is, as the name would suggest, bored to .410in (10.41mm). The bore at the point of the choke is smaller than the nominal bore. The amount of constriction varies according to how the choke is made and from maker to maker. The old rule was that the full choke was constricted .040in (1.01mm), the three quarter .030in (0.76mm), the half choke .020in (0.50mm), and the quarter choke or improved cylinder .010in (0.25mm).

Having decided on the best type of shotgun for the task in hand the next decision is the size of shot to be used. The shotgun cartridge varies in the weight and size of shot that it carries. Thus the length of the shotgun cartridge, be it $2\frac{1}{2}$, $2\frac{3}{4}$ or 3in (63.5, 69.8 or 76.2mm) allows different weight of shot to be contained for any given size. This can be $1\frac{1}{8}$oz (32g) or even $1\frac{1}{2}$oz (42.5g).

The size of the shot is referred to as the number. A small size, the number 10, is .07in (1.77mm) in diameter and has 870 to the ounce. A large size, the number 2, is .15in (3.81mm) and has only 90 to the ounce. Obviously there is a balance between shot size and killing power and the amount of shot that will determine the density of the pattern for any given choke boring. The type of target dictates the type of shell. The game shot may use the number 6 and the clay pigeon shot the number 8.

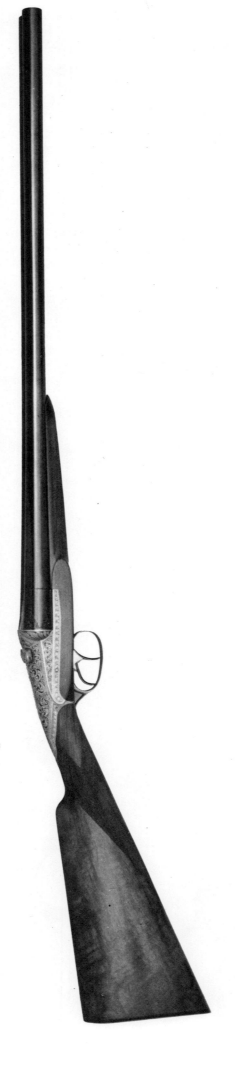

Glossary

ACP

Automatic Colt Pistol. When John Browning developed the range of Colt automatic pistols he also developed cartridges. The Colt company was the sole supplier of Browning designs in the United States so they used the name on the cartridges as well.

ACTION

The mechanical assembly that controls the function of the weapon. See also blowback, recoil.

Double Action/Single Action

The operation of a revolver by first cocking the hammer indicates the single action type; when the hammer is cocked by the action of the trigger it is double action.

ALARM GUN

A gun that fires a blank cartridge and is actuated by a trip wire. The gun firing acts as an alarm for intruders.

AMMUNITION

The cartridge or shell for use in firearms or guns. Also used to cover the bullet, propellant and primer when separate as in a muzzle-loader.

ARQUEBUS/HARQUEBUS

This is literally a hook gun. Normally an early type of portable firearm often fired from a rest.

AUTOMATIC

Although technically a weapon that fires continually at one pull of the trigger, the expression is now almost universally applied to the self-loading pistol. Automatic fire means continuous fire.

BALLISTICS

The science of the study of projectile and propellant behaviour.

External Ballistics

The study of the projectile while between barrel and target.

Internal Ballistics

The study of the projectile, propellant and primer behaviour while the bullet is in the barrel.

Terminal Ballistics

The effect of the projectile against its target.

BANDOLIER

A container worn or carried for cartridges. It is often of light cloth with pockets for clips of cartridges.

BARREL

The tube through which the bullet is driven by the propellant. See also rifling, Damascus.

BATTERY CUP PRIMER

See Primer.

BELT

A cartridge belt is a means of loading cartridges for a machine gun. The cartridges are contained in loops or clips in a belt of metal or cloth.

Disintegrating/Non-Disintegrating Belt

Some machine guns have a belt that passes through the gun. Modern machine guns often use the cartridge itself as part of the belt and therefore the belt disintegrates on firing.

BENCH REST

The sport of bench rest shooting consists of shooting at long ranges resting the rifle on special benches. Also used to check the sights of a weapon for zero.

BERDAN PRIMER

See Primer.

BLACK POWDER

The original propellant manufactured from sulphur, saltpetre and charcoal. On firing it produces a large amount of smoke.

BLANK CARTRIDGE

A cartridge which contains no projectile and is used for a noise effect only.

Grenade Blank

A blank used to launch grenades from a rifle.

BLOWBACK

A type of action with no locking system but relying on the weight of the components and the spring force to keep the breech closed until the pressure has dropped to a safe limit. The breech is then 'blown' open by the reduced gas pressure. This system is generally limited to low-pressure cartridges.

Blowforward

A system similar to blowback except that the action works by moving forward.

Delayed Blowback

To enable the blowback system to function with high-pressure cartridges, the opening of the breech is delayed by mechanical or gas means before being allowed to open. The system is at no time locked.

BLUING

A chemical rusting that gives a blue or blue/black finish to metal. The finish is resistant to corrosion. Browning is a similar finish.

BLUNDERBUSS

The Blunderbuss or Thundergun was an early form of shot-firing weapon. Typically it was a flintlock having a brass barrel with a belled mouth.

BOLT ACTION

An action where the locking is accomplished by the longitudinal movement of the breech block by a handle.

Straight Pull

A bolt action which is operated by a simple longitudinal motion.

Turnbolt

A bolt action where the locking is accomplished by a rotary movement of the bolt.

BORE

The hole in the barrel down which the projectile travels. Also a term applied when indicating the size of the barrel, i.e. 12 bore.

BOTTLENECK CARTRIDGE

See Cartridge Case.

BOXER PRIMER

See Primer.

BOX LOCK

A type of lock that is contained within the body of the weapon; usually applied to shotguns.

BREECH

The rear face of the barrel and often used to indicate the area at the rear of the barrel.

Closed Breech Firing

The normal type of breech operation for the majority of firearms. The breech is closed and a round chambered when the gun is ready to fire.

Open Breech Firing

The firing of a weapon that has the breech open in the normal position to aid cooling. The breech block moves forward when the trigger is pulled and chambers a round on the way.

Standing Breech

The rear face of the breech area or frame that acts as a support to the chambered ammunition.

BREECH BLOCK

The part of the action that closes the end of the barrel at the breech end of a breech-loader.

BREECH LOADER

A gun that is loaded from the breech as opposed to the muzzle. A cartridge is normally used.

BROWNING

See Bluing.

BULLET

The projectile fired from a gun.

Armour Piercing (A.P.)

A specialist bullet designed with a hard core, typically tungsten, that has the specialist function of penetrating armour.

Ball

The standard anti-personnel bullet.

Dum-Dum

A name adopted from an Indian arsenal that is commonly used to indicate a bullet that expands on impact. This is achieved by using a soft lead exposed point or a hollow point.

Incendiary

A bullet that contains a fire-producing compound such as phosphorous.

Tracer

A bullet that has an element that burns, giving an indication of its trajectory.

Wad Cutter

A target bullet that has a blunt front to cut a clean hole in the target.

BULL PUP

A term that is applied to a rifle or machine gun that has no butt. The feed and action are thus directly against the firer's shoulder and the trigger and grip towards the front of the weapon.

BUTT

The grip of a pistol, the stock of a rifle or shotgun, that extends from the action to form a rest for the shoulder.

CALIBRE

The dimension across the bore of a gun. In a rifled weapon this is measured across the lands of the rifling.

CANE GUN

A rifle or shotgun disguised as, or in the form of, a walking cane.

CAPPER

A device for putting the percussion cap on the nipple.

CARBINE

A shortened version of a rifle. Originally a special short weapon for the cavalry.

CARTRIDGE

Ammunition that contains the primer, propellant and projectile as a unit. This is normally accomplished by using a cartridge case. Experiments have dispensed with the case and bonded the propellant as a unit.

Centrefire

A cartridge with the primer set in the centre of the base.

Needlefire

The primer is detonated by the use of a needle rather than a firing pin. The primer in a needlefire cartridge is often between bullet and powder rather than behind the powder.

Pinfire

The primer on the pinfire is detonated by a pin set at approximately right angles to the bore. This pin protrudes through the side of the cartridge case at the rear.

Rimfire

The priming compound is situated in the recess of the rim of the cartridge case.

CARTRIDGE CASE

The means of holding the primer, propellant and projectile as a unit.

Belted

A cartridge that has a raised belt near the base for strength and head space.

Bottlenecked

A case that has a reduced diameter at the bullet compared to the base.

Rimmed/Rimless

The construction of the rear of the cartridge case to facilitate extraction and head space.

CHAMBER

The part of the barrel (or, on a revolver, the cylinder) that holds the cartridge.

CHARGER

See Clip.

CHOKE

The reduction in the bore size near the muzzle of a shotgun. This restriction is graded to provide a tighter control on the shot pattern, eg quarter choke, half choke, full choke. The shotgun with a perfectly cylindrical bore is called true cylinder bore.

CLIP

A clip or charger is a means of holding cartridges ready to be loaded, typically in units of five or 10. Some pistols and many rifles have 'clip guides' to allow the gun to be loaded from clips.

COCK

To cock a gun is to pull the firing pin striker or hammer into a position ready to fire.

Half Cock

Some revolvers and automatic pistols have a position between the hammer being forward and cocked, a throwback to flintlock and percussion weapons where this was the safe position for the hammer. Even today, some revolvers use this position for loading.

COMBINATION GUN

There are two types of combination gun. The first is the gun, normally a pistol, that combines with another article such as a knife or lance. The second has a shotgun barrel and a rifle barrel on the same weapon.

COOK OFF

The firing of a weapon by the residual heat retained after extensive firing. The propellant ignites from the heat after a time and the firing is not controlled by the user.

CRIMP

A means of holding either a projectile or a primer in a cartridge case.

CUT OFF

A device fitted to the magazine of military rifles so that the gun can be loaded with single cartridges while retaining the magazine in a fully loaded state.

DAMASCUS BARREL

A barrel that is manufactured by the hammer-welding of strips of metal round a mandril. Careful intertwining of iron and steel rods and then etching the finished barrel with acid results in a most attractive pattern.

DERRINGER

A small concealable pistol often of single or double barrel construction that takes its name from an early inventor of the type.

DISCONNECTOR

A component of the trigger that prevents a self-loading weapon from firing more than one shot per pull of the trigger.

DOUBLE ACTION

See Action.

DRILLING

A combination of a shotgun and a rifle in a variety of different ways, e.g. two shotgun barrels, one rifled one, or one shotgun and one rifle.

DUCK'S FOOT PISTOL

A multi-barrelled pistol in which the barrels point outward in an arc to provide a spread of fire.

DUELLING PISTOL

A pistol specially designed to provide the best possible chance in a duelling match. Normally cased in pairs, one for each contestant.

EJECTOR
The component that throws the cartridge or cartridge case clear of the action after firing.

EXTRACTOR
A component that pulls either a live round or a fired case from the chamber.

FALSE MUZZLE
A device used to protect the muzzle from wear and ensure the centring of the components when loading a muzzle-loader.

FLASH HIDER
A device fitted to the muzzle of a weapon to diminish the flash when the weapon is fired.

FLINTLOCK
A lock in which the means of ignition is a shower of sparks caused by striking a flint against part of the lock.

FLUTED CHAMBER
To assist the extraction of a cartridge in a blowback weapon flutes are cut in the chamber so that gas can bleed back from the action and float the case off the chamber walls.

FOLLOWER
See Magazine.

FORESIGHT
See Sight.

FRAME
The body of a revolver.
Hinged Frame
A frame that is hinged so that it can be opened for loading.
Open Frame
A frame that has no connection at the top between the barrel and the breech face.
Solid Frame
A frame which is continuous.

FRIZZEN
The component of a flintlock against which the flint is struck.

GAS OPERATION
The operation of a self-loading gun by using the gas from the burning propellant.
Direct Gas
Some actions notably that of the M16 dispense with the piston and cylinder and use the gas fed via a tube in the action itself.
Gas Piston/Cylinder
Arrangement whereby the gas energy is transferred to the action by a piston and cylinder.
Gas Port
The hole in the barrel through which the gas is taken. In some cases there is a means of adjusting the amount of gas to regulate the weapon in different conditions.
Short/Long Stroke Piston
The short stroke piston travels only far enough to give an impulse to the mechanism. The long stroke piston travels the full action length after it has been actuated.

GROOVE
The part of the rifling that has been cut out, i.e. the hollows in the barrel.

GUN POWDER
See Black Powder.

HAIR TRIGGER
See Trigger.

HAMMER
The part of the mechanism that imparts a blow either direct to the primer or percussion cap or to a firing pin. So-called because it is similar to the domestic hammer and pivots at its base.
Concealed Hammer
A gun that has a hammer but incorporates it inside the mechanism. A typical pistol is the Colt .32 acp.
Hammerless
Hammerless guns in the true sense are fired by a striker rather than a hammer. The term is often applied incorrectly to concealed hammer guns.

HAND CANNON
A hand-held cannon ignition firearm.

HANDGUN
A hand-held weapon, i.e. a pistol or revolver.

HANGFIRE
When the firing of the propellant charge is not immediate on firing the weapon.

HARMONICA GUN
Any weapon, either rifle or pistol, that uses a slide containing the charges in a row. Normally this was in a horizontal direction.

HEAD SPACE
The distance between the bolt face and the supporting point of the cartridge, typically the mouth, rim or neck. This ensures that the cartridge is a correct fit in the chamber.

HOLLOW POINT
A hollow point on a bullet is used to aid expansion in game when shot.

JACKET
The outer covering of a bullet. Usually of guilding metal but for economic reasons or for special purposes it can be of steel coated with copper to protect the bore.

KICK
The recoil effect felt by the firer.

LANDS
The raised parts of the rifling.

LEVER ACTION
A type of action that is operated by the movement of a lever, typically the Winchester 66/73.

LOADING GATE
A hinged cover for either the magazine or in the case of a revolver the cylinder.

LOCK
On early weapons the lock included the firing mechanism. Today the term is often applied to the complete breech system.

LOCKING LUGS
The lugs that hold the breech closed by engaging in corresponding cut-outs in the breech or barrel extension.

LR
Long Rifle. A description applied to one of the two standard rimfire rounds in common use. The other is the .22 short.

MACHINE GUN
Any weapon that fires a continuous stream of projectiles at one pull of the trigger.
General Purpose Machine Gun (GPMG)
A machine gun that is able to meet the requirements of both a LMG and MMG. At best it is usually deficient in one of these roles.
Heavy Machine Gun (HMG)
A machine gun similar to the medium type but firing a special cartridge such as the .50 Browning or 12.7mm Russian.
Light Machine Gun (LMG)
An easily portable machine gun, e.g. the Bren Gun.
Medium Machine Gun (MMG)
A machine gun that is belt fed and capable of sustained fire. Normally of rifle calibre.
Submachine Gun
A machine gun firing essentially a pistol type cartridge, and of very portable size and weight.

MAGAZINE
In the context of small arms a storage device for cartridges.
Box Magazine
A detachable or fixed magazine in the shape of a box. The box magazine is of two types, the single column and the double column, a term that applies to the layout of the cartridges in the magazine.
Drum Magazine
A magazine normally either fitted vertically or horizontally and containing the cartridges in a drum-shaped container.
Magazine Follower
The component in the magazine that transmits the force of the spring to the cartridges.
Rotary Magazine
A magazine that has the cartridges contained in a spool which rotates as the rounds are used. A good example is the Steyr Mannlicher type.
Tube Magazine
The tube magazine has the cartridges contained in a tube normally positioned under the barrel of the firearm.

MATCHLOCK
An early form of ignition that used a slow-burning cord called a match which was lowered into the touch hole or pan.

MIQUELET LOCK
A type of flintlock that has the pan cover and the frizzen integral. There is usually a

large externally mounted V-shaped main-spring.

MUSKET
Originally a single shot smoothbored long-arm, but when rifling became prevalent the term rifled musket was used.

MUZZLE
The front end of the barrel.
Muzzle Brake
An attachment to the muzzle to lower the recoil by diverting the gases that leave the muzzle.
Muzzle Energy
The energy of the projectile as it leaves the muzzle derived from the mass and the velocity of the projectile.
Muzzle-Loader
A weapon that is loaded solely from the muzzle, or front of the chamber of a revolver.
Muzzle Velocity
See Velocity.

NIPPLE
A small tube that is screwed into the firearm to link the flash of the percussion cap, which fits tightly over it, to the propellant.

OPEN SIGHTS
A sight that has no optical aid such as an aperture or scope.

ORGAN BATTERY
A multi-barrelled volley gun with the barrels arranged in the form of a horizontal array of organ pipes.

OVER AND UNDER
A double-barrelled gun that has the barrels mounted in a vertical plane.

PALM PISTOL
A pistol, normally mechanically operated, that fits into the hand rather than being gripped.

PAN
The pan or priming pan is a pan shaped hollow in which the priming charge is placed.
Pan Cover
A cover to keep the priming protected from wind and rain.

PATCH
A piece of material, usually cloth or paper, that is wrapped round the bullet of a firearm to assist in gripping the rifling and prevent a build-up of fouling on the bore.

PEPPERBOX
A revolving-type firearm in which a number of barrels revolve in their entirety as opposed to the action of a revolver where only the cylinder revolves.

PERCUSSION CAP
There are a number of percussion caps ranging from tubes to the common children's cap gun type, but the type normally associated with a percussion firearm is similar to that fitting over the nipple.

PERCUSSION IGNITION
A firearm that is designed to be fired by a percussion system uses a compound that is very sensitive to percussion as the means of igniting the propellant.

PILLAR BREECH
The Tige breech system invented by Colonel Thouvenin of France. It uses a pillar set in the centre of the breech face to expand the projectile as it is hit by the ramrod.

PISTOL
Any hand-held firearm which is designed to be fired with one hand. Often applied to the self-loading pistol as a generic term.

PISTOL GRIP
A pistol-type grip fitted to a long arm in addition to the normal stock.

PRIMER
The self-contained unit that contains the priming charge which is sensitive to percussion.
Battery Cup Primer
The primer in a shotgun case requires, because of the case's weaker construction, additional support. So the battery cup primer is a unit that contains the primer and a separate anvil. The unit or cup fits into the hole in the case.
Berdan Primer
A primer which relies on an anvil built into the cartridge case and thus uses one or more flash holes offset in the case.
Boxer Primer
A primer that has the anvil built into the primer itself and uses a case with a centrally located flash hole.

PROJECTILE
Technically any object that is in flight from a gun barrel, but normally used to indicate the bullet even when in the cartridge case.

PROOF
From the 16th century it became general in some countries to test the gun after manufacture and before sale. This test involved, as it still does today, the firing of an over charge or proof load to see that the firearm is safe. Proof marks are then stamped on the gun to show that it has passed the test.

PROPELLANT
An explosive that burns in a slow, controlled manner and can thus be used to propel projectiles from firearms.

PUMP ACTION
A firearm which uses as its method of operation a grip fitted under the barrel which is pulled and pushed in a motion parallel to the barrel.

PUNT GUN
A type of shotgun of massive proportions used to shoot a group of sitting birds from a punt or boat.

PYRITES
An early type of mineral used before true flint in wheellocks, etc.

RAMMER/RAMROD
A metal or wooden rod used to load a muzzle-loading firearm. Sometimes incorrectly applied to a cleaning rod.

RAMP SIGHT
See Sight.

REAR SIGHT
See Sight.

RECEIVER
The portion of a firearm that contains the action.

RECOIL
The opposite reaction to the firing of a cartridge. The projectile moves forward and the gun back. The recoil is often referred to as the kick.

RECOIL OPERATION
The use of the recoil energy to operate the action of a self-loading weapon.

RECOIL SPRING
The spring that returns the action to the ready position after firing.

REVOLVER
A pistol that uses a cylinder with multiple chambers in it which can be rotated to present a fresh charge aligned with the bore.

RICOCHET
A projectile which on impact with an object does not cease to move but glances off and continues its flight.

RIFLING
A series of spiral grooves cut in the bore of the barrel to impart a spin to the projectile. This spin gyroscopically stabilizes the projectile.

SAFETY
A means of locking or making safe the hammer-firing mechanism or trigger on a firearm.
Grip Safety
Some firearms are fitted with a safety device that the firer has to grip before they can be fired.

SALOON PISTOL/GALLERY PISTOL
A single shot pistol of very low power which was used for indoor target practice.

SCENTBOTTLE LOCK
The earliest form of percussion ignition, so named because the percussion compound was contained in a scentbottle-shaped vessel.

SEAR

A lever or group of levers that are used to control the action of the trigger by connecting it with the hammer or firing pin.

SELF-LOADING

A firearm that carries out the reloading cycle without recourse to the firer.

SELF-LOADING PISTOL

The correct name for the so-called automatic pistol.

SEMI-AUTOMATIC FIRE

A self-loading weapon in which the fire is restricted to one shot per pull of the trigger.

SET TRIGGER

See Trigger.

SHOT

The round, small pellets which are fired from a shotgun. They vary in diameter from approximately .03in to .36in.

SHOTGUN

A smoothbored weapon specifically designed for the firing of shot. In certain countries a technically incorrect rule is applied to the barrel length.

SIGHT

An aiming device fitted to a firearm.

Aperture Sight

A rear sight that uses a small, often adjustable, hole or aperture to improve the sight image.

Front Sight

The portion of the sight fitted to the front of the firearm near the muzzle.

Leaf Sight

A type of sight that uses a hinged leaf which can be raised to accommodate different ranges.

Open Sight

A sight that has no form of optical device such as an aperture or magnification.

Optical Sight

Any form of sight using a series of lenses whether to magnify the image or merely to impart an aiming mark or other information to the firer.

Post Sight

A front sight in the shape of a post.

Ramp Sight

A front sight that is fitted on a ramp raised from the barrel.

Telescopic Sight

An optical sight that uses a lens system to increase the image size.

SILENCER

A device fitted to a firearm to reduce the amount of noise given on firing. It could more correctly be called a sound moderator.

SLIDE

The top cover often integral with the breech block of a self-loading pistol.

SLIDE ACTION

See Pump Action.

SLING

A leather or webbing strap attached to a weapon to facilitate carrying and firing.

SMALL ARM

A definition normally applied to any weapon that is portable by man. It includes heavy machine guns and light anti-tank guns.

SMALL BORE

A term normally applied to weapons firing the .22 LR cartridge. It is also applied in certain countries to other small-calibre types.

SMOKELESS POWDER

The term applied to any propellant other than black powder. This came into being because black powder emitted a dense cloud of smoke while the nitrocellulose type powders burnt with little or none.

SMOOTH BORE

A firearm that has no rifling in the barrel. While this originally applied to any firearm it is now often used to denote a shotgun.

SNAPHANCE/SNAPHAUNCE

A flintlock in which the pan cover and frizzen are separate.

STOCK/BUTT STOCK

In a pistol the stock is the covering of the grip area to provide a comfortable hand hold. In the longarm the stock or butt stock is the extension from the rear of the action to the shoulder of the firer. The stocks were, and still are, on top-class firearms made of wood, but plastic and nylon have become universal where price and durability are prime considerations.

STRIKER

When a firearm is fired without the use of a firing pin/hammer combination, a striker is used. The striker is a component that is controlled by its own spring and the action of the trigger. The firing pin can be an integral part or attached to it.

SUBMACHINE GUN

See Machine gun.

SUICIDE SPECIAL

A term of opprobrium used to indicate the poorest quality of small handgun.

TAKE DOWN FIREARM

A firearm, normally a rifle, or shotgun, that can be easily dismantled for transport and quickly assembled for use.

TARGET PISTOL/RIFLE

A pistol or rifle that is especially adapted for target shooting.

TOUCH HOLE

The hole that connects the pan to the barrel, down which the ignition of the propellant takes place.

TRAJECTORY

The path taken by a bullet during flight.

TRIGGER

A lever that is used to actuate the firing mechanism of a firearm. It is normally pulled, but can be pushed, released or squeezed by a finger.

Hair Trigger

A term used to denote a trigger that requires little pressure to actuate it. Sometimes applied to a set trigger.

Set Trigger

A trigger specially designed to be ultra-sensitive and requiring a separate lever to 'set' it ready for firing.

TRIGGER GUARD

A component that protects the trigger from damage or accidental movement.

TUBE LOCK

A percussion lock that uses a tube filled with the percussion compound rather than the normal cap.

TURRET GUN

A firearm in which the chambers are arranged in the manner of the spokes of a wheel rather than in the manner of a revolver.

TWIST/PITCH

The rate of the twist in the rifling. This is expressed as 'one turn in so many units of measurement (inches or mm)'.

UNDERHAMMER GUN

A firearm in which the operation of the hammer is under the action.

VELOCITY

The speed of the bullet.

Muzzle Velocity

The velocity of the projectile as it leaves the muzzle of the firearm.

VERY PISTOL

A flare pistol named after the inventor of a signal system of coloured lights projected from a pistol.

VOLLEY GUN

A gun that fires a volley of shots at one discharge.

WHEELLOCK

The lock that uses a stationary flint which is held against an abrasive wheel that is spun by a clockwork-type spring to produce the spark.

WINDAGE

The lateral drift of a bullet usually used when compensating for a crosswind.

ZERO

The sight setting which, with a given cartridge type, range and weather conditions, etc. will ensure a hit at the point of aim.

Collections

BELGIUM
Musée Royal de L'Armée et d'Histoire Militaire (The Royal Museum of the Army and Military History), Brussels – The collection concentrates on arms particularly from World War I and II.
Le Musée d'Armes (The Army Museum), Liège – The collection consists of all systems of firearms, from 1350 to the present day.

CZECHOSLOVAKIA
Vojenshé Muzeum (Military Museum), Prague – Illustrates military history to 1918, and the history of the Czech army and firearms in particular are shown.

DENMARK
Tøjhusmuseet (Royal Arsenal Museum), Copenhagen – Illustrates the development of arms and military equipment up to the present day.

FINLAND
Sotamuseo (The War Museum), Helsinki

FRANCE
Musée de l'Armée (Army Museum), Paris

GERMAN DEMOCRATIC REPUBLIC
Deutsches Armemuseum (German Army Museum), Potsdam – Includes weapons of the German armies from the 18th century until today.

GERMAN FEDERAL REPUBLIC
Bayerisches Armeemuseum (The Bavarian Army Museum), Ingolstadt
Wehrgeschichtliches Museum (Museum of Military History), Rastatt – Weapons and military equipment from mediaeval times to the present day.

GREAT BRITAIN
Imperial War Museum, London
National Army Museum, London
The Armouries, HM Tower of London, London
The Rotunda Museum, London
The Pattern Room, RSAF, Enfield Lock
The School of Infantry, Warminster, Wilts

NETHERLANDS
Het Nederlands Leger en Wapensmuseum 'General Hoefer' (The Dutch Army and Arms Museum 'General Hoefer'), Leiden

NORWAY
Haermuseet (The Army Museum), Oslo – The main part of the collection consists of Norwegian arms up to the present day.

SPAIN
Museo del Ejército Español (The Spanish Army Museum), Madrid – Since 1933 this has been organized as the central museum of the Spanish Army.

SWEDEN
Kungl. Armémuseum (The Royal Army Museum), Stockholm

USA
Wadsworth Atheneum, Hartford, Connecticut – Includes an arms collection mainly of Colt firearms and of Samuel Colt's personal arms collection.
Winchester Gun Museum, now at the Buffalo Bill Cody Museum, Wyoming – Early Winchesters a speciality.
The War Memorial Museum of Virginia, Newport News, Virginia – Large collection of World War I and II weapons.
The United States Marine Corps Museum, Quantico, Virginia – The weapons collection traces the evolution of infantry arms in general and automatic weapons in particular.
Springfield Armory Museum, Springfield, Massachusetts – One of the world's most complete collections of modern small arms.
The West Point Museum, West Point, New York
Ordnance Museum, Aberdeen Proving Ground, Maryland
US Army Infantry Museum, Fort Benning, Georgia

Index

Page numbers in italics refer to illustrations.

Acknowledgements

Illustrations by: Steven Clark, Stuart Perry, Graham Rosewarne

Special photography by: Sally Chappell, Paul Forrester, Angelo Hornak, K. F. J. Jackson, Eileen Tweedy

The publishers would like to thank the Pattern Room at Enfield; Mr Keats at Holland and Holland Ltd; the Tower of London Armouries; and the Victoria and Albert Museum, for their help. Also the owners, authorities, trustees and individuals for their kind permission to reproduce the following photographs in this book

By Gracious Permission of Her Majesty The Queen 39; Army Museum, Ingolstadt 13; Beretta 34; Bodleian Library, Oxford 10 above; Cooper-Bridgeman Library 19 above, 24 below, 26 centre and below, 26–27 above, 71, (QAD/(ORD) Pattern Room, Enfield) 94–95 centre, 146; A. J. R. Cormack 24 above, 42, 83, 101, 140–141 below, 156 above, 156–157 centre, 157 below, (Angelo Hornak) 70 above, 72, 73, 74, 75, 76, 77, 78 below, 79, 95, 96, 100, 102 below, 102–103 above, 108–109, 110 below, 111, 145, 147, 148–149, 150–151, 151 above, 152, 153, 154–155, 158, 160–161, 162 above, 162–163, 164–165, 166–167, 168, 169, 170–171, 172, 173, 174–175, 176, 180 above; Euro Colour Library 15; FN 142 below; Gower Guns, Hemel Hempstead 182 above; The Gun Digest Company (A. C. Coopers) 87, 89, 90, 179 below; F. N. Herstal, Belgium 32, 36 above; Holland and Holland Ltd (Angelo Hornak) end papers, half title, title, contents, introduction, 65, 80, 84–85, 104–105, 110–111 above, 180–181 centre; The Robert Hunt Library 88 below; Imperial War Museum, London 97, (Eileen Tweedy) 86, 93, 144 below; Kelvingrove Art Gallery and Museum 178 below; MAS 50; National Army Museum 52; QAD/(ORD) Pattern Room, Enfield 41, (Angelo Hornak) 35, 37, 45, 47, 51 below, 59, 107, 113 below, 114–115, 118 left, 118–119 right, 120, 121, 123, 124–125, 126, 127, 131 above and below, 134–135 below, 136, 137, 139, 143, 160 below, 192; Quarto Books (Burgerbibliothek, Bern) 8, (University of Gottingen) 10 below, (Munich State Library) 11, (Ambrosiana, Milan) 16, 51 above, 58 left and right; The Royal Artillery Institution, Woolwich 14 above, 14–15, 31 above, 70 below; SIG 57 above; Smithsonian Institute, Washington 43; Sturm-Ruger 60; C. Thompson 115 centre; The Tower of London Armouries (Angelo Hornak) 21 below, 24 centre, 30, 30 inset, 31 below, 66 above, 66–67 below, 67 above and below, 68, 68–69 below, 98 below, 98–99, 177 (Paul Forrester) 178–179 above; The Tower of London Study Collection (Paul Forrester) 78 above; Victoria and Albert Museum 17 above, (Gallery Photography & Co (K. F. Jackson)) 12–13, (Sally Chappell) 16–17 below, 17 above, 18 below, 18–19, 20 below, 23 below, 25, 27 below, 28–29, 69 below; The Wadsworth Atheneum, Hartford, Connecticut 38; The Trustees of the Wallace Collection (John R. Freeman & Co (Photographers) Ltd) 20–21 above, 22–23; Winchester 64

The author would also like to thank Victoria De Korda for helping to compile the list of collections